THE POLITICS OF
Presidential Impeachment

SUNY series in American Constitutionalism

Robert J. Spitzer, editor

THE POLITICS OF
Presidential Impeachment

Daniel P. Franklin
Stanley M. Caress
Robert M. Sanders
Cole D. Taratoot

SUNY
PRESS

Published by State University of New York Press, Albany

© 2020 State University of New York

For information, contact State University of New York Press, Albany, NY
www.sunypress.edu

Library of Congress Cataloging-in-Publication Data

Names: Franklin, Daniel P., Caress, Stanley M., Sanders, Robert M., Taratoot, Cole D., authors.
Title: The politics of presidential impeachment. / Daniel P. Franklin, Stanley M. Caress, Robert M. Sanders, Cole D. Taratoot, authors.
Description: Albany : State University of New York Press, [2020] | Series: SUNY series, American Constitutionalism | Includes bibliographical references and index.
Identifiers: ISBN 9781438480039 (hardcover: alk. paper) | ISBN 9781438480046 (pbk. : alk. paper) | ISBN 9781438480053 (ebook)
Further information is available at the Library of Congress.

10 9 8 7 6 5 4 3 2 1

Contents

CHAPTER ONE

Impeachment

Safeguard or Political Weapon?

In a democracy we trust the will of the people. If public officials betray the public's trust, there must be a mechanism to hold them to account. The obvious remedy is periodic elections. However, for those officials whose misbehavior is at the beginning or in the middle of their terms or for those officials, such as judges, who serve for life, there must be another remedy. That mechanism is provided for in the Constitution through impeachment.

The problem, however, with impeachment is that it is often a matter of opinion whether an alleged transgression is a betrayal of the public trust or simply a decision out of the ordinary. How can we be properly governed if leaders are limited to doing what is only conventional or popular? We must, after all, trust our elected and top appointed officials to do the right thing, even if it is unpopular in the moment. As Edmund Burke once said, "Your representative owes you, not his industry only, but his judgment; and he betrays instead of serving you if he sacrifices it to your opinion." That is why James Madison made it very clear in the Federalist Papers that set terms between elections were essential because they would allow elected leaders sufficient time to make decisions that at the moment seemed mistaken, even negligent, but might in the long run be in the nation's interest.[1] This illustrates why impeachment under the Constitution is such a controversial procedure. Impeachment and removal at its most basic level represents no less than a subversion of the electoral will of the people, and it must be deployed rarely and judiciously if it is not to undermine the legitimacy of democratic governance.

Consequently, in the interim between elections, or after appointment in the case of federal judges, impeachment is the final resort to be used against treasonous, criminal acts or even gross negligence by elected officials.

But it is precisely because of periodic elections and the care with which we vet our appointed officials that actual impeachments are relatively rare.

Regardless of the original intent, impeachment has also been used as a political weapon. The ability to bring charges against an officeholder and force a trial for possible removal can be a devastating blow to a political opponent. An impeachment conviction is the equivalent of a political death sentence, and even the mere threat of impeachment can greatly weaken an adversary or affect their behavior. Thus, impeachment can be used to intimidate an otherwise powerful officeholder. In the intensely and increasingly combative conditions that frequent American politics, impeachment can even be used as a strategy to advance a political agenda.

Since impeachment is both a safeguard and a political weapon, an important question needs to be asked: Has the impeachment power been used in accordance with its original intent, or has it evolved into something far beyond the desires of the founders of our government?

The wording of the Constitution clearly indicates that impeachment is a method for protecting the American system of government from those who seek to abuse it. There is no question that the impeachment mechanisms created by the Constitution were designed to remove public officials who violated the public's trust by committing serious criminal acts; however, did the Constitution also intend that impeachment be used as a tool to incapacitate or harass a political opponent? Has the impeachment power been used as it was intended in American history?

Under the Constitution impeachment is described in the following manner:

Article I, Section 2 (5)

The House of Representatives shall chuse their Speaker and other Officers; and shall have the sole Power of Impeachment.

Article II, Section 4

The President, Vice President and all civil Officers of the United States, shall be removed from Office on Impeachment for, and Conviction of, Treason, Bribery, or other high Crimes and Misdemeanors.

Article I, Section 3 (6, 7)

The Senate shall have the sole Power to try all Impeachments. When sitting for that Purpose, they shall be on Oath or Affirmation. When the President of the United States is tried, the Chief Justice shall preside: And no Person shall be convicted without the Concurrence of two thirds of the Members present.

Judgment in Cases of Impeachment shall not extend further than to removal from Office, and disqualification to hold and enjoy any Office of honor, Trust or Profit under the United States; but the Party convicted shall nevertheless be liable and subject to Indictment, Trial, Judgment and Punishment, according to Law.

As is the case in much of the Constitution, the wording in regard to impeachment is at times straightforward and in some instances vague, leaving room for interpretation. Impeachment, the power to bring charges for possible removal from office, is given solely to the House of Representatives in Article I, Section 2. If the House of Representatives, by a simple majority vote, approves the impeachment, Article I, Section 3 gives the Senate the sole authority to try the impeachment. The only requirements are that the senators, when sitting for the trial, must be under oath or affirmation[2] and that a two-thirds affirmative vote of the members present is necessary to convict. The same section also requires that, in the case of presidential impeachment, the chief justice of the United States Supreme Court presides over the trial. Additionally, Article II, Section 4 states that the president, vice president, and all civil officers of the United States can be removed from office if impeached and convicted, and that the impeachable offenses include "treason, bribery and other high crimes and misdemeanors."

The only other clarification in the Constitution concerning impeachment is in Article I, Section 3, which states that the punishment for conviction cannot extend beyond removal and disqualification in the future from holding public office.[3] However, once removed, the convicted individual could still be subject to criminal indictment, trial, and punishment in a court of law.

Since the ratification of Constitution in 1789, the House has impeached nineteen individuals: fifteen federal judges, one senator,[4] one cabinet member, and three presidents (Richard Nixon resigned before he was impeached). The Senate has conducted sixteen full impeachment trials. Of these, eight individuals, all federal judges, were convicted.[5]

These judicial precedents are important because they serve to clarify some of the ambiguous language about the impeachment process outlined in the Constitution. Among the issues resolved are which "officials" are subject to impeachment: basically, judges and federal officials with a policy-making portfolio.[6] It appears that impeachment can only relate to activities during an individual's time in office and in relation to the official responsibilities of that office. So, for example, if an official engaged in a cover-up while in office of criminal activities that took place before he or she came into office that would be an impeachable offense. However, it is not the case that an official convicted of a crime committed before taking office would be subject to impeachment for that crime.[7] However, if individuals violate the law in pursuit of office, the question remains as to whether this would be grounds for impeachment.

But while the text of the Constitution makes it plain that impeachment is designed to remove criminals and traitors ("treason and bribery") from the government, what constitutes "high crimes and misdemeanors" is not clear.

Is the meaning of high crimes and misdemeanors limited to criminal conduct or can other activities justify an impeachment (and conviction)? Alexander Hamilton fairly definitively answers this question in Federalist 65:

> A well constituted court for the trial of impeachments, is an object not more to be desired than difficult to be obtained in a government wholly elective. The subjects of its jurisdiction are those offenses which proceed from the misconduct of public men, or in other words from the abuse or violation of some public trust. They are of a nature which may with peculiar propriety be denominated POLITICAL, as they relate chiefly to injuries done immediately to the society itself.[8]

Furthermore, later in the same essay, he provides other reasons to regard impeachment as something other than a criminal procedure. First, the trial for impeachment is held not in the courts but in the Senate. Because of the partisan and ideological nature of this body, the standards by which the Senate decides will inevitably be political. In addition, an official who is impeached could still be subject to criminal charges. While the Constitution makes it clear that double jeopardy is not allowed in criminal cases, an official who has been impeached, removed, or even acquitted by the Senate can still be formally charged with a crime. Therefore, impeachment is, from a constitutional perspective, different from a criminal charge.

Thus, if an officeholder obtained his or her position through fraudulent means but broke no actual law, could that still be considered a political crime even if falling below the standard of a crime or a "misdemeanor"? If a president acted in a reckless manner that jeopardized the security of the United States or disregarded the Constitution, for example, in ignoring a direct order of the court, would that individual be subject to impeachment? It appears that this judgment is at the discretion of the House of Representatives.

Obviously, the Constitution is relatively vague in this regard. But sometimes in that respect, vice is virtue. The Constitution is flexible enough to adapt over time. When the Constitutional Convention considered this provision, it used a phrase that was in common usage at the time. Impeachment had been in existence in England since the fourteenth century. There is some reason to believe that the "high" in high crimes and misdemeanors referred not to the classification of the crime, but to the position of the transgressor.[9] After all, impeachment was in form and substance not to be restricted to common crimes and misdemeanors. Those transgressions were handled in different venues, the common courts, and by different standards, requiring that a jury hold that a crime had occurred beyond a reasonable doubt. Whereas, as noted above, impeachments are tried in a different venue, by a different process, and conviction is based on a different standard.

High-ranking officials in the performance of their duties can commit "high crimes." "Crimes" obviously refers to criminal behavior including but also other than treason and bribery. "Misdemeanors" seems to refer to actions taken by officials that make them unfit to serve, for example in violation of their oath of office. In the modern context we have a rather narrow definition of the word "misdemeanor" (something in between a crime and a tort), but it is not the equivalent of what was meant by the Framers in the context of the impeachment clause.[10]

In his ""Notes of Debates in the Federal Convention of 1787," Madison recounts the convention's debate on July 20, 1787 on this provision:

> **Mr. MADISON** thought it indispensable that some provision should be made for defending the Community agst. the incapacity, negligence or perfidy of the chief Magistrate. The limitation of the period of his service, was not a sufficient security. He might lose his capacity after his appointment. He might pervert his administration into a scheme of peculation or oppression. He might betray his trust to foreign powers. The case of the Executive Magistracy was very distinguishable, from that of the Legislature or of any other public body, holding offices of limited duration. It could not be presumed that all or even a majority of the members of an Assembly would either lose their capacity for discharging, or be bribed to betray, their trust. Besides the

restraints of their personal integrity & honor, the difficulty of acting in concert for purposes of corruption was a security to the public. And if one or a few members only should be seduced, the soundness of the remaining members, would maintain the integrity and fidelity of the body. In the case of the Executive Magistracy which was to be administered by a single man, loss of capacity or corruption was more within the compass of probable events, and either of them might be fatal to the Republic.

The fact that Madison quotes himself gives particular weight to the sentiments expressed. He clearly meant the provision for "high crimes and misdemeanors" to mean something other than that to which we make modern reference in the classification of crimes (i.e., felonies and misdemeanors).

As a result, the House and Senate, as elected bodies, can be the judge of what constitutes a high crime or misdemeanor rising to the level of impeachment. Thus, impeachment, to a considerable extent, can be considered a political process. There are limits beyond which the House cannot go in initiating an impeachment if there is any hope for a conviction. After all, to convict in the Senate requires a two-thirds vote and that won't happen unless a considerable number of senators from the president's party are convinced to go along. Of course, as we shall see in the case of the impeachment of Bill Clinton, removal from office never seemed to be the intent of the congressional opposition at all. Rather impeachment, in this case, was applied, or more accurately misapplied, as a political tool.[11]

American Impeachment's English Roots

Impeachment is not a uniquely American constitutional artifact as impeachment had been a British governmental practice since the fourteenth century.[12] Impeachment was often deployed by the Parliament for partisan reasons and was seen as a practical instrument to be deployed in struggles for power. The British monarch could not be impeached, but impeachment was often used by Parliament at the behest of the king to remove and even punish political enemies. The king could order the House of Commons to initiate impeachments against anyone inside or outside the government, and then order the House of Lords to convict and punish the accused individual. The charges varied but often resembled the familiar American variant of "high crimes and misdemeanors."

Gradually, impeachment became a more formal power exercised independently by the British Parliament, with the House of Commons using the process to bring charges against a wide assortment of public and private citizens, often with little hard evidence. At times this was done to punish political enemies or in the battle between political parties. Indictments from the House of Commons were sent to the House of Lords, which had a higher standard for evidence and usually would only proceed if the case had a possibility of conviction. Often the House of Lords would disregard the House of Commons' indictment and not hold a trial at all.

English impeachment practices had many similarities to the procedure eventually written into the United States Constitution, but there were several critical differences. The English version differed markedly from the process described in the Constitution because it could be used not only against judges, royal ministers, and other government officials but also against private individuals. While the Parliament usually preferred that commoners be tried in regular courts, there were many notable exceptions, usually involving political motives. Furthermore, English impeachment convictions could result in severe punishments, whereas American impeachments can only result in removal and disqualification from office. But English impeachment practices did provide the model for impeachments that took place in the American colonial period.

Colonial Impeachment

In the absence of any way to discipline, vote out of office, or remove colonial officials, Americans under British rule impeached the king's representatives with some regularity. As early as 1635, the Virginia General Assembly attempted to impeach its governor, John Harvey. After the General Assembly charged Harvey with malfeasance, he was sent to England for trial. However, King Charles's Privy Council refused to hold a trial and sent Harvey back to continue service.

Impeachments were common in colonial Maryland, which had a bicameral legislature. Similar to the English system, the legislature in Maryland accused officials of wrongdoing in one house and tried them in the other. However, these cases were again subject to appeal to the English authorities, who often reinstated the officials. Among the other colonies to have impeachment provisions in their colonial charters were Virginia, Rhode Island, and Pennsylvania.[13]

Despite these early colonial impeachments, the British government never completely accepted their legitimacy, but also never ordered their cessation. The colonists believed that these actions were their only recourse against corrupt or abusive officials, but they were also careful not to overstep their bounds. While the colonial governments adopted much of the British model, there were several significant modifications. Impeachments in the colonies were solely used against government officials with the only punishment, subject to the approval of the Crown, being removal from office. These early cases thus set the precedent that impeachments under the U.S. Constitution are also not to be used against private individuals and do not carry a penalty beyond removal and disqualification from office.

Several other colonial governments including Pennsylvania, Massachusetts, South Carolina, and North Carolina began conducting their own impeachments with the English Privy Council as a court of appeals.[14] As the Revolutionary War neared, impeachment was increasingly used as a means of protest against colonial rule. Efforts to oust objectionable royal appointees were seen as statements of the superiority of locally controlled representative governments over the distant Crown. Some colonies further defied the homeland government by refusing to implement decisions to reinstate impeached officeholders. Most colonial governments, however, eventually relented.

The last colonial impeachment before the Revolutionary War took place in the Massachusetts colony in 1774 when Chief Justice Peter Oliver was accused of accepting an illegal payment from the king. That payment was a supplement to his salary and was paid for by the Crown. Colonists were outraged that they were to be judged by a justice in the pay of someone other than themselves (other judges refused the pay). John Adams served as one of the principal prosecutors for impeachment, a role that helped establish his revolutionary credentials. He argued that even though the money came from the Crown, the judge should be removed from office for accepting it. This case illustrated how far colonial impeachment had evolved from its origins. American impeachment had now been transformed from a method to remove a government official for blatant malfeasance into a means of making a rebellious statement. In short, impeachment in America had become a political weapon.

After independence from England was secured, the newly formed states, which had previously used impeachment, continued the practice and included similar measures in their new state constitutions. Therefore, many of the delegates to the Constitutional Convention in Philadelphia in 1787 came to the Convention with experience from their states. These delegates who were knowledgeable about the subtleties of impeachment in practice were also the individuals who took the lead in the debate.

In addition, at the time of the convention, a well-publicized impeachment case was taking place in England. Many Americans read the news accounts of this case, and it had considerable influence on the Constitution's authors. This impeachment charge was made against Warren Hastings, governor general of the East India Company, which had colonial authority over the Indian subcontinent. He was accused of having a corrupt administration and of having conducted an unauthorized war. To many, the case was viewed as a political witch hunt, a punishment for unpopular policies rather than actual malfeasance. The details of the trial tantalized the American public and made the newly independent American citizenry acutely aware of the use and potential misuse of impeachment.[15]

In following the Hastings trial, the authors of the Constitution, learning from the British example, were conscious of the abuse of impeachments for partisan purposes. Hastings, who was ostensibly on trial for personal malfeasance, was actually the subject of a political debate (orchestrated by Edmund Burke) over the policies of colonial administration in India.[16] Requiring a two-thirds vote in the Senate for conviction was a protection against that problem. But also, unlike the British system, the U.S. Constitution did not allow for the imposition of criminal or civil penalties. Hastings potentially had been facing substantial criminal penalties, and even though he was eventually acquitted, he bankrupted himself in his defense.

The Purpose of Impeachment

In order to better understand the role impeachment was supposed to play in American government, it is useful to look back at the deliberations of the Constitutional Convention of 1787 and other formative writings of the time. This convention created the basic governmental structure that remarkably still exists today and is a logical starting point for any effort to comprehend the intended purpose of impeachment. Convention proceedings were not open to the public and no official record exists, but numerous accurate reports and personal accounts of the deliberations were distributed and give valuable insights into the creation of American government and the intended function of impeachment. James Madison kept a journal of the convention, which has become one of the most valuable original sources of information on the thinking of the founders of American government.[17]

The authors of the Constitution clearly thought impeachment was a useful means of preventing high-ranking officials from abusing their authority. Like many features of the newly formed Constitution there was considerable discussion about the nature and extent of the impeachment power. During the constitutional debate, impeachment was a recurring subject that came up numerous times and went through several iterations. However, while there was some controversy over the structure of impeachment, there was little objection to including it in the final document. After all, given the fact that elected officials were allowed set terms and judges would potentially serve for life, there needed to be some method for a midterm corrective. Thus, even if impeachment hadn't existed in Britain and the states, it probably would have had to be invented.

Fortunately, as a point of reference, a variety of impeachment procedures were already in use in many states, so there was quite a bit of detailed knowledge about which features to retain and which to discard. As an essential component of checks and balances, many convention delegates were ardent supporters of impeachment. George Mason of Virginia, in particular, had an expansive view of impeachment and was instrumental in having the modifier "high crimes and misdemeanors" added to the charges of treason and bribery as a justification for impeachment. He further wanted to include "maladministration" as another charge. Mason believed that the new national government should have the means to remove incumbent officials who were grossly negligent or derelict in their duties. His underlying assumption was that blatantly inept officials could pose such a danger to the state that there had to be a means to remove them from office before the end of their terms.

While Mason contended that maladministration was a justifiable cause for removal from office and that this charge was necessary to protect the American people, others disagreed. Other delegates believed the problem with this rationale was that it was too subjective. Maladministration could be interpreted as simply performing a job poorly or even pursuing a policy that while unpopular in the short term was essential for the long-term public good. While committing a criminal or treasonous act could be proven beyond a reasonable doubt, poor performance in office was a matter of opinion. After considerable conversation, maladministration as a standard for impeachment was rejected as being too vague. Impeachment was to be reserved for criminals, traitors, and other miscreants.

Benjamin Franklin added his considerable prestige to the impeachment debate and was a strong supporter of an impeachment clause. He was quoted by Madison as saying that he believed that impeachment was absolutely necessary because it would be a deterrent to assassination! History had taught him that if there were no means to remove an incumbent before the term of the office expired, some would be tempted to use extreme measures. He believed that the impeachment power was a reasonable alternative that even at the height of emotion would be enough of an alternative to prevent violent acts.[18] Franklin's argument was unusual, but it would have made sense to a student of the founding of the Roman Republic. In the rule of empire, the only remedy for misrule would be the death of the king. Therefore, impeachment makes quite a bit of sense if public officials are to serve for set terms or even for life, as is the case with the federal judiciary or for presidents who, under the original constitution, did not face term limits. Franklin's support for impeachment all but ensured that impeachment, in some form, would be included in the new American Constitution.

Other Early Opinions on the Proper Use of Impeachment

To more fully grasp the role impeachment was intended to play in the American government, it is important to examine the contemporary writings of the individuals who were instrumental in the Constitution's ratification. The Federalist Papers are the most frequently cited source of knowledge on the thoughts of the delegates who created our government.

Impeachment is discussed in a number of these papers.[19] While these papers give a lengthy discourse on some of the more troubling concerns about impeachment, they also make clear why it was necessary to include the provision in the Constitution. On the one hand, impeachment was a most serious recourse, only to be used as a last resort. After all, the effect of conviction and removal, particularly of an elected official, was a subversion of the will of the voters. On the other hand, for judges and for officials who serve lengthy terms protected from removal in any other way, impeachment is an essential check against the abuse of power.

As noted above, the most thorough discussion of impeachment was written by Hamilton in Federalist 65. In that essay, he makes a clear distinction between impeachment and a criminal trial, not just in the procedural sense, not just in the type of charges that could be brought, but also in the fact that the target of an impeachment could still be held over for a criminal trial. Thus, impeachments become under the Constitution an essential check on the governing activities of the other branches of government by the legislature.

Hamilton, reflecting his own worries and those of others, attempted to allay grave concerns about the improper use of impeachment. In Federalist 66, Hamilton reassures the readers that the Constitution has provisions that will prevent the abuse of the impeachment power by any particular faction. He describes how the more judicious Senate will need to have a two-thirds vote before an official is convicted of any charge, saying, "As the two thirds of the Senate will be required to a condemnation, the security to innocence, from this additional circumstance will be as complete as itself can desire."[20] In Hamilton's mind, the supermajority requirement in the Senate would prevent a large, even majority, faction or party in the House from dominating the government and abusing the impeachment power.

Besides Federalist 65, in Federalist 69 Hamilton discusses impeachment specifically as one of the most significant checks on the president. In other essays, Federalist 47, for example, Madison mentions impeachment as an example of how the checks and balances would be expected to work in the new American government.

The concerns expressed in Federalist 65 leave no doubt that Hamilton worried extensively about the misuse of impeachment. His writings in this paper clearly illustrate that he had grave concerns about impeachment being used as a political weapon by factions in Congress seeking domination. Hamilton believed, however, that impeachment was absolutely necessary to protect against corruption and treason, and that the constitutional provision mandating a trial by the more judicious Senate with a two-thirds majority needed to convict was a sufficient protection.

While there were no presidential impeachments until after the Civil War, judicial impeachments in the early years of the Republic seemed to indicate what was the proper use of that power by Congress. The first ever impeachment and removal of a public official was in 1804. Prior to that time, District Judge John Pickering had been showing signs of mental deterioration for several years. The Senate voted to convict and remove Pickering for drunkenness and unlawful rulings. While drunkenness was one of the charges, it may well have been that Pickering suffered from dementia, but the Senate couldn't use that as an excuse for removal. Mere incompetence doesn't seem to qualify as a given reason for impeachment. Because Pickering had been appointed by President John Adams, Federalists still howled in protest over what they saw as a partisan prosecution, but nevertheless there seemed to be real evidence of incompetence in that case.

On the other hand, the same year there was a failed attempt to remove (Federalist) Supreme Court justice Samuel Chase from the bench. At Representative William Randolph's urging (Randolph had been a strong advocate of impeachment at the Constitutional Convention), the House adopted eight articles of impeachment, all of which were based on fairly frivolous claims.[21] Despite the fact that the Senate had more than a sufficient number of Democratic Republicans to convict, Chase was acquitted even though a majority of the Senate voted to convict on three out of eight of the charges but by less than a two-thirds vote. Being a political opponent of the administration was not, it seems, enough for a number of Democratic senators to convict.

Presidential Impeachment

The impeachment power vested in the legislative branch by the Constitution can be used against any officeholder in the executive or judicial branch. It was even briefly considered as an appropriate way for the legislative branch to remove one of its own members, but this was quickly rejected in the early years of the republic in favor of expulsion.[22] While the most frequent use of impeachment in American history has been against federal judges, its most critical and controversial uses have been against sitting presidents.

The significance of a presidential impeachment is undeniable. A successful impeachment and conviction can overturn the outcome of a legitimate presidential election, so the stakes are enormously high. A presidential impeachment grips the nation and brings into focus all the prevailing political emotions of the time. Even an effort in the House of Representatives to adopt articles of impeachment is filled with intense drama, only to be exceeded by an impeachment trial in the Senate. The spare description of impeachment in the Constitution is laid bare as trials are not conducted behind closed doors but are visible to the entire nation. Presidential impeachments therefore are not only a vital function of government; they are also a fascinating and passionate public spectacle. When they have occurred, they have been some of the most critical events in American history.

The power to impeach, convict, and remove a president from office gives Congress the potential ability to dominate the nation's chief executive *as long as Congress is strongly united in opposition to the president.* While that kind of unity in Congress is exceptionally rare, the use and even the threat of this awesome power against a sitting president has become much more common in the modern political context. With increasing partisan polarization, in the case of divided government (one party controlling the presidency and the opposite party controlling one or both chambers of Congress) it is much easier to conceive of the possibility of impeachment if not removal. It is not enough to just stand in opposition, it is tempting and quite common in the modern era to criminalize the actions of the other party. And while in a polarized political environment it is much less likely for the Senate to convict, with a two-thirds vote being required, it is much more likely for the House to impeach. Such were the conditions that led to the impeachment and trial of President Bill Clinton. The Republican House was anxious to impeach, but given the nature of the charges (which did not involve gross abuse of the power of the office) it was quite unlikely that the Senate would ever vote to convict.

In the first fifty-three years of the House of Representatives, there was not a single attempt to pass articles of impeachment against a sitting president. By the 1840s, however, as partisan divisions began to harden, some members of Congress began considering the use of impeachment as a political weapon.

The emergence of political parties and the aggressive presidency of Andrew Jackson began to create a climate wherein conflicts between the president and the leaders of Congress were more intense. Novel assertions of presidential authority over Congress with the use, for example, of the veto intensified a hostile partisan environment, which gradually resulted in serious congressional consideration of impeachment. By the mid-nineteenth century, with the rise of divisive partisan feelings in both the electorate and their congressional representatives, presidential impeachment seemed to become a more acceptable option. While an actual attempt to remove a president from office was at first more of a subtle threat than a serious possibility, as circumstances compounded partisan differences, impeachment seemed to become more likely.

The presidency of John Tyler marked the first attempt at presidential impeachment. Tyler, the tenth president of the United States, was the first vice president to assume the presidency as the result of the death in office of the president. Just weeks after he was inaugurated as president, William Henry Harrison died in 1841. Because Tyler was picked as a running mate by Harrison primarily to create regional balance on the ticket, Whig leaders were neither familiar nor comfortable with the possibility of Tyler actually serving as president. Tyler had been chosen because he, like Thomas Jefferson, James Madison, and James Monroe, was a Virginia planter. But the Virginia planters had been Democrats, in opposition to the Whigs. Therefore, to the Whigs, Tyler was suspect.[23]

While historians have mixed opinions on Tyler's performance in office, there is little doubt that he attempted to be a strong president in the mold of Andrew Jackson. But he never managed to be as popular as Jackson. The fact that Tyler managed to antagonize nearly everyone in Washington in just a couple of years meant that he was destined to serve no more than the rest of Harrison's term.[24]

Tyler antagonized Congress right from the start. A president had never died in office before, and the Constitution was ambiguous as to presidential succession. With no prior precedent, congressional leaders believed that Tyler was to be no more than a caretaker until such time as the next election. Tyler, however, interpreted the Constitution differently, believing he was the new president, with full power and authority, and he acted accordingly. He insisted on being called "Mr. President" and moved into the presidential mansion even though his detractors constantly complained that he had never been elected to the presidency. Furthermore, in his first year as president he vetoed attempts by the Whigs in Congress to reinstate a national bank (abolished by Democrat Andrew Jackson) and aggressively promoted policy objectives such as the annexation of Texas, which many Whig leaders opposed. Eventually all of his cabinet members, Harrison appointees, resigned with the exception of Daniel Webster, who stayed on as secretary of state.[25]

The filing of articles of impeachment against President Tyler took place in 1843 after his veto of a tariff bill supported by the Whigs. He was never actually accused of treason, bribery, or any other criminal behavior, but the impeachment articles accused him of corruption and misconduct. In reality, however, Tyler's actual transgression was his antagonism to the majority party in the House.

In the meantime, the Whig Party had suffered badly in the midterm election of 1842, losing almost half, sixty-nine, of its 142 seats. Consequently, the Democrats would, as of March 1843, hold a majority in the new House of Representatives. Despite their losses, the lame-duck Whigs moved quickly, and articles of impeachment were introduced during the last few months of the lame-duck congressional session as a final attack on Tyler. Clearly, this impeachment was an effort to discipline Tyler for political actions and was not in any way motivated by a desire to remove a criminal or traitor from office. Furthermore, even though the Whigs held a comfortable majority in the Senate, thirty of fifty-two, they could command nowhere near the two-thirds majority to convict. Thus, the first use of presidential impeachment was simply an exercise in raw power politics and in no way resembled the use of impeachment according to the founders' intent. After a raucous debate, the House of Representatives voted 127 to 83 against impeachment, as even many Whigs sided with Tyler.

The Tyler impeachment was the only example of an attempted presidential impeachment before the Civil War. Congress's use of the impeachment power to attempt to remove Tyler, however, set the stage for the more contentious impeachment of Andrew Johnson. The Tyler impeachment, if anything, set the precedent of an attempt by Congress to remove a president over basic policy disagreements. But it wasn't until the Johnson impeachment that a policy dispute as the basis of an impeachment fell into disrepute.

The Johnson impeachment took place under far more strained circumstances created by the lingering bitterness over the Civil War and the shocking assassination of Abraham Lincoln. Johnson, like Tyler, was never elected president, taking office on the death of a sitting president. Like Tyler, the tragedy of his succession to office tended to delegitimize Johnson's presidential authority. And, also like Tyler, Johnson's primary problem was a set of significant policy disputes with congressional leaders over matters mainly associated with Reconstruction. Johnson, however, also suffered the disadvantage of being a lifelong Democrat serving concurrently with an overwhelmingly Republican Congress. And while his impeachment has other minor similarities to the Tyler case, it was complicated by the extremely harsh feelings that were ugly remnants of the war. The Republicans in Congress were in no mood to moderate their policies of Reconstruction. What had the war been fought for, anyhow, if not to reform the South? Johnson's subversion of policies of Reconstruction, along with his evident Southern roots (regardless of his support for the Union), explains why the move against Johnson was so much more successful than the one against Tyler.

The Johnson impeachment was another example of impeachment used as a political tool. It was used by congressional leaders to try to remove an obstacle to their policy objectives, in this instance the aggressive pursuit of Reconstruction. As was the case with Tyler, there was never any hint that Johnson had committed any real criminal act or engaged in any treasonous behavior. Ostensibly, the articles of impeachment against Johnson were based primarily on his failure to abide by the recently passed Tenure of Office Act. Johnson thought that the law, which forbade him from firing his appointees, was unconstitutional. It turns out he was right.[26] Nevertheless, even if congressional leaders disagreed, this type of dispute should have been settled in the courts. But, in reality, the Tenure of Office Act was only an excuse. Congressional leaders wanted to remove Johnson from office for policy reasons. They weren't willing to give Johnson the kind of authority wielded by Lincoln, especially after the end of the war.[27] The fact was that Johnson was not Lincoln, and maybe Lincoln was the only leader who could have had the moral authority to go easy on the South. But Johnson was no Lincoln. He didn't have the stature, wasn't even elected, and was suspect because of his Democrat leanings and the fact that he was from the South. In Johnson's conduct of Reconstruction, Republican leaders could see the sacrifice of the war slipping away (and it turns out they were right). They were desperate to remove Johnson and, short of waiting until the next election, impeachment was all they had.

The articles of impeachment against Johnson passed the House of Representatives by a wide margin, despite every Democrat voting against them. The Senate trial was a battle for the votes of moderate Republicans against the Radical Republicans. With every Democratic senator voting to acquit, Johnson was successful in getting enough moderate Republican votes to avoid conviction and removal by a single vote.

The actual prospect of removing a president from office over what was obviously a policy disagreement again brought into stark contrast the intent of the Framers and the goals of the congressional leadership. While political disagreements can rise to the level of heated debate or even adjudication in the courts, impeachment is not the solution to problems that clearly do not involve criminal, negligent, or treasonous behavior. Even though Johnson was wildly unpopular in Congress and in the North, his removal from office could await the next election. Moderate Republicans who voted against impeachment realized this and allowed Johnson to continue, albeit without support in Congress and, thus, severely handicapped in office. Ultimately, Johnson, who wanted to run for president in his own right in 1868, was denied the nomination by *both* the Republican and Democratic Parties. With his political career in tatters, on the day of the inauguration, Johnson boycotted the ceremony, got in his carriage, and returned to Tennessee. It was a fitting end to an unpopular presidency.

After being dormant for over a century, presidential impeachment reemerged in the 1970s with the contentious Nixon presidency. While the proposed Nixon impeachment had some similarities to the Johnson case, it had significant differences as well. Richard Nixon is the only American president to be forced from office because of an impeachment investigation. Nixon, like Andrew Johnson, served in tumultuous times under difficult circumstances with the opposing party firmly in control of the Congress. But unlike the nineteenth-century presidential impeachment cases, Nixon had been elected first by a narrow margin and then reelected by a landslide. There was no sense that he was an illegitimate president in any way. Rather, Nixon was charged by the House Judiciary Committee with criminal acts and his fate was sealed with his own words, by the release of tape recordings of conversations in the Oval Office.[28]

Richard Nixon was the only American president to resign from office because of the political fallout from the impeachment effort, but, ironically, he was never impeached or convicted. In the Nixon case there was an actual crime: a break-in and burglary of a political party office. Nixon, however, was not a participant in the original criminal act. He did not plan it, nor was he even aware of it before it happened. Impeachment charges were brought against Nixon because he was accused of withholding crucial evidence related to the crime. Articles of impeachment were approved by the House Judiciary Committee, but Nixon resigned before the articles were even voted on by the full House of Representatives. By the time he decided to step down, Nixon knew that the articles would certainly pass the House and that two-thirds of the Senate probably would vote to convict.

But there were still those who saw the Nixon impeachment as a partisan witch hunt. As such, the episode left a bitter residue that set the stage for another impeachment years later. Bitter enmity associated with the impeachment of President Bill Clinton exists to this day and was reflected in the confirmation hearings of Supreme Court justice Brett Kavanaugh who had served on the staff of Whitewater prosecutor Kenneth Starr.[29]

The Nixon case opened a floodgate with the once unmentionable use of impeachment becoming far more plausible and more common. In some ways the Nixon hearings set a pattern for contemporary presidential impeachments. In the decades following the Nixon experience, a president was actually impeached and tried, while another president labored under its shadow and evaded it only through skillful maneuvering. During the second term of the presidency of Bill Clinton, articles of impeachment were approved by the House of Representatives and the case actually went to trial. In his second term, Ronald Reagan had to confront a scandal that burst forth with many of the same conditions that characterized Nixon's Watergate. In both cases, history seemed to be repeating itself.

Reagan had been reelected by a wide majority, just like Nixon, and he also was burdened with at least one house of Congress controlled by rival Democrats. The Iran-Contra Affair seemed enough like Watergate to prompt some journalists to refer to it as "Contragate," and while impeachment articles were introduced but never acted upon, they seemed a plausible outcome.[30] Reagan, however, handled the situation with greater political dexterity than Nixon. In addition, the national mood was much different in the 1980s than during Nixon's second term. Nevertheless, after Nixon, the Iran-Contra Affair demonstrated that presidential impeachment, even when merely implied, was now a real weapon that members of Congress were no longer afraid to use.

The presidency of Bill Clinton, however, showed that impeachment could be more than just a mere threat. Ironically, when President Clinton was impeached by the House of Representatives in 1998, some of the same circumstances that surrounded both the Nixon and Reagan cases were evident, but in reverse. Instead of a Republican president being investigated by a Democratically controlled Congress, a Democratic president was under the scrutiny of a Republican controlled House. Also, ironically, unlike Nixon and Reagan, Clinton actually was impeached and tried before the Senate, a dubious honor he shared (until the recent impeachment of President Trump) only with Andrew Johnson. Also, like Johnson, while both men were acquitted, unlike Johnson, the fate of Clinton's Senate trial was never in doubt. While the House of Representatives had a Republican majority at the time and the Senate was also firmly in the hands of the GOP but with only fifty-five votes, the Clinton defense team made sure that the trial was "spun" as a partisan affair. Consequently, as the Senate vote was largely along party lines, Clinton was easily acquitted and served out the remainder of his term. Clinton, never accused of treason or bribery, was impeached for lying under oath. While he had been investigated extensively by a special prosecutor, the only wrongdoing alleged was a charge of lying in his sworn testimony to a grand jury about an extramarital affair and obstruction of justice in trying to cover up his lie. Ironically, even with the scandal, Clinton, like Reagan, but unlike Nixon, remained popular with his supporters and a majority of the general public.

The virtually predetermined outcome of the Clinton trial made many political observers come to the conclusion that his impeachment was more of an effort to embarrass and to gain a measure of revenge against the Democrats for their actions taken against Nixon and Reagan. This case, however, clearly illustrated how impeachment has become firmly established in the modern partisan arsenal. Unlike the century that followed the Johnson case, when impeachment went dormant, impeachment has become a fact of political life in the twenty-first century.

Impeachment Today

The debate surrounding a presidential impeachment has always been characterized by high-sounding rhetoric claiming that impeachments are intended to protect the people from an incumbent who grossly and unscrupulously misuses the powers of office. Upon reflection, however, the truth is generally more complex. Almost always, presidential impeachment is driven by partisan or ideological animosity. And with increasing partisan polarization, the potential for presidential impeachment, once extremely rare, is likely today to be a recurring element of modern American politics.[31] In fact, as we will point out, polarization is likely to make impeachments at the same time more likely and less formidable.

While the founders had grave concerns that the impeachment power could be misused or abused, they still believed that impeachment was a necessary safeguard. The impeachment actions against recent American presidents clearly show that the framers' fears were not without foundation. The examples of presidential impeachment discussed above indicate that impeachment has never been used to remove an incumbent because of treachery or treason. It is abundantly clear that the most likely context for a presidential impeachment has never been overt criminal behavior, but instead has been a hostile partisan division between the president and Congress.

After the Nixon, Reagan, and Clinton experiences, it is apparent that presidential impeachment will remain a feature of American politics for the foreseeable future. The likely possibility of presidential impeachment will continue for as long as divided government, enhanced by partisan polarization, continues to be the rule. There is an irony in this situation, however. While the chances of impeachment are higher, so is the likelihood of acquittal. In a sharply divided political environment, it is that much easier to convince members of the opposition party to charge a president with malfeasance than it is to convince a significant number of senators from the president's own party to convict. Thus, while there was some concern at the Constitutional Convention that the impeachment power might be abused, it was never anticipated that the impeachment power might become irrelevant.

Throughout much of the twentieth century when presidential impeachment was dormant, single-party government, with the same party in control of both executive and legislative branches, was the norm. Presidents could reasonably expect that their party would have the majority of seats in both the House of Representatives and the Senate. Presidents typically had long coattails as voters would cast their ballots for a presidential candidate and at the same time vote for members of his party running for Congress.[32] With the luxury of unified government, presidents could expect considerable support for their agenda. These executive/legislative governing coalitions served presidents well. Even after midterm elections, when the number of congressmen and senators from the rival party could increase, presidents usually retained the backing of a majority of the members in both chambers of Congress.[33]

Voting patterns, however, began to diverge in 1968 when the Republican, Richard M. Nixon, was elected president but the Congress remained solidly Democratic. Since that time divided government has become more common than unified government.[34] Presidents can no longer expect that the executive and legislative branches will be controlled by the same party and that their agenda will be advanced by supportive congressional leaders. With divided government, presidents must anticipate that they will encounter latent hostility in Congress. This antagonism always has the potential to escalate and reach a point where members of Congress want to intimidate or even damage a presidency. As long as the American electorate continues to elect a majority of members of Congress from the rival party, the potential use of impeachment will become a more common fixture of the American political system.

An Overview of This Book

This book provides a comprehensive analysis of the politics of presidential impeachment using a sample of major cases in American history. It scrutinizes the details surrounding the impeachments of Andrew Johnson, Richard Nixon, and Bill Clinton. But the decision not to impeach is important as well. This book also examines in depth the investigation of the Iran-Contra scandal during the presidency of Ronald Reagan. Why in that case did Congress choose not to impeach? These cases suggest a conceptual framework that identifies the major contextual factors that contribute to the likelihood that a president will be impeached. In developing this framework, we will identify the occasions in which it is likely that impeachment will be used as a political weapon.

What is different about this book is that we take a social science approach to the subject of impeachment. Most other books that deal with impeachment approach the topic from a constitutional/legal or historical perspective.[35] But to the extent that impeachment is not a judicial process at all renders legal interpretations generally moot. After all, the House of Representatives is responsible for what, in form, is similar to an indictment, but it is not a judicial institution at all. It is a political institution and as then Congressman Gerald Ford once said, "An impeachable offense is whatever a majority of the House of Representatives considers it to be at a given moment in history."[36]

There have been many fine historical studies of impeachment and a number of them are cited in this book.[37] Historians typically try to uncover the details of past events and tell fascinating stories about how they occurred. This book takes a different approach. In the academic discipline of political science, scholars engage in comprehensive analysis that pairs specific political phenomena with expected political outcomes. This type of analysis goes beyond descriptive.

In presenting the data for this project, we will use a case study approach. However, our case studies are not exhaustive. They can't be, given the limits of the goals of the book. Each case of presidential impeachment, to be done right from a historical perspective, deserves its own and probably several books. What we are looking for in our cases are patterns, and for that purpose they are largely adequate. As John Gerring notes in his guide to the use of case studies in political analysis:

> A *case study* may be understood as the intensive study of a single case for the purpose of understanding a larger class of cases (a population). Case study research may incorporate several cases. However, at a certain point it will no longer be possible to investigate those cases intensively. At the point where the emphasis of a study shifts from the individual case to a sample of cases we shall say that a study is *cross-case*.[38]

Ours is a cross-case analysis.

This method of scholarship endeavors to uncover that combination of factors that produce an important political event. It seeks to explain why something happened and the primary factors that could cause it to happen again. This is an inexact science, but it does help us understand the nature of political events more fully. This type of scholarship is at the heart of the study of presidential impeachment in this book.

Chapter 2 presents an analytical framework for understanding presidential impeachments. This framework identifies the most important factors that contribute to a presidential impeachment. It then places them in a logically constructed matrix that illustrates under what conditions a presidential impeachment is most likely to occur. This matrix provides a clear and orderly way to view the political factors that are the most significant in creating the circumstances that can produce an impeachment. This type of analysis makes it possible to view all the cases of presidential impeachment in American history in a comparative manner. This contextual analysis makes it easy to see the similarities and differences in the various cases and can help the reader develop general conclusions about why presidential impeachments take place. This matrix ultimately can help answer the question: What combination of political realities create the conditions for a presidential impeachment to occur?

Chapter 3 looks at the impeachment of Andrew Johnson. Since Johnson was the first American president impeached, his impeachment proceedings set several important precedents for the use of impeachments to follow.

Chapter 4 similarly examines impeachment actions that led to the resignation of Richard Nixon. Even though he was not actually impeached, Nixon has the unenviable distinction of being the only president forced out of office because of an impeachment investigation. Additionally, the impeachment procedures of the House of Representatives are examined to see why his case was both similar and different from the other presidential impeachments in American history. This chapter also discusses why the Nixon case differed from the Johnson impeachment and created a political environment where impeachment was no longer considered an unthinkable act.

The events surrounding the Iran-Contra scandal in the presidency of Ronald Reagan are covered in chapter 5. There was never any follow up by the House leadership of articles of impeachment introduced by a small number of House members against President Reagan. This chapter explains why the impeachment pattern created by the Watergate scandal that plagued Richard Nixon was similar, but also critically different, from Iran-Contra. This chapter attempts to answer the question of why under some circumstances evidence of malfeasance can be fairly obvious but still not amount to an impeachable offense.

President Bill Clinton's impeachment is the subject of chapter 6. This chapter traces the development of President Clinton's political career and shows how it eventually led to an impeachment investigation. This chapter focuses on the ironies of the Clinton impeachment and illustrates why he became the second American president to stand trial in the Senate. It also shows how this impeachment will probably fit the paradigm of modern impeachments.

Chapter 7 synthesizes the preceding historical cases and develops a social science approach to understanding presidential impeachments. It summarizes the findings revealed by the framework presented in chapter 2 for each of the substantive cases listed above. This analysis suggests that there are certain structural and political elements necessary for an impeachment to occur. It also explains what circumstances ultimately could lead to a presidential impeachment in the future. This chapter then revisits the fears expressed by the founders about the possible misuse of impeachment and assesses the validity of their concerns. It is the case that impeachment is a potent political weapon that has become an established fixture of American politics. But perhaps impeachment is the wrong tool even if it is the only tool available to address a very real problem. Perhaps the use and abuse of impeachment reveals a weakness in a constitutional scheme that is unable to remove in any other way presidents for which the public's confidence is hopelessly lost.

Finally, we have included a postscript on the impeachment of President Trump. It now becomes clear that in adding the impeachment provision to the Constitution, framers may have gotten it wrong. Impeachment is not dangerous in its misapplication, it is dangerous in its irrelevance. Whether or not President Trump committed an impeachable offense, at the start of his trial he was no more likely to be convicted and removed than was President Clinton. If impeachment cannot realistically be imposed on the president, and if President Trump is able to advance even in part his novel argument that the Congress has no power to investigate impeachments, a significant check has been lifted on presidential power. If that were to be the case, we are likely to see an even further expansion of the imperial presidency.

CHAPTER TWO

Methods

Analyzing Presidential Impeachment

The review of American presidential impeachments in the preceding chapter illustrates how the impeachment power granted in the Constitution has been used as a political weapon. It also suggests how, after a full century of disuse, the impeachment of a president became more acceptable during the last half of the twentieth century. Historical accounts, however, only give a partial picture of political events. Presidential impeachments don't just happen. They are the result of a complex set of interrelated institutional factors that combine to produce the action. To fully understand why presidential impeachments occur, a comprehensive analysis is needed. This analysis must go beyond simply assembling facts and retelling historical accounts of the events surrounding presidential impeachments. It must scan the political landscape and recognize the key elements that produce a desire in Congress to seek to remove a president from office. It also must identify what other conditions create the belief that a presidential impeachment is a justifiable and legitimate action. A valid analysis needs to be systematic in its examination of the factors that could produce an impeachment. Such an analysis should ultimately produce a framework that can be used to assess when and under what conditions presidential impeachments are likely to occur.

Methods of Study

Political scientists utilize a variety of methods to analyze political phenomena. When examining presidential impeachments, some of these methods make sense, while others are not appropriate. Typically, political scientists make use of quantitative research that relies on large amounts of statistical data to analyze political events and behavior through elaborate mathematical testing. This methodology allows political scientists to move beyond historical accounts and to provide information on the probabilities of specific events or behaviors occurring, the specific effect of one phenomenon on another, and to create models that not only explain but predict.[1] This type of quantitative methodology, however, does not lend itself well to studying presidential impeachments. Quantitative research gathers data from observing a large number of cases and aggregating it for assessment,[2] but there have been only a handful of presidential impeachment cases in American history. This makes quantitative study of impeachments difficult.

To illustrate this point, one only needs to look at the small number and subject matter of the quantitative studies that have been done by political scientists relating to presidential impeachments. These studies can be grouped into three primary categories: studies that examine the factors that affected how individual members of Congress voted in impeachment cases,[3] the effects of public opinion on the Clinton impeachment,[4] and the effect of impeachment on subsequent elections.[5] So while quantitative research also uses statistical modeling practices that make it possible to make generalizations within broad parameters,[6] because presidential impeachments are so few in number a more suitable form of analysis is through the use of qualitative methodology.

Qualitative research that uses informed knowledge of a subject can be very useful in understanding a political institution or process.[7] Qualitative research often successfully uses comparative case studies to help conduct an effective analysis of political events. While this method of study does not produce the hard numbers of quantitative methods, it provides a more in-depth look at each case than quantitative methodology. Comparative case studies can be systematic and can provide a thoughtful and comprehensive analysis that will yield defensible conclusions. In order to produce these conclusions, however, effective case studies must go beyond the surface and uncover the consistent and systematic factors that explain why an action, such as an effort to impeach a president, took place and whether such an effort was successful. This method of study, therefore, if successfully applied, has the ability to explain why presidential impeachments have become a political tool in modern American politics.

As will be evident from the following case studies, several features of the American political system that can surround an impeachment keep reappearing in case after case. These features, which can be considered impeachment commonalities, can then be analyzed to help develop an understanding of the impeachment process. One does not expect that every commonality will be present in all cases, but recognizing which factors play a consistent role in impeachments is the first step in developing a framework for understanding the dynamics of the impeachment process.

Recognizing commonalities, however, is only the beginning of an effective analysis. There needs to be an effort to show how, when, and why these commonalities actually bring about an impeachment. An effective analysis, therefore, must go beyond merely identifying which political factors surround an impeachment and attempt to distinguish between factors that directly contribute to it and those that have no real association with it. There is no foolproof method for uncovering the linkage between factors and an event. Even statistical tests only show an association and not a causal connection. Developing an understanding of what causes what involves logical reasoning using a basic knowledge of the American political system. If the factors identified as contributing to an impeachment appear in case after case, an assumption can be made that there is a connection. Continuous co-occurrence of a condition or factor provides good evidence for drawing conclusions.

Once the most important commonalities have been identified and their potential connection to impeachment has been explained, they can be considered contributing factors and placed into a matrix chart. The matrix chart will apply all of the contributing factors to each historical example of presidential impeachment. This chart will be useful in visually illustrating the contributing factors and in showing which characteristics of the political process are most likely to create conditions favorable for an impeachment or an attempted impeachment. The contributing factors can be easily viewed and used for the creation of an overall theoretical framework for understanding presidential impeachment. Ultimately, this framework explains what factors make an impeachment more likely to happen, why the idea of presidential impeachments has become far more acceptable in the past few decades than at any other time in American history, and why most impeachment attempts are likely to fail in the Senate. In this regard, the analysis can have predictive power that can be applied to future presidencies.

Theoretical Basis for Analysis

To comprehend how the impeachment power has been used in American history and provide a comprehensive analysis of when that power is likely to be used, it is necessary to explain why presidential impeachment is now considered a legitimate political weapon and not just a constitutional check used to punish extraordinary abuses of presidential power. Constitutional scholar Keith Whittington created a valuable theoretical basis for understanding what factors can lead to a presidential impeachment.[8] He believes that while the Constitution restricts the actions of governmental officials, it simultaneously empowers them to create new strategies that can be used to pursue policy objectives. Whittington uses the impeachment power as a primary example of this practice. As was argued in chapter 1 and as was foreseen by Hamilton in Federalist 65, Whittington maintains that impeachment has evolved far beyond its original purpose of protecting the nation from traitors and criminals into a way to promote a political agenda. His investigation of the Andrew Johnson and Richard Nixon impeachment cases as well as the case of the impeachment of Supreme Court justice Samuel Chase led him to conclude that politics creates (constructs) the meaning of the Constitution. He argues that the vagueness of the wording of the Constitution enables those in positions of political power (political actors) to move beyond simply interpreting the Constitution to actually creating their own new meaning of what the Constitution means. He concluded that while the Constitution limits some political actions, it also has been shaped by politics. The concept that politics defines constitutional governmental power suggests that political factors are the key ingredient in the use and success of presidential impeachment.

The notion that presidential impeachments are the result of political factors and not a reaction to a criminal or traitorous president therefore shapes the framework for analysis developed in this chapter. In searching for an explanation of what is necessary for a presidential impeachment to happen, this chapter's focus is on identifying the political forces that are the primary contributors to an impeachment. The contributing factors of an impeachment are not to be found in historical/legal volumes or accounts of the original intent of the framers, but in the characteristics of the American political system. Some of these factors can be traced to the origins of American government, but many have evolved over time. While some factors are a product of the political environment of a specific time in American history, many are enduring characteristics that are integral parts of American politics. By examining the major cases of presidential impeachment, this book's analysis will show which political realities fit only a particular case and which reoccur and are continuous features of the impeachment process. The book will also show that while the use of impeachment is a political weapon, the removal of presidents from office through this power is very unlikely.

As previously stated, every event in American politics has unique elements, but some patterns of conditions and circumstances that can potentially lead to impeachments are visible. The comprehensive analysis of presidential impeachment that will be used in this book, therefore, will first identify the major factors in the American political process that contribute to the possibility of an impeachment taking place. While a complex combination of factors can influence the possibility of an impeachment, our analysis strives to focus on the most significant and influential factors. The identification of these factors enables the development of a framework for understanding the sequence of events that typically impact the likelihood of the initiation of an impeachment occurring. Unlike the hard sciences, there are no universal laws to explain political events, but a comprehensive analysis, if done thoughtfully, can have predictive power and help explain the conditions that could increase the likelihood of a future presidential impeachment. This allows us to move beyond simple historical accounts of presidential impeachments and to derive a model that can have predictive power, one of the primary goals of scientific research.

Factors Potentially Influencing the Likelihood of a Presidential Impeachment

The following aspects of the American political system can be considered potential contributing factors to a presidential impeachment. Each is examined in detail to show why it can contribute to a presidential impeachment.

Potential Impeachment Contributing Factors

1. Divided Government

2. Ideological Distance between Congress and the President

3. Time of National Crisis/Social Upheaval

4. Personal Animosity between the President and Congressional Leaders

5. Presidential Popularity

6. Presidents in Their Final Term

7. Accused of Criminal Behavior—Actual

8. Accused of Illegal Behavior—Procedural

9. Accused of Illegal Behavior—Political

Divided Government, Political Ideology, and Ideological Distance

Political scientists use the term "divided government" to refer to instances in which one political party controls the presidency and the opposite party controls Congress. The opposite, when the same political party controls both the legislative and executive branch, denotes unified government. Sometimes, however, there are instances in which one political party controls the presidency and one chamber of Congress, while the opposite party controls the other chamber of Congress, known as quasi-divided government. Because this book asserts that impeachment is the result of political forces, it is important to consider party control of these institutions as this will play a large role in shaping the political landscape and relations between Congress and the president that may impact the use and success of impeachment. Additionally, because each chamber of Congress plays a different role in the impeachment process, knowing whether the chamber is of the party of the president is a crucial factor that will impact the potential success of the impeachment process in each chamber.

The study of divided government has been an important topic of consideration for political scientists as divided government has become the norm, not the exception, in modern American governance. However, Joel Silbey points out that in forty-four of sixty elections between 1832 and 1952, 73 percent of the time, the same political party controlled both the presidency and both houses of Congress.[9] Since the beginning of the modern presidency under Franklin Roosevelt in 1936, divided government has occurred in forty of the eighty-two years (48.7%). More startling is that, since 1970, divided and quasi-divided government has occurred in thirty-three of the forty-eight years (68.75%). This provides more opportunities in which the president and Congress will have differing policy positions. But partisan differences are only the beginning of potential differences between the president and Congress that may lead to the use of the impeachment power. Leroy Rieselbach adds that policy gridlock may be traced to divided government, leading to only moderate legislation, an inadequate solution to the problems of the day. Interestingly enough, however, a study by David Mayhew of the period from 1947 to 1990 indicates that this may not always be the case. He states that about as many major pieces of legislation have evolved under divided control as during unified control.[10] However, the nature of divided government would make removal of a current president unlikely, given the needed sixty-seven yes votes in the Senate.

Casual observers of American politics often think that partisanship and political ideology are synonymous, but they are not one and the same. Partisanship refers to a psychological connection to a particular political party, while political ideology is a consistent set of ideas and beliefs surrounding politics and public policy. Common partisan identifications in the United States are Republican or Democrat, while the most common ideologies include conservatives and liberals. However, a partisan may identify as Republican or Democrat while having a conservative or liberal ideology, but a Republican is not necessarily a conservative, nor is a Democrat necessarily a liberal. Throughout American history, the two major parties have shifted their ideological beliefs, causing voters to change their partisan affiliations in order to maintain their ideological and policy preferences. However, since a realignment of the two major parties after the civil rights movement of the 1960s, Republicans have been the brand of conservatism while Democrats have been the face of liberalism, leading to the seemingly synonymous nature of partisanship and ideology.

Because ideology and partisanship are not the same, divided government provides only a partial picture of the policy differences between presidents and Congress that may lead to an impeachment. Divided government will certainly lead to disagreements between the branches if for no other reason than "winning" and "losing" has meaning in the political context in and of itself. But understanding the ideological differences between the parties and the depth of those differences helps to further our understanding of the conditions that can provoke the use of the impeachment option.

Political scientists have developed measures of ideology on a liberal-conservative spectrum to help pinpoint the exact ideological preferences of presidents, Congress, and individual members of Congress. The most widely used measure, developed by Keith Poole and Howard Rosenthal, ranges from −1 to 1, where a move toward −1 represents a more liberal actor and a move toward 1 represents a more conservative actor, while actors around 0 are considered moderates. The use of such measures allows political scientists to measure the exact ideological distance between actors, or, said differently, the extent to which actors are ideologically opposed.[11]

This measure provides unique insight into the ideological landscape of the political world of American government. Poole and Rosenthal report that since the 1970s there has been a continually increasing gap in the ideological distance between the two major parties in Congress. This increasing ideological polarization means that differences in views on policies of the two major parties are growing. As of the 113th Congress (2013–15) there are no Republicans whose ideology moves in a negative direction and no Democrats whose ideology moves in a positive direction. In addition, Poole and Rosenthal report that less than 10 percent of Democrats and Republicans are considered moderates, with the number continuing to decrease.[12]

An examination of each chamber of Congress will further illustrate why the increasing prevalence of divided government and growing ideological differences between the parties is an important factor in the use and the threat of the use of the impeachment option. We will also provide analysis to help understand why impeachments may be initiated but may not ultimately be successful.

Opposition in the House of Representatives

As stated above, partisanship is an undeniable characteristic of the American two-party system. Whether the majority of members of the House of Representatives belong to the same party as the president or not can influence the potential of a presidential impeachment occurring. Although the authors of the Constitution had a strong distaste for political parties and hoped the disruptive influence of "factions" would not affect the new government they were creating, political parties nevertheless emerged and have been a permanent feature of American politics since the early nineteenth century. The two-party system quickly developed because constitutional election requirements discouraged multiple parties, and for over a century and a half the division of members into two partisan groupings has been the main way of organizing authority in both the House of Representatives and the Senate. With the increase in the pervasiveness of divided government and quasi-divided government, this makes parties and party differences all the more important as it pertains to the role of each chamber in the impeachment process.

The Constitution vests all power to originate presidential impeachments in the House of Representatives. While the promoters of an impeachment action always seek bipartisan support, the reality is that an impeachment is unlikely to ever start without the firm backing of members of the majority party in the House. The party that has the most House seats will determine who serves as Speaker of the House and who will chair the various committees. Without the enthusiastic support of the House leadership it is highly unlikely that the impeachment process would ever begin. The Speaker is always from the majority party, and he or she controls the chamber's agenda. Without the support of the Speaker it is unlikely that an impeachment could progress through the chamber. Additionally, since the development of the modern committee system in Congress, an impeachment must first pass through the House Judiciary Committee before it can be considered by the entire House.[13] If the chairman of this committee, always a member of the majority party, opposes an impeachment, it probably would never get on the committee's agenda and the issue would simply disappear. Therefore, the party in the majority and thus in control of the House of Representatives' leadership and committees is a significant contributing factor to the possibility of an impeachment taking place.

The party with the most members in the House of Representatives, therefore, will have an enormous impact on the possibility of a presidential impeachment. While members of the same party in Congress may not always be united on all matters, the partisan label is still a strong indicator of a member of Congress's inclination to support or oppose an impeachment vote. Therefore, the partisan balance in the House of Representatives is vital in determining the likelihood that an impeachment effort will occur or not. Given that divided government has become the norm and not the exception, this means there will be more opportunities for Congress to be of the opposite party from the president, thereby increasing the likelihood of the use of impeachment.

In addition to the partisan makeup of Congress and divided government, it is important to consider the extent of the ideological divisions between the president and Congress. Having a party that opposes the president provides the initial motivation for invoking impeachment. But as the ideological divide between the president and Congress grows, there becomes an increasing motivation for members of the majority party to seek to remove the president. However, we distinguish between broad policy differences and differences on key policies, which will be discussed below.

Opposition in the Senate

As in the House of Representatives, party control of the United States Senate is a vital factor in the impeachment process and the increasing prevalence of divided government exacerbates the importance of this factor.

As in the House, the two-party system is firmly established in the Senate. While senators have a reputation for being more independent and less under the influence of party leaders than members of the House, party label is still one of the best indicators of a senator's voting pattern. This points back to the growing ideological differences between the two parties, even in the Senate. While the House can act on its own and approve an impeachment, the potential for conviction and removal by the Senate may influence the House's actions. In other words, members of the House might be forward thinking in considering the use of impeachment based on the partisan makeup of the Senate. The Constitution designates the Senate as the only institution that can try an impeachment. Unlike the House of Representatives, which only needs a simple majority vote to approve articles of impeachment, the Constitution requires a two-thirds vote in the Senate to convict and remove an officeholder. When examining the partisan makeup of the Senate, which party has the majority of seats is important, but of far greater importance is if that party also has a supermajority of two-thirds of the members necessary for conviction. It is for this reason that we believe that the use of the impeachment power may be invoked as a political weapon by the House, but will not likely result in conviction in the Senate, as it will be difficult to gain a supermajority in the Senate that will ultimately remove the president.

If the House approves the impeachment, the Senate must conduct the trial even if the Senate is of the opposite party of the House. Even though the Senate has no choice about holding a trial, party control of the Senate is still an important determinant. Like the House, party balance will determine who the Senate's leaders are. While not as dominating as the House leadership, the Senate leaders still have an important influence on how the trial is conducted. They can determine the type and number of witnesses, the length of arguments, and other procedural matters. The Senate leaders can greatly limit the duration of the trial if they do not favor conviction or opt to draw it out if they want to embarrass the president and maximize the possibility of conviction. The only constitutional requirements are that the senators be under oath or affirmation and that the chief justice of the U.S. Supreme Court presides over the trial.

Thus, party control of the Senate, like that of the House of Representatives, is critical in explaining the potential for a presidential impeachment. If a president belongs to the party opposite the majority of the Senate, he can expect much different treatment than if he shares the same party affiliation. Congress always finds it far easier to be harsh on presidents who belong to the opposition party, while it is much more forgiving of a president who is one of their own.

As is the case for the House, party control only provides an important first step toward determining the use and outcomes of the impeachment power. While opposition parties will follow the general trend discussed above, greater ideological difference between the president and Congress may exacerbate the dynamics of the impeachment process. When the ideological distance between the Senate and the president grows, we should expect the Senate to be more aggressive in the use of trial procedures. Said differently, not all opposition parties will be the same. There will great variance in the degree to which opposing parties disagree with the president, and the level of disagreement may impact the Senate's role in the impeachment process.

Critical Policy Differences between the President and Congressional Leaders

Regardless of the party affiliation of the president, the majority party of the House and Senate, or the ideological differences between Congress and the president, there are times when a major issue emerges that can be so divisive and emotionally charged that the leaders of Congress feel that it justifies extraordinary action. Issues of this magnitude would not be simple, routine ideological differences in policy, but are rather an expression of a profound disagreement on a matter that has far-reaching consequences. Thus, these types of issues are differentiated from the basic ideological differences discussed in the above section. Issues of this nature would be much rarer and not emerge in every presidency, but only when a new issue dimension develops that is of national importance.

A president's agenda will never be identical to that of every member of Congress. It is not unreasonable for even harsh disagreements to arise. However, if congressional leaders believe that the president is an intractable obstacle in the path of a critically important policy goal, they could be more inclined to feel that the president must go. This policy goal must generate such emotional intensity that the congressional leadership believes it justifies a disruption in the balance of power between the branches of government. The desire to accomplish this goal would need to have such power that it overwhelms the leadership's normal concern for routine matters such as passing the budget or enacting constituent-friendly legislation. A single issue or set of issues that are considered so critically important that they greatly exacerbate partisan differences between a president and congressional leaders is therefore a contributing factor to an impeachment.

Presidential Success and the Use of Impeachment

While all presidents have the same authority outlined under Article II of the Constitution, not all presidents have the same amount of power. Power refers to a person's ability to influence others so as to get them to do what he or she wants. Presidents that exert more power are, on average, going to be more successful than presidents who have less power as a result of their ability to influence others into helping achieve the president's policy agenda. In this regard, in spite of an equal playing field of authority, some presidents have been quite powerful and others have not. Political science scholars have attributed a number of factors that contribute to the amount of power that presidents possess. Some of these factors have already been discussed, such as the nature of the policy issue and relations with Congress. But other factors, such as the stage of the president's term, public opinion, and current events, such as national crises or social upheaval, can affect the president's power. Each of these factors is discussed below.

TIME OF NATIONAL CRISIS/SOCIAL UPHEAVAL

Governments must always deal with controversies, and there have been few times in American history that can be considered tranquil. There have been times, however, when American society is confronted by several destabilizing problems, and the entire nation seems to be in crisis. These times could result from economic turmoil or some other kind of calamity, such as a war, acts of terror, economic crisis, or civil insurrection. Regardless of the cause, these time periods are characterized by some type of major strain on the nation that disrupts normal societal behavior.

During times of social stress, the public could experience a sense that something is fundamentally wrong with the country and place pressure on the government to take decisive action. If these conditions persist, members of Congress could begin to feel that extreme measures are justified. Under such circumstances members of Congress, feeling frustrated with their inability to resolve the issues confronting the nation, could begin to search for ways to pacify the public. This situation could affect the likelihood of members of Congress considering presidential impeachment as a viable option. While some members of Congress could be motivated by a desire to shift blame to the president, others could honestly believe that in some undefined way the president is either symbolically associated with the turmoil or even contributing to it.

Time periods characterized by social upheaval or disturbance create a widespread sense of national unease; therefore, they could increase the possibility that the public would be more willing to support or at least to accept a presidential impeachment. Presidents virtually never cause these types of national crises, but, as head of state and unitary actor, they can be saddled with the responsibility for them. While members of Congress could be sincere in their desire to fix the problems and mend society, their hostility toward a president could increase if, despite all efforts, the national crisis continues for a prolonged period of time. This would be especially true if the crisis persisted despite presidential attempts to resolve it. If conditions actually worsened, members of Congress might start to feel that a presidential impeachment is necessary.

But not all national crises may lead to impeachment of a president as not all national crises are necessarily detrimental to the president. Some national disruptions may actually benefit the president. For example, it is said that during times of war presidential powers expand. This expansion of power may enable the president to accomplish more of his policy objectives. After the attacks on the World Trade Center on 9/11, President George W. Bush saw the highest approval rating of any president during the era of modern polling.[14] After an attack on the home soil of the country, the nation rallied around the president, thereby making a crisis into an advantage for the president. As a result, there is a strong connection between crises and the popularity of a president, which is another potential contributing factor to the use of the impeachment power by Congress.

PRESIDENTIAL POPULARITY

The public popularity of a president can have a profound impact on the possibility of an impeachment occurring and a conviction being rendered. Congress is a representative body that at least in theory reflects the will of the public. When members of Congress consider impeaching a sitting president, they always claim they are listening to the voice of the people, even if in reality their actions are based more on their own views than on the opinions of their constituents. However, the general public's attitude toward a president can potentially influence the Congress's willingness to initiate an impeachment. If members of Congress believe that the public supports and even demands the removal of the president, they are far more likely to act. If members of Congress feel the president has widespread public support, they may be far less inclined to take steps toward impeachment. Thus, there would be an inverse relationship between presidential popularity and the use of the impeachment power.

Presidential popularity is complex and has not always been easy to judge. Prior to modern polling techniques, the American people's opinion of a president's performance in office could only be roughly estimated. The views of the public on a president could be measured by reading news reports written in more professional newspapers and journals, but even the most legitimate publications were not reliable sources for determining national public opinion. Letters to the editor or editorials may reflect the more extreme views of more politically active members of the public or newspapers engaged in yellow journalism. The occurrence of large demonstrations and protests could be used as illustrations of opposition to a president, but they at best are only indications of the views of a small segment of the population and not necessarily of overall public attitudes. Therefore, before the development of random sampling survey research, measuring a president's public popularity between elections was almost impossible.

In the modern era, however, advanced polling techniques are available, and a president's popularity is continuously measured. Public approval ratings of a president's performance in office are now a fixture of American politics and can be used to further understand the reasons an impeachment occurs. Public opinion polls have become so sophisticated that their findings are normally dissected into demographic categories and policy areas. It is now common to have different questions to determine not only general approval levels but also the public's prevailing opinions on the president's performance on different policy issues. It is not surprising, for example, to see such measures of the opinion of ethnic minority males on the president's performance on economic issues. Likability rates are also frequently measured separately from performance ratings. A president could conceivably have a likeability score that differs greatly from the performance in office score.

Despite the widespread use of presidential approval polls, pundits often remark that the only poll that counts is the tally of votes cast on Election Day. Given the potential volatility in polling results, this statement seems to hold a great deal of truth. In regard to a presidential impeachment, the election that has the most significance is a midterm election. Congressional elections held between presidential elections are frequently viewed as a barometer of the public's approval of the president's performance. This notion is based on the assumption that if the public supports the president's actions, it will vote for congressional and senatorial candidates of the same party in the midterm election, commonly known as the "coattails effect." If the public is unhappy with the president, then it will vote for congressional candidates of the rival party.

Members of Congress are not just motivated by national trends, however. Richard Fenno suggests that members of Congress pay attention to the demands and nature of their constituencies as a result of their primary goal of getting reelected.[15] The abilities and characteristics of House and Senate candidates certainly affect the likelihood of their successful election to office, but local factors also influence congressional election outcomes. Local matters can attract a great deal of public interest in some congressional elections where the candidates' positions will influence the vote of some people. This means that candidates must pay attention to both national and local trends as they pertain to decisions related to impeachment. Local issues, therefore, could play a role in the outcome of midterm House and Senate elections.

Ingrained party loyalty also creates habitual voting habits that make many congressional districts predominately Republican or Democrat. Partisan voting patterns are especially evident in lower-visibility House of Representatives elections. Some congressional districts, however, have a virtually even number of Republicans and Democrats, and the votes of a relatively few swing voters can determine the outcome of elections. Which party's candidates win these "contestable" districts often determines the partisan balance in the House of Representatives. These districts often are considered the bellwether of the national public mood. If the public's mood in these districts turns against a president, it can be expected that many of them will elect representatives from the opposite party. If this happens, conditions for an impeachment improve.

Today, despite the potential influence of local issues, midterm elections are often considered presidential referendums. If, in a midterm election, candidates from the president's party lose many of the contestable seats, it is considered a public vote of no confidence in the president's policies and decisions. In early American history, these midterm elections served as a good proxy for public opinion polls. In modern American politics, if these election outcomes coincide with very low presidential approval ratings in public opinion polls, the majority in Congress could feel more emboldened to challenge a president, which could even lead them to consider an impeachment.

THE STAGE OF THE PRESIDENT'S TERM

One of the most counterintuitive notions regarding presidential power and success has to do with the stage of the president's term. Political scientists use two primary terms to describe the stage of a president's term: the honeymoon period and a lame duck. The honeymoon period is the time in the president's term just after election or reelection. Presidents are often judged by how they perform in the first one hundred days, which is typically the time period in which the president has the most power, as the president will assert that he is acting on the will of the electorate. Oddly enough, for newly elected presidents, this is also the period in which presidents have the least knowledge about the job.

The lame duck, on the other hand, is the president who has not been reelected or is serving out the final portion of their second term. Because the president is on their way out of office and a successor has already been selected, this is when presidents usually enjoy the least amount of power and success. Again, this is counterintuitive as this is also the time in which the president has the most experience in the position. Nevertheless, for members of Congress, this is usually when presidents pose the least amount of "threat" as they do not possess the political capital to accomplish goals during their presidency as the nation awaits the newly elected president.

The question then becomes, why does the stage of the president's term matter for impeachments? If you recall from chapter 1, impeachment provided a safeguard by which to remove an unsatisfactory president or a president who engaged in acts forbidden by the Constitution in the middle of their term. For presidents in the honeymoon period, it is unlikely that they would be so unpopular as to warrant impeachment efforts because they are riding the coattails of electoral victory. Additionally, for presidents who are already on their way out, the motivation for Congress to invoke the impeachment process seems very low. In instances in which elections are in the distant future, impeachment seems a more likely tool for Congress to deal with a problematic president. Thus, presidents who are past the honeymoon period and in the middle of their terms would be most likely to be subjected to impeachment, all else being equal.

There is one unique situation in American history that is worth addressing as it pertains to the president's term and places a slight caveat on the above arguments. Eight times in U.S. history the vice president of the United States has had to assume the office of the presidency because of the death of the president. In one of the most extreme examples, the vice president succeeded a president after the president died of pneumonia only thirty-one days into his presidency. In these unique circumstances, the president did not assume office under normal conditions or even sometimes by election. Being elevated to the presidency in this manner may bring into question the legitimacy of the new president and cause ideological disagreements between the president and Congress. Furthermore, while it is now commonplace for the presidential candidate to select a vice-presidential nominee of the same party, this has not always been the case.

Prior to the passage of the Twelfth Amendment of the Constitution in 1804, the person who obtained the second highest number of electoral votes earned the position of vice president of the United States. This meant that there were instances in which the vice president would not be of the same party as the president. Even after the passage of the Twelfth Amendment there were instances in which presidents selected vice presidential running mates from other parties to increase their electoral chances of victory. Republican Abraham Lincoln selected Democrat Andrew Johnson as his running mate in order to gain support in the South. This again means that a presidential successor may not enjoy the popularity of the elected president, nor have the same relations with Congress as his predecessor. Thus, presidents who assume office in this manner are more likely to be subjected to impeachment.

The Types of Accusations against the President

ACCUSED OF CRIMINAL BEHAVIOR—ACTUAL

This category encompasses behavior that would be a crime if committed by any American citizen. Theft, intentionally harming another person or their property, and other actions that would be considered serious criminal offenses fit this category. It is likely that engaging in this type of behavior would fit the Constitution's definition of a "high crime and misdemeanor." A person guilty of this type of crime would have violated a basic, universally accepted principle of behavior and would be branded a criminal in any modern national or cultural context. Impeachment would certainly be appropriate for a government officeholder accused of a crime of this nature, and, if found guilty, removal from a position of public trust would be justified. Conviction for this type of criminal activity would in fact warrant punishment beyond simple impeachment and removal from office: indeed, impeachment would be only the first step—a precursor to an actual criminal trial.

Treason and bribery are the only two offenses specifically mentioned in the Constitution as reasons for impeachment in addition to high crimes and misdemeanors. While the legal definition of treason can vary, it is generally understood to be betraying one's country by aiding a national enemy. Bribery is also a clear-cut offense defined as supporting a policy in return for some type of financial payment or reward. There was no doubt that the authors of the Constitution felt that these were inexcusable crimes and that they demanded punishment. If there was ample evidence that a public official was guilty of treason or bribery, impeachment was justified. If the official was found guilty, removal from office was necessary.

In addition to the constitutionally prescribed crimes of treason and bribery, the other high crimes are not clearly defined, but they would certainly include the deliberate taking of a human life or the outright theft of either public or private property. It is reasonable to conclude that impeachment was designed to protect the nation from a government official who committed murder or embezzled public funds for personal enrichment.

The authors of the Constitution undoubtedly hoped that the new institutions they created would attract only people of the highest character, but they also realized that men are not angels and that a person with criminal tendencies could rise to a high and influential position. During the time when the Constitution was written, violence was more common in the affairs of state. In European monarchies, political rivals were known to murder their opponents or align themselves with a foreign power in pursuit of their own ambitions. Therefore, the founders of our government, recognizing that a person capable of grossly criminal actions could gain a high governmental position, wanted to establish a way to protect the nation.

While in modern fiction authors are fond of creating stories filled with presidential intrigues and misbehavior, in reality it seems unlikely that an American president will have obvious criminal tendencies. Presumably, the vetting process for getting elected will expose the sinister peccadillos of a habitual criminal. And even if the voters willfully ignore the criminal tendencies of a candidate, the American political system seems designed to prevent a person from succeeding in criminal acts in the highest office. Nevertheless, the impeachment power is the final line of defense protecting the country from this kind of individual.

ACCUSED OF ILLEGAL BEHAVIOR—PROCEDURAL

It is important to note that public officials can commit illegal acts that, while not criminal, are, nonetheless, impeachable offenses. The law recognizes that not all illegal acts rise to the level of a crime. So that if a citizen commits a misdemeanor or even a tort, the result would be some form of punishment, usually a fine or, in the case of a civil proceeding, a payment in compensation. This is the point at which an impeachment differs from a criminal trial. The essence of what government officials do is to make and carry out the law. If an official will not carry out or subverts the law, then while that may not be a criminal offense, it could be an impeachable offense.

Modern government officeholders are subject to a wide range of complex laws that govern both their election and behavior in office. At the presidential level, violation of these procedural statutes could include a deliberate violation of an act of Congress. But for their part, presidents accused of disregarding an act of Congress could argue that they were not breaking a law but, in fact, obeying the law by disregarding an unconstitutional restriction on executive authority. The decision to impeach would then belong to Congress.

But there are many options available to Congress before this confrontation triggers an impeachment. Congress could pass legislation that presses the president to act, either through horse-trading appropriations, exchanging something the president wants in exchange for compliance, or by simply ordering the president to act in the clearest terms. Of course, such legislation in the latter case would have to pass over the president's veto. But if it did, if Congress did override the president's veto, then that would be a clear indication that there were probably enough votes to impeach in the House and for removal in the Senate.

Finally, and most likely, Congress, or some party with standing, could sue the president in court to require compliance with the law. It is often the case that the courts demur on disagreements between the executive branch and Congress, falling back on the doctrine of "political questions." But if the courts did order the president to comply with the law and the president ignored the court order, Congress would then have cause to impeach.

Thus, there are situations in which the president could act in a way that while not criminal would still be impeachable. That is why impeachment is not the same as a criminal proceeding.

Accused of Illegal Behavior—Political

In order to get and hold office, politicians have to please the voters. But, at the same time, candidates are required to follow the law. These laws can involve anything from campaign finance to patronage. Even if a candidate violates the election laws in a way that doesn't rise to the level of a criminal offense, and even if that behavior took place before the president took office, the violation could still be considered an impeachable offense.

Blatant dishonesty is an example of a political crime. Using false information in an election campaign may not be a violation of the law, but it can be considered a political crime. Candidates for public office frequently exaggerate and create their own interpretation of facts, but fabricating completely false stories that support or damage a candidate could be considered a political crime. This type of crime is typically investigated and revealed by the media, with the most critical punishment being loss of one's reputation. However, it is possible that a candidate's lies will only be found out after being elected to office. In that case impeachment is a viable option.

There are a myriad of ways a president can use the office for a political purpose. Political appointments are almost always made in exchange for some type of political favor. That is the essence of patronage, and patronage is completely legal. However, it is possible that an appointment or regulatory decision, or a presidential pardon or some other type of perk, can be offered for some kind of unethical reason. A lot of these "pay for play" decisions are prohibited under the law. But, as noted above, impeachments are not criminal proceedings. It is possible that nepotism, or exchanging a pardon for political or personal benefit, might not in the strictest sense be illegal, or there would be insufficient evidence to prove the crime in a court of law, but could still be considered an impeachable offense.

Thus, a political crime might not even be an illegal act. However, if there was evidence or at least a strong suspicion that a president was guilty of this kind of behavior, it could exacerbate the tension between Congress and the president. That could lead to the view that the person in the White House lacks good character and does not deserve to hold the highest office in the land. Thus, political crimes must be considered a contributing factor to the potential for an impeachment.

Hypotheses and Framework for Analysis

The nine potential contributing factors are arranged in the table below, which will be used to assess each example of presidential impeachment. It will be revisited in the final chapter after all the cases of presidential impeachment have been thoroughly scrutinized.

Table 2.1. Impeachment Contributing Factor Matrix

	Andrew Johnson	Richard Nixon	Ronald Reagan	Bill Clinton
Divided Government				
Ideological distance between president and Congress				
Major Personality Conflicts with Congressional Leaders				
National Crisis/ Social Upheaval				
Unpopular President				
Presidents in Their Final Term				
Accused Criminal Behavior—Actual				
Accused Illegal Behavior— Procedural				
Accused Illegal Behavior— Political				

HYPOTHESES

Now that the most important factors have been outlined in the above matrix for identifying the conditions under which impeachments may occur, the next step for the framework of analysis is to outline the expected relationship between each factor and the likelihood of impeachment. For each factor we hypothesize the following:

1. Divided Government:

   a. Impeachments will be most likely to occur under divided government, more likely to occur under quasi-divided government, and least likely to occur under unified government.

2. Ideology:

   a. The greater the ideological distance between the president and the House and the president and the Senate, the more likely an impeachment will occur.

   b. The greater the ideological distance between the two major parties, the more likely an impeachment will occur.

3. Policy Differences

   a. The presence of a major policy difference between the president and Congress on an emergent, divisive issue will increase the likelihood that an impeachment will occur.

4. National Crises and Presidential Approval

   a. National crises will generally work against sitting presidents and increase the likelihood of the use of impeachment by Congress.

   b. Presidents who are more unpopular (i.e., have lower approval ratings) will be more likely to be impeached than presidents with higher approval ratings.

5. Stage of the President's Term

   a. Presidents in the middle of their terms will be more likely to be impeached than presidents who are in the honeymoon period or are lame ducks.

6. Impeachment Charges

   a. Presidents who engage in actual criminal behavior will be more likely to be impeached.

   b. Presidents who engage in controversial procedural behavior will be less likely to be impeached.

   c. Presidents who engage in controversial political behavior will be less likely to be impeached.

In each of the case studies to follow, these contributing factors will be discussed and applied to see whether they had the predicted effect. In the last chapter, these findings will be compiled and weighted to gain a better understanding of what conditions paved the way for previous impeachments and what combination of factors would be the most likely to produce a presidential impeachment in the future. Finally, we would expect to find that the process of presidential impeachment is a political weapon and not necessarily a tool by which to remove presidents who have committed criminal, unconstitutional, or treasonous acts. Thus we will demonstrate that impeachment should not be thought of as a constitutional and legal proceeding, but more accurately as a political process, an essential component of checks and balances.

CHAPTER THREE

The Impeachment of Andrew Johnson

Our goal for this book is to analyze the impeachment of previous presidents through the lens of social science to be able to make predictions about the conditions under which future impeachments are more likely to occur. This analysis begins with the impeachment of President Andrew Johnson. The Johnson presidency was the first instance of the impeachment and trial of a sitting president. And it will be used to support our central hypothesis that impeachment is largely wielded as a political weapon when used against presidents. The Johnson impeachment represents the first point, in a larger data set, used to demonstrate a point that impeachment is often not so much a constitutional check as a process used by political opponents to weaken a president.

In 1868, the trial of President Andrew Johnson was the first time the impeachment of a president resulted in a Senate vote to determine whether a sitting president should be removed from office. While the trial fell one vote short of the two-thirds needed for conviction, the entire process closely followed the procedure described in the Constitution. The House of Representatives, by a majority vote, approved articles of impeachment, which set in motion the Senate trial presided over by the chief justice of the Supreme Court. But while there were procedural norms that were easily established, even more important was consideration of the propriety of removing a duly elected vice president from office upon assuming the presidency. As outlined in chapter 1, the power to impeach, granted by the Constitution, was intended by the framers to negate the will of the voters when certain extraordinary circumstances arise. In the case of Johnson, there certainly was the political context necessary as Congress was in the hands of a large and determined majority, the president was extremely unpopular, and because Johnson wasn't even elected as president, there was a question about his legitimacy in office. But, even so, was removal the right thing to do under the terms of the Constitution? As we will suggest, the Johnson impeachment was really about disagreements over policy. Ultimately, the subtext of those policy disagreements were so much more important than the behavior of the president in office.

The Civil War was won at a horrendous human cost, with 620,000 Americans dead and hundreds of thousands wounded. What followed was the widespread desire among many in the North to punish those in the South who were responsible. Additionally, there was also the matter of Reconstruction. Allowing Reconstruction to be subverted would be to dishonor the dead. This sentiment was evident in the U.S. Congress as many of its members wanted to adopt a harsh Reconstruction policy that would bury once and for all the antebellum South.[1]

Reconstruction contained two essential components for remaking the South: civil and voting rights for the newly freed slaves and land reform. Without both, the South would revert to form. The problem was that Southern society wasn't going to voluntarily reform itself. If such a thing was even possible, it would require an ongoing and active intervention in the South by the national government.[2]

The problem was that, as a practical matter, an extended occupation of the South by federal troops was logistically difficult and politically impossible. After the Civil War, the professional army of the United States was quite small, and its services were needed elsewhere, particularly on the frontier. During the war, the ranks of both sides were swelled by draftees who were signed for the duration of the war. The draft had always been controversial, but to draft soldiers or extend their enlistments so that they would act as an occupying army was basically out of the question.

President Lincoln recognized this and hoped that generous terms of surrender might convince Southerners to return to the Union as a changed region. But a seamless transition was going to be a stretch no matter who the president was or how great his veneration, to say nothing of the opposition he faced to leniency in both his government and even his own party.[3]

Even before President Lincoln was assassinated, a stalemate had begun to form on the issue of Reconstruction as Radical Republicans began to push back against Lincoln's plan for a lenient postwar transition. Before the end of the war, Lincoln had proposed his so-called ten percent plan, which allowed former Confederate states to be readmitted to the Union if a mere 10 percent of residents in that state pledged their loyalty to the United States. Congress refused to act on that plan but instead passed a much harsher bill of its own, the Wade-Davis Bill, which the president, in turn, vetoed.[4]

On the crucial issue of land reform, in 1862 Congress had passed, and Lincoln had signed, the Freedman's Bureau Act, which created, among other things, a provision for land redistribution. Pursuant to this law, land that had been abandoned (mainly by Confederates fleeing the Union Army) would be distributed to freed slaves in forty-acre plots, *but only until the death of the original owner* (then the land was to revert to its original heirs). Congress tried to fix the latter portion of the provision in 1865 but couldn't come to an agreement between the chambers. Later, when Johnson became president, he basically invalidated the original provision of the law by simply having administrators rule that the land had never been abandoned. Thus, land reform, and the resulting reorientation of Southern society, was stillborn.

So when President Lincoln was assassinated, a mere seven days after Robert E. Lee's surrender, it was already clear that winning the peace might be as hard as winning the war. Even Lincoln's veneration might not have been enough to carry the day. Therefore, it was inevitable that, after Lincoln died and despite a wave of good will in favor of the new president, there would be tensions between Congress and the president. And regardless of his initial support, Johnson was in the political sense no Lincoln.

Johnson's Life and Career

The political career of Andrew Johnson was one of remarkable upward mobility. His success was both a reflection of his personal abilities and a tribute to the openness of American society at a time when people from extremely humble origins could rise to high office. In fact, his upbringing was remarkably similar to that of Abraham Lincoln.[5]

Andrew Johnson was born in 1808 in Raleigh, North Carolina to an impoverished family. Johnson's father died when he was three and his destitute mother apprenticed him to his brother as a tailor. His early life was one of hard work and no formal education, but he gradually picked up basic reading and writing skills. After six years of servitude, he ran off to return home as a teenager and move his family to Greeneville, Tennessee, where he opened a small tailoring business. At age eighteen he married Eliza McCardle, a local girl who assisted him in furthering his education. He read her textbooks and she tutored him to help develop his writing abilities.

Johnson's tailor shop prospered and became a focal point for community discussion as he encouraged local students from Greeneville College to visit and discuss their classes with him. Many of the faculty and administrators of

Greeneville College at the time were abolitionists and this shaped Johnson's early thinking on the issue of slavery. He never enrolled in the college but participated in its debating society where his verbal abilities soon became apparent. He engaged students and other local community people in lively conversations on a broad range of issues as his shop became a public gathering place.

From this modest community base, he entered local politics and was elected a town alderman in 1829. After serving five years, he was elected mayor of Greeneville. His career in local government inspired Johnson to turn his attention to politics at the state level. In a remarkable path of political ascendancy, he was elected as a representative to the Tennessee legislature in 1835 and later to the state senate. He moved into national politics when he successfully ran for the U.S. House of Representatives in 1843. After serving in Congress for several terms, his district was drastically reconfigured during reapportionment and seemed far less winnable, so he decided to run for governor of Tennessee in 1853. He was elected and two years later reelected, and after completion of his second term of office, the Tennessee legislature chose him to be the state's United States senator where he served in that position through the outbreak of the Civil War.

During his early political career Johnson was supported by members of the local Whig Party, but he soon moved into the Democratic Party. His ideology fit the nineteenth-century Democratic Party emphasis on a weak central government. Johnson believed in a strict interpretation of the Constitution with, as he saw it, more authority reserved for the states. He saw the Whigs as too elitist, not serving the best interests of the small independent farmers who were his main constituency. Later in his career, this view shaped his position on slavery. He didn't oppose slavery so much on principle, but on the belief that slavery, as an institution, almost exclusively benefited an aristocracy of wealthy plantation owners. Because wealthy plantation owners made up a small portion of the population in the South, slavery was of no value to most Southern citizens. In fact, after the onset of the Civil War, Johnson made speeches advocating emancipation at the state level as a military tactic and became a Southern spokesman against slavery.

Even though Johnson remained completely loyal to the Union and spoke out for the abolishment of slavery, he was still perceived by many as a defender of the South. The fact that he was never elected president but took office only after the assassination of Abraham Lincoln only added to questions about the legitimacy of his authority. In the wake of the bloody war and Lincoln's death, the intensity of emotions in the nation was so great that Johnson's impeachment seemed an acceptable political option. As time passed, however, and the acrimony lessened, most scholars and ordinary Americans began to think of Johnson's impeachment as an abnormal event produced by an abnormal time.[6]

By the outbreak of the war, Johnson had become very prosperous; ironically, he owned several slaves, which was hypocritical considering his public stance on the issue. He later justified his ownership by saying that he purchased the slaves to preserve family units that otherwise would have been broken up were they to be bought by large commercial slave combines.[7] He eventually freed all his slaves when, during the war, he was appointed military governor of Tennessee.

In the years leading up to the Civil War, Johnson strongly opposed secession and adamantly supported the idea that the U.S. Constitution provided a solid framework for resolving disputes between the states. He believed that the issue of slavery had to be resolved within the Union, and that breaking the nation apart would be a terrible mistake. Johnson's view represented the pro-Union sentiment that was prevalent in the mountain-ous eastern region of Tennessee that was Johnson's home. This region, with its small family farms, had an identity at odds with that of many other Southern areas that had large plantations worked by vast slave populations.

Johnson's strong pro-Union views motivated him to become a leading national voice against secession. His strong desire to keep the nation unified, however, was soon overwhelmed by events in other parts of the South. In 1861, just before Tennessee seceded from the Union, Johnson helped organize a pro-Union convention in Greeneville that opposed secession, but Johnson was forced to flee to Washington after the governor of Tennessee dispatched the state militia to put down Johnson's anti-Confederacy movement.[8]

Johnson's beliefs about the importance of maintaining the Union were unique in the United States Senate. He was the only Southern senator to remain in Washington at the outbreak of the Civil War as all his Southern colleagues resigned. As the war progressed and Union forces invaded and occupied large sections of Tennessee, President Lincoln appointed Johnson military governor of the state. As military governor, Johnson helped organize regiments of soldiers, which included several African American regiments, to fight for the Union. As previously noted, while serving as governor, Johnson freed his own slaves. The following year he preceded the national govern-ment when he issued an executive order freeing all slaves in the state even though President Lincoln's Emancipation Proclamation had not technically included slaves held in Tennessee as the state was no longer considered in rebellion. Again, although not necessarily opposed to slavery in principle, Johnson made clear his belief that freedmen would be better workers than slaves, and that the end of slavery would benefit the South.

In 1864, with the presidential election approaching, Lincoln faced three problems. First, Lincoln faced a strong challenge from Democrat George McClellan. With the outcome of the war still in doubt and the nation wearying of the conflict, McClellan was running as the peace candidate. Second, Lincoln had to think what he could do to facilitate the end of the war. And, finally, he had begun to consider the integration of the Southern states back into the Union. Lincoln needed a running mate with impeccable Unionist credentials who would have appeal across party lines. Andrew Johnson seemed the perfect choice for a running mate as Johnson had the experience and had distinguished himself as a loyal Unionist in his actions as the military governor of Tennessee. Furthermore, Johnson was also a Democrat, thereby allowing Lincoln to reassure Southerners who had not completely bought into the Confederacy that reuniting with the North would not be completely to their political disadvantage. Furthermore, Johnson had experience with Reconstruction in Tennessee and had by all accounts been enormously successful.[9]

The capitulation of Atlanta in September 1864, two months before the election, sealed the fate of the Confederacy and, by association, the McClellan candidacy as well. Then, with just the non-Confederate states voting, the Lincoln-Johnson ticket won over the Democratic ticket by a substantial margin.

After the inauguration the following March, Johnson assumed the duties of vice president with no idea about the events that would soon place him in the White House. In the spring of 1865 the Civil War was ending, and Lincoln planned to implement the postwar plan that he had been working on since 1863 for reuniting the nation. Lincoln had developed a nonretaliatory amnesty plan for the South, which Johnson supported. Lincoln wanted to embrace the South and hasten its return to the Union without malice. His amnesty plan would require each of the rebellious Southern states to prohibit slavery, and then allow them to rejoin the Union and hold congressional elections after 10 percent of the number of voters who cast ballots in 1860 signed an oath of allegiance to the Union. In effect, this plan would give full citizenship, including voting rights, to former Confederate soldiers and their families if they pledged loyalty to the Union.

Five weeks after he was sworn in to his second term in office, Lincoln was assassinated on April 14. A shaken Andrew Johnson recited the oath of office in front of a small gathering and became America's seventeenth president. When Johnson took over the presidency, he soon began implementing Lincoln's amnesty plan to assimilate the former Confederate states back into the Union. Within months after the end of hostilities between the North and South, most Southern states had rejoined the newly reunified nation.

Road to Impeachment

When President Johnson was sworn in as president, Congress was adjourned and did not come back into session until December 1865. At first, upon return, it seemed that congressional Republicans were willing to cooperate and work with Johnson. His early meetings with Republican congressional leaders were cordial even if a bit tense. There was still some doubt about Johnson's commitment to the establishment of the full rights of citizenship for the former slaves. The Republicans knew that Johnson's emancipation credentials were well established, but there was more to ending slavery than just emancipation. The new president found favor particularly with moderate congressional Republicans because he supported giving voting rights to freed slaves, but only those who were literate or who owned property. His idea of the gradual establishment of civil rights for all blacks also fit the views of many (mostly moderate) Republicans.[10]

Before Congress came back into session, Johnson began to implement Lincoln's amnesty plan, and most Southern states were readmitted. They then held congressional elections in the fall of 1865. Former supporters of the Confederacy were by and large allowed to vote, but most former slaves still had no voting rights. As a result, given the makeup of the new Southern electorate, many of the candidates elected to Congress were either pre–Civil War congressional incumbents or other prominent members of the Confederacy. This result was condemned by many Republican leaders who feared that the South was returning to its antebellum roots. Johnson was also concerned that many of the newly elected members of the Southern congressional delegation were not totally committed to the Union. He made his concerns known to Southern governors, but he did nothing to overturn election results.

The troubles that Johnson would have with Congress began to emerge when the newly elected Southern congressmen arrived at the Capitol when Congress reconvened in December 1865. The Republican leadership opposed the inclusion of Southern congressmen who had served in the Confederate government or who had previously taken other anti-Union stands (which as a practical matter included almost all of the new members). Most of the members of Congress considered the Southern congressmen disloyal and not worthy of service in Congress. Many members elected from the South were not allowed to leave their state and if they arrived in Washington, the majority refused to even seat them. Johnson opposed the failure to seat newly elected members from the South, but there was nothing he could do.

Furthermore, given the size of the Republican congressional majority, Johnson's relationship with Congress became increasingly strained. After the election in 1866, the House of Representatives remained politically lopsided with 175 members of the Republican majority to only forty-seven Democrats. The Republicans, however, were divided along ideological lines into moderate and radical factions. The moderate faction wanted the immediate enfranchisement of all former slaves and the ratification of the Fourteenth Amendment. They, however, also desired the rapid reattachment of Southern states to the Union with the restoration of full rights to former Confederates once they swore allegiance to the Union.

This inclusion of voting rights for all former Confederate soldiers separated moderate Republicans from the so-called radical faction that desired a more punitive approach. The radical faction, led by such men as Congressman Thaddeus Stevens of Pennsylvania, Senator Charles Sumner of Massachusetts, and Senator Ben Wade of Ohio, had an entirely different idea of how to treat the formerly rebellious Southern states. They shared the desire to enfranchise former slaves but viewed the Southern states as conquered territory that should remain under military rule. Their opposition to restoring voting rights to any participant in the rebellion, which meant most white Southerners, was a critical issue that separated them from their more moderate Republican colleagues and the president.

The moderate Republicans, such as Senator Lyman Trumbull of Illinois and Senator William Fessenden of Maine, originally sought a working relationship with President Johnson as they believed that they could work with the new Democratic president. In 1866, Congress passed two bills concerning the South, the Freedmen's Bureau Bill and the Civil Rights Bill of 1866, and hoped that Johnson would support both. Johnson, however, found sections of both bills objectionable. The first bill established military courts for Southern civilians, which Johnson thought unconstitutional. The second bill granted immediate voting rights to all former male slaves and allowed them to testify in court and serve on juries. Johnson believed these provisions were unwise and premature and, as a result, he vetoed both bills.

The veto of the Freedmen's Bureau Bill was sustained, but the Civil Rights Bill veto was overridden. Congress later passed a modified version of the Freedmen's Bureau Bill that Johnson also vetoed, but this time that veto was also overridden. After these two vetoes, Johnson's conflict with Congress began in earnest. Johnson would eventually veto a total of twenty-nine bills, of which fifteen were overridden.[11]

While Johnson's early vetoes alienated the moderate congressional Republicans, they infuriated the radical faction. His desire to return voting rights to former supporters of the Confederacy and his opposition to the same rights for most former slaves set the stage for intense conflict with the Congress. While it was clear that Johnson believed that the assimilation of former slaves into mainstream society would eventually take place, he believed it had to be a gradual process. His continued opposition to giving former slaves full citizenship rights eventually put him at odds with virtually all congressional Republicans. His previous antislavery background became more and more irrelevant as Radical Republicans increasingly saw him as an opponent who needed to be defeated, and even more moderate Republicans began to think of him as an obstacle to their policy goals.

There are two related interpretations of what, at that point, led the House Republicans to choose the course of impeachment. The more traditional theory suggests that Johnson was faithful to Lincoln's wish that the South be integrated as quickly and seamlessly as possible back into the Union. And if that meant a delay in land reform and civil rights, so be it. The Radical Republicans, seeing the fruits of their victory slipping away, overreached in attempting to remove Johnson.[12]

We add an institutional twist to the traditional interpretation. We supply the motive and the means. As to motive, very early in his term, Johnson decided that he wanted to run for president in his own right. The problem was that there wasn't a clear path to the nomination, much less to a majority in the electoral college. It was highly unlikely that he would get the Republican nomination; he was a Democrat and a Southerner. But he also had a problem with the Democrats. He had run as a vice presidential candidate against the Democratic nominee in 1864. It was unlikely that he would get that nomination either, so he had to thread a needle.

If he could manage to reintegrate the Southern states back into the Union by 1868 on terms that would put the Democrats in control (read the old order), he might be able to grab the Democratic nomination carried by a united South.

Therefore, he went beyond going easy on the South. In his opposition to land reform, the Freedmen's Bureau, and civil rights, he not only went against the Republicans in Congress, he went against his own beliefs, which apparently were not so deeply held.

As to the means of impeachment, because for the most part the South was still not represented in Congress, and because the parties were roughly sectional (there were very few Democratic congressmen from the North), the Republicans enjoyed an unusual absence of opposition. That made impeachment all the more realistic as an option. Republicans could easily get a majority for impeachment in the House and they even had a good chance of getting enough votes to convict (the Republicans held a majority in the Senate, forty-five to nine, which was more than the two-thirds vote needed for impeachment).

The Midterm Election of 1866

The midterm election of 1866 was pivotal to President Johnson's relationship with Congress.[13] While there was a Republican majority in both congressional chambers before the election, the Republicans lacked the two-thirds' majority in both houses necessary to override all presidential vetoes, which was a critical issue during the campaign. Just as important, however, was the growing ideological split between Johnson and the Republicans. Johnson's perception of the new unified nation, with white Southerners reclaiming their rights that were at the same time being denied most former slaves, was in sharp contrast with Republican beliefs. Republicans demanded immediate voting rights for former slaves, while the radical faction of the Party went even further in demanding a punitive approach to the South, including military rule and white disenfranchisement.

Even though Johnson maintained that he supported Lincoln's plan for reconciliation and full citizenship for former Confederates in the weeks leading up to the 1866 election, events favored the Radical Republicans. There were a growing number of reported cases of white assaults on the rights and persons of former slaves by the newly reconfigured Southern state governments. These stories, which received wide publicity, seemed to confirm the Radical Republican claims, and fueled Northern voters' fears that leniency toward the South would mean a return to the old Southern pattern of racial exploitation.

The 1866 election's outcome gave the Republicans a convincing victory with at least a two-thirds majority in both houses of Congress. This not only meant that Congress could consistently override Johnson's vetoes, but it also set the stage for the eventual impeachment of the president. The Radical Republicans felt that the election had validated their position that the South needed to be punished during Reconstruction and that Andrew Johnson was an obstacle that needed to be removed. Their victories in the 1866 election made impeachment all but a certainty.

Tensions Increase as Impeachment Nears

The conflict between President Johnson and the Republican majorities in the House and Senate dramatically worsened in 1867. Johnson, aware of the increasingly partisan hostility toward him and the possibility of an impeachment, vetoed the Colorado and Nebraska statehood bills. Bringing these two new states into the Union would have undoubtedly resulted in four new Republican senators and several new Republican congressmen, which would have weakened Johnson's authority even more. In 1867, he also vetoed the first Reconstruction Bill, which would have placed the South under military rule and required that, as a precondition for readmission to the Union, the former rebellious states ratify the Fourteenth Amendment. Johnson believed this bill was unconstitutional because, in his opinion, the South had never left the Union and therefore was not a conquered territory as Radical Republicans seemed to think. His veto of the Reconstruction Bill, like so many others, was overridden by Congress. Eventually, Johnson was able to negate the effects of the Reconstruction Act through administrative action and his power as commander in chief. But what he wasn't able to stop was a number of congressional elections in the South in 1867 that resulted in the election of even more Republican congressman (Southerners who had served the Confederacy were largely excluded). Thus, in 1867 Johnson's problems with Congress only got worse.[14]

President Johnson's difficulties with a member of his own cabinet further compounded his troubles with Congress. Edwin Stanton, appointed by President Lincoln as secretary of war, had long been hostile to most of Johnson's policies. Stanton originally supported military courts for trying civilian matters in the South, which Johnson opposed, and he also favored the adoption of the Reconstruction Bill, which would divide the South into military districts. Stanton favored complete voting rights for blacks while denying voting rights for the formerly rebellious white population. On all of these issues, Stanton took a position that was in complete opposition to the president he served.

Adding to this conflict between Stanton and Johnson were belated revelations about Stanton's involvement in the 1865 trial of those accused of conspiring to murder Abraham Lincoln. Stanton, as secretary of war, oversaw the trial that followed the assassination of the Lincoln and he was intent on swift revenge. Four people were accused and eventually convicted of conspiring with John Wilkes Booth in Lincoln's death. One of the defendants, a woman named Mary Surratt, after her conviction had written a letter to President Johnson with what might have been exculpatory information related to her case. The letter never reached Johnson, and it was learned later that Stanton had withheld the letter until after Johnson had signed the warrant for her execution. This revelation outraged Johnson and gave him even more reason to want to remove Stanton from office.[15]

Johnson's anger grew as he learned of other actions taken to either deceive or discredit him. There had been rumors that some members of Congress had attempted to smear Johnson almost as soon as he took office. These rumors were later verified when reports were uncovered that two Republican congressmen had plotted to falsely implicate Johnson in the murder of President Lincoln. The congressmen had secretly contacted a defendant convicted in the Lincoln assassination trial and encouraged him to say that Johnson was somehow involved in the assassination plot. Johnson didn't learn of this congressional intrigue until two years after it occurred. The knowledge of this type of secretive activity increased his resolve to purge his administration of enemies who sought to undermine him. It became well known in 1867 that Johnson was planning to fire Stanton, setting the stage for the presidential impeachment. Johnson began searching for a replacement while at the same time Congress began to take steps to prevent him from firing any member of his cabinet.

Two men outside of Congress were critically important in the events that led to Johnson's impeachment. Both were well known and had their own base of support outside the government. Frederick Douglass and Ulysses S. Grant had developed influential public reputations in the country but for very different reasons; both were pivotal to the Johnson presidency.

Frederick Douglass was the most prominent African American citizen in the nation during the Civil War era. As a respected leader of the abolitionist movement, he had written and spoken widely against slavery and for racial equality. When he met with President Johnson a few months after Lincoln's assassination, he insisted on complete citizenship for all former slaves including voting rights. This position put him at odds with Johnson who favored voting rights only for former slaves who were literate or property owning.[16] Johnson said he supported a gradual expansion of voting rights as former slaves became more adjusted to their new freedom, but Douglass insisted on full rights immediately. Many Republicans in Congress had originally favored Johnson's position, but were convinced by Douglass's advocacy to adopt his call for immediate voting rights. Johnson later attempted to appease the increasingly hostile Congress by offering to appoint Douglass head of the Freedmen's Bureau, but Douglass turned down the appointment because of Johnson's consistent opposition to universal black suffrage.

After Lincoln's assassination, Ulysses S. Grant was probably the most popular person in the United States. Johnson believed that if he could somehow associate himself with or include Grant in his administration, his presidency would have enough popular appeal to lessen tensions with Congress (and also aid Johnson's candidacy for the presidency). Grant grew increasingly uncomfortable with what he perceived to be the president's use of his service as a prop for a political campaign. But, on the other hand, Johnson was commander in chief and Grant, who was still on active duty, was obligated to follow the president's commands. Consequently, Grant resented the fact that Johnson had used him as a political pawn.

Nevertheless, when Johnson sought to replace Stanton as secretary of war he appointed Grant, which he hoped would pacify Congress. Grant temporarily accepted the position, but as he became more aware of the hostility between Johnson and the Republicans in Congress, he wanted no part of the conflict, particularly on Johnson's side. When the Senate ordered that Stanton be reinstated, Grant resigned.[17] That decision further enhanced Grant's popularity and improved his chances of being elected president in 1868. For Johnson, however, Grant's lack of support was a disaster that paved the way for the president's impeachment by the House of Representatives.

Impeachment

The intention of the Radical Republicans became clear as early as January 1867 when the House Judiciary Committee began deliberations on the impeachment of President Johnson. This was even before the new Congress in which the Republicans achieved a net gain of twenty-nine seats (out of

174) was sworn in.[18] As stated earlier, the 1866 congressional election had elected enough new Republicans to the Congress that they had a two-thirds majority in both chambers. With their numbers strengthened, the Radical Republicans felt emboldened enough to initiate the removal of Johnson from office. The House Judiciary Committee initially drafted articles of impeachment focusing on Johnson's refusal to allow the confiscation of a railroad company from its Southern owners. They even investigated the president's finances, but to no avail. What was left were charges for which there was no actual criminal conduct.

Thus, the debate at that time, as it has been ever since, was the meaning of "high crimes and misdemeanors." Without a strong "hook" (criminal behavior or gross incompetence) on which to hang their charges, many House members were reluctant to vote for impeachment. Hence, when the articles were presented to the entire House in the late fall of 1866, they were voted down. But this did not deter the Radical Republicans who began a second effort based on Johnson's violation of the recently passed Tenure of Office Act.

The Tenure of Office Act was passed March 2, 1867 over Johnson's veto. The law was in fact passed and Johnson's veto overridden two days before the new Congress came into session. It appears that this legislation was a deliberate trap to provide legal grounds for impeachment, because it was well known that Johnson wanted to fire Secretary of War Stanton. This act would require Senate approval for the removal of any presidential appointee who had previously received Senate confirmation. The reasoning was that since the Senate confirms presidential appointments, it should have a say in their removal.[19] Johnson believed this act was unconstitutional mainly because Stanton had been appointed by Lincoln and not himself and, thus, a new president could not be bound by the choices of predecessor. The bill passed over Johnson's objections and his eventual veto.

Johnson ignored the Tenure of Office Act and on August 12, 1867 proceeded to fire Stanton, replacing him, as noted above, temporarily, with Grant. The firing occurred while Congress was in recess, but when it returned Congress immediately ordered Johnson to reinstate Stanton, which he refused to do. Grant soon realized he was in the middle of the conflict between Johnson and Congress. He was unwilling to stay in the office and returned the position to Stanton in January 1868.

Then, on February 21, Johnson, undeterred, appointed former Civil War general Lorenzo Thomas to fill Stanton's position. When Thomas informed Stanton that he was replacing him, and that Stanton should vacate his office,

Stanton locked himself in his office and refused to leave. The reaction in Congress was immediate and forceful. The Senate went into an executive session and passed a resolution ordering Stanton to retain his office, while the House began to move on a second bill of impeachment. The Radical Republicans in the House now felt they had a strong enough case and a lopsided enough majority to remove Johnson. The argument was that Johnson had willfully violated an act of Congress and had therefore engaged in an act (in the meaning of the Constitution) that justified impeachment and removal from office.

Normally, a president's refusal to enforce an act of Congress (based on the president's belief that the act was unconstitutional) would go to the courts. After all, a mere disagreement between the two branches of government is not sufficient cause for impeachment as there are other remedies. But it was clear that the majority of Congress was looking for any reason to rid themselves of Johnson.[20]

Furthermore, what made the Tenure of Office Act unusual is that it included criminal penalties for noncompliance. So what Congress had done in passing the law was to criminalize a policy disagreement between the president and Congress. Congress was obviously anticipating impeachment when it stated in Section 5 of the law that anyone acting contrary to provisions of the act either in the performance of their duties or serving in a nonapproved appointed role will "be guilty of a high misdemeanor" and subject to a fine of up $10,000 and prison sentence of up to five years.[21] It is no wonder that Grant yielded the War Department back to Stanton at the insistence of Congress (he would have faced legal sanction too) and that Johnson stood trial when he refused to accede.

The Constitution states that a "high crime or misdemeanor" is a justifiable cause for impeachment but gives no additional clarification or definition. In criminalizing the policy disagreement between Johnson and Congress over who could serve in his cabinet, Congress had made removal of Stanton an impeachable offense. The House majority felt that Johnson's violation of the Tenure of Office Act was sufficient to be considered a "high misdemeanor" in the meaning of the Constitution and a justifiable reason for impeachment. But not everyone, not even all the Republicans, agreed.

On February 24, 1868, eleven articles of impeachment were filed, eight of which were related to the Tenure of Office Act. The stage was set for the impeachment vote when the House Judiciary Committee presented the articles of impeachment to the entire House of Representatives. The debate was highly partisan with the small House Democratic minority calling it a disgraceful overreach and a majority of the Republican members strongly in support. The articles passed the full House of Representatives on March 17, 1868, by a vote of 126 to 47. Andrew Johnson then became the first American president forced to stand trial in the United States Senate for possible removal from office.[22]

The Senate trial began on March 30, 1868 and lasted several weeks. The news accounts coming out of Washington captivated the attention of the nation as the public wondered if Johnson would be convicted. The outcome of the trial was initially unknown because it was not clear at the beginning whether two-thirds of the Senators would vote for removal. There were fifty-four senators representing twenty-seven states with forty-five Republicans and only nine Democrats.[23] Thus, thirty-six votes were needed to convict (and nineteen to acquit). All the Democrats announced their intention to vote for acquittal even before the trial began. There were also three moderate Republicans who were open about their opposition to conviction, but there were thirty-five others in their party who clearly favored removal. Seven moderate Republicans, however, were undecided and held the key to conviction.

Johnson aggressively courted the undecided Republicans, hoping to prevent the two-thirds vote that could remove him from the presidency. As the trial progressed, the suspense grew, with the undecided Republicans holding Johnson's fate in their hands. Johnson's lawyers went to great lengths to extol the president's bravery during the war when he put himself in peril by accepting President Lincoln's appointment to serve as military governor of Tennessee. They also made the case that the Constitution requires grievous criminal behavior to warrant impeachment and removal and that a squabble between the Congress and the president over a cabinet appointment was far from the "high crime" necessary to justify such a conviction.[24]

Johnson's defense was aided by the efforts of Republican Senator William Fessenden who had favored a moderate approach to Reconstruction. Fessenden never liked Johnson, but here is where the potential of Senator Benjamin Wade as president made a difference. Fessenden along with other moderate Republicans had been at odds with Wade throughout the war and after.[25] It also should be noted that Fessenden was Wade's main rival and that he lost to Wade in the Senate vote for president pro-tempore.

Fessenden used his influence to help persuade six other Senate Republicans to vote for acquittal.[26] He felt that the conviction of Johnson would set a dangerous precedent that would threaten all future presidents and destroy the constitutional separation of powers. In his mind, Johnson was not a traitor nor a criminal and did not deserve to be impeached. By the time of the impeachment trial, Johnson's hopes for a presidential term in his own right had all but evaporated. He wasn't going to get the nomination from either political party. He was going to be out of office soon anyhow. Eventually, Johnson prevailed by a single vote in the Senate with Edmund Ross of Kansas casting the deciding vote.[27] Ross had been considered a radical, but he believed that he could not, in good conscience, cast a guilty vote for removing a president based only on politics.

In fact, there may have been as many as four more votes for acquittal. Any time a resolution in Congress prevails by a single vote, it is likely that there are more votes in the wings waiting to be cast if necessary.[28]

At the end of the trial in May, the group of Republicans who opposed conviction evidently knew they had enough votes, but they wanted Johnson to be acquitted by only a single vote. If Johnson won by several votes it would not have the same impact as a one-vote victory, which would send a powerful message that Congress had regained its dominance over the presidency. Some who opposed conviction, therefore, only voted to remove Johnson to keep the final margin razor thin.

The conventional view is that Ross voted on principle, that he believed that removing a president over policy differences, no matter how great, would set a dangerous precedent for the future and destroy the constitutional separation of powers.

The reality is probably a bit more nuanced. Ross had also had his differences with Wade, in this case over patronage. He saw an opportunity to gain favor with Johnson by voting for his acquittal. And, in fact, Johnson returned the favor by appointing a friend of Ross's to a federal position after the trial. Whatever the reason for his vote, Ross realized that his vote would enrage many of his constituents back home in Kansas and he never ran for office again.

President Johnson stayed in office to serve the remainder of his term and on Christmas Day, in 1868, after Ulysses Grant was elected president, he issued a general amnesty to all participants in the Confederacy.[29] The power to pardon is one of the few powers granted to the president in the Constitution that is basically unchecked. This final act of defiance toward the Republican-controlled Congress demonstrated that Johnson was undeterred by his impeachment and was still firmly committed to his views on implementing Reconstruction. With the election of Ulysses S. Grant to the White House, however, the Radical Republicans' ideas on Reconstruction prevailed for the following eight years without any interference from a disapproving president. However, the "damage" had already been done as Union troops no longer remained in most of the South and most of the states in the region had begun to return to their antebellum roots.

Impeachment Analysis

The information about the Johnson presidency discussed above provides a good case through which we can analyze presidential impeachments so as to identify patterns and contexts that increase the likelihood of an impeachment event. We demonstrate below that the Johnson impeachment fits very neatly into our institutional analysis and the framework proposed in chapter 2. Because of the Civil War and the exclusion of congressional members from the South, there was, at the end of the war, an unprecedented absence of an opposition party. While there were some doctrinal differences within the Republican Party, they were not severe enough to short-circuit the attempt to impeach, especially after Johnson decided to reincorporate the South on the easiest possible terms. However, it is a testament to the Framers' beliefs that impeachment and removal should be rare and only occur under the most extreme conditions that the Republicans couldn't muster the necessary two-thirds vote to convict in the Senate even when they held 83 percent of the seats (forty-five to nine). The Johnson impeachment demonstrates why presidential impeachments are so rare, but it also demonstrates how impeachment can be used as a political weapon. Although Republicans were not successful in their efforts to impeach Johnson, they were successful in derailing Johnson's bid for another term in office.

If we examine the metrics of impeachment provided in the matrix in chapter 2, we can see that many of the factors necessary for impeachment were present.

1. OPPOSITE PARTY CONTROL OF THE HOUSE

In chapter 2, we propose that divided government is a necessary precondition for presidential impeachments. This is the case, as we indicated in chapter 1, because the House of Representatives must pass articles of impeachment by a majority vote. Thus, it is a crucial condition of impeachment that the House be controlled by the opposite party of the president, and by a substantial margin at that. While it might seem that this is a constitutional condition, it really is a condition of political necessity.

During Lincoln's first term, the president and the majority in Congress were from the same party, a unified government. The Republican-controlled Congress acted in concert with the president. However, because Johnson as a Democrat had been brought onto the ticket primarily to form a unity coalition, we see a change to divided government just as Johnson assumed the presidency. This dynamic was accentuated by the fact that Johnson was seeking to be elected president in his own right and his path to the nomination did not include policies favored by the Republican majority.

The Republicans, for their part, were ready to cut Johnson loose. Johnson, who was from the South, was always suspect with regard to his dedication to the ideals for which the Civil War had been fought. Furthermore, as noted above, the absence of the South from Congress (to the extent that there was Southern representation, it was elected under the occupation of Union troops) added to the fact that the Republicans further expanded their majority in the midterm elections of 1866. This meant that not only did divided government exist, but that after 1867 the Republicans enjoyed essentially unchallenged unified control of both chambers of Congress.

In the United States, it is very rare for one party to have this level of control in Congress. Thus, the extreme and unusual nature of divided government in this instance created conditions that forced Johnson to maneuver on a very short leash. Despite these conditions, Johnson wanted to be president in his own right, but his path to the presidency didn't lie with a Republican Party that would certainly reject his candidacy. Johnson quickly realized that his only path to a nomination for the presidency existed within the Democratic Party; as such, he had to promote policies in line with the minority party. This created more tension with Congress.

Considering Johnson's political ambitions, his move toward the Democratic Party made perfect sense. Additionally, the Republicans' response to Johnson's policy decisions also made perfect sense. This, plus the size and motivations of the Republican Party, created the necessary conditions that would make impeachment almost inevitable. This was a House of Representatives, given the power to impeach, that was implacably hostile to and completely under the control of the party opposite that of the president.

2. OPPOSITE PARTY CONTROL OF THE SENATE

As was the case with the House, party control of the Senate was also a critical factor in the impeachment of Andrew Johnson. While the House of Representatives is responsible for adopting articles of impeachment, the

Senate is charged with conducting the impeachment trial. Thus, another necessary condition to impeach a sitting president is when that president is not from the party that controls the Senate.

The House can always adopt articles of impeachment, but without a Senate supermajority likely to vote for removal, what is the point? At the very least, without some assurance that the Senate will vote for removal, a good case can be made against impeachment in the House.

While the Senate was already controlled by the Republicans by a large margin when Johnson assumed office, the Republicans achieved an overwhelming majority in the new Congress seated in 1867. At that point, after the midterm elections, they held more than 80 percent of the seats. Given the overwhelming majority the Republicans held in the Senate, House Republicans could move on articles of impeachment with a reasonable expectation of success. Furthermore, as Johnson had no vice president, they could replace a Democrat in the presidency with a Republican, and a Radical Republican at that. However, what Republicans didn't count on was the degree to which there was still an ideological division in the Senate, regardless of their overwhelming partisan majority.

In spite of the ideological division, Republicans ultimately accomplished their political goals without setting a dangerous precedent. By the time senators voted on impeachment, Johnson's term was almost over and it was clear that he was not going to be nominated by either party. Members of Senate who wanted to vote against Johnson agreed to let him survive by one vote. In other words, while the goal of impeachment could have been removal, the larger political goals had already been accomplished, making impeachment unnecessary. The Senate had wielded this weapon to derail a presidency.

3. Critical Policy Differences between the President and Congressional Leaders

Another contributing factor to the likelihood of a presidential impeachment is the existence of critical policy differences between the president and the congressional majority. While there are always policy differences in the case of divided government, the existence of divided government alone is not enough to ensure the conditions necessary for impeachment. Often, presidents and Congress can compromise on key policy differences, and even if they can't, if the Johnson impeachment demonstrates anything it is that legitimate policy disagreements between the branches of government cannot constitute the basis for an impeachment. Presumably there will be enough members of the party opposite to the president of good will and conscience who will refuse to subvert the will of the voters. This was clearly the case with the Johnson impeachment. Even as the end of the Civil War brought with it many difficult policy issues that needed to be addressed, and even though the Republicans held a majority sufficient in both houses to impeach and remove the president, they didn't do it.

That fact highlights a central feature and perhaps weakness of impeachment under the U.S. Constitution. No matter what policy differences exist between the parties, there is an even bigger issue involved in the decision to impeach and that involves the integrity of the democratic design of our political system. Perhaps it is a flaw in the system that the only way to remove presidents before the end of their terms, short of death or incapacity, is through impeachment. What that leaves is a space between physical incapacity and criminal behavior. What is the remedy for simple incompetence? Johnson was on a course to subvert Reconstruction. What is the constitutional procedure to remedy that?

The issues that separated Johnson and the Radical Republicans were far more than mere disagreements over public policy. For the issues involving the end of the Civil War and policies of Reconstruction, time was of the essence. As Union troops began to withdraw from the South, the window of opportunity for Reconstruction began to close. Not only that, the enormity of the costs of the war weighed heavily on the consciences of all the members of Congress. Were the South to be reintegrated into the Union with no consequences, in some sense the purpose of the war would be lost. The Republicans were aware of these conditions and were forced to manufacture criminal charges against a political opponent who was undermining the goals central to the war. The Constitution provided them with no other alternative.

The historical analysis presented above demonstrates that President Johnson did not share the Radical Republican view that the South should be punished for starting the war. While President Lincoln also did not share the opinion that the South should be punished for starting the war, Johnson was not Lincoln and did not enjoy the benefit of having been popularly elected. In addition, he could not paper over his policy differences with Congress—policy differences, as noted above, that were of unusual and timely import.

In addition to crucial policy differences surrounding the Civil War and Reconstruction, Johnson and Congress also did not see eye to eye with regard to the Tenure of Office Act. Despite Congress making it clear that it did not support the removal of the secretary of war, Johnson challenged the law by removing Stanton and appointing Grant. It turns out that Johnson was right. The Tenure of Office Act was unconstitutional. He did what he thought right and so did the Republicans in Congress; in the meantime, Reconstruction failed. What was the remedy for that?

These critical policy differences strained the relationship between branches and made impeachment almost a certainty. The fact that the branches were controlled by opposite parties only accelerated the process.

4. TIME OF NATIONAL CRISIS/SOCIAL UPHEAVAL

During times of national crisis, presidents tend to enjoy higher levels of popularity among the electorate. This popularity, in turn, provides presidents with the political capital necessary to influence other branches and accomplish policy goals. However, national crises also present challenges to a president that can result in a sharp decrease in popular support in the long run and, thus, a loss of political capital. For Johnson, it was the latter of the two scenarios as a popularly elected Republican Congress saw the understudy Johnson mismanaging Reconstruction.

Perhaps, excepting the American Revolution, the Civil War was the greatest crisis in American history. The human costs of the war were staggering. Because so many families in the North and South had lost loved ones, the consequences of the war were felt on a personal level throughout American society. Consequently, policy disagreements over the Reconstruction of the South were magnified by the sense that were the causes of the war not resolved, the losses suffered would have been in vain. Furthermore, there was a very limited window of opportunity. The ranks of the Union Army had been swollen by the draft and with the end of the war came a massive demobilization. Southern soldiers went home and so did troops from the North. But the Northerners were still needed to keep order in the South. The regular army wasn't large enough, and it had responsibilities elsewhere, so the occupation of the South ended very quickly—probably, in fact, too soon.

In the absence of an occupying force, the South quickly reverted to its antebellum roots. The Republicans in Congress realized this while it was happening and believed that they had to act fast. The fact that President Johnson was uncooperative, even after he lost the ability to sustain a veto, made impeachment seem a necessity. Even though by 1868 it was very clear that Johnson would be leaving office soon anyhow, he could do a lot of damage in the interim. At that point, the Republicans in Congress believed they had no choice but to impeach (and the fact that Johnson would be replaced if removed by a Republican, a Radical Republican at that, was a bonus).

Thus, one of the greatest crises in the history of the United States was not only being mismanaged, but Johnson was squandering the opportunity to quash the antebellum South forever. This, in and of itself, was an additional crisis created by Johnson that would further the conditions necessary for impeachment. As a result, we find that the motivation for impeachment was largely political in nature, not having to do with anything but superficial constitutional and legal disagreements.

5. Personal Animosity between the President and Congressional Leaders

Another factor that can contribute to the likelihood of impeachment is personal animosity between the president and congressional leaders. This will exacerbate any existing ideological, partisan, or policy differences. In the case of Andrew Johnson, he suffered from a major deficit: he was no Abraham Lincoln. To quote from Professor Elizabeth Varon's description of Johnson:

> For the most part, historians view Andrew Johnson as the worst possible person to have served as President at the end of the American Civil War. Because of his gross incompetence in federal office and his incredible miscalculation of the extent of public support for his policies, Johnson is judged as a great failure in making a satisfying and just peace. He is viewed to have been a rigid, dictatorial racist who was unable to compromise or to accept a political reality at odds with his own ideas. Instead of forging a compromise between Radical Republicans and moderates, his actions united the opposition against him. His bullheaded opposition to the Freedmen's Bureau Bill, the Civil Rights Act of 1866, and the Fourteenth Amendment eliminated all hope of using presidential authority to affect further compromises favorable to his position. In the end, Johnson did more to extend the period of national strife than he did to heal the wounds of war.[30]

Whether or not Johnson's opposition to Reconstruction was principled is a matter of some debate and the interpretation has changed across time. In the modern interpretation of history, through the lens of modern civil rights, Johnson is seen as a racist Neanderthal. In reality, his opposition to an effective Reconstruction was simply a ploy for winning the presidency in his own right. Prior to World War II, however, through the lens of the prewar attitude toward race relations, Johnson was seen as someone committed to constitutional principles that led him to take reasonable positions on critical issues. Accordingly, this position placed him on the middle ground between extremes where he advocated moderation, or what was moderation in the context of the day. Unfortunately, his public life took place during a time that was anything but accommodating to a moderate.

Johnson's differences with the leaders of both the House and Senate, however, seem to have been based more on partisanship and ideology than on personality. There were certain members of Congress who deeply disliked Johnson, but their views undoubtedly were influenced by their opposition to issues he supported. There were no complaints from the Democrats in Congress that Johnson was inflexible or stubborn, and, in fact, many found him likable. Johnson had a reputation for having a very sociable personality tracing back to his youth in Greeneville, Tennessee. It was only in the heat of intense disagreements with other strong-willed politicians that Johnson came to be considered stubborn and oblivious to the opinions of others.

But in what was his most serious error, Johnson had alienated one of the most popular Americans of his time, Ulysses S. Grant. Grant resented the president because he believed that Johnson had abused his position as commander in chief. By using Grant as a campaign prop,[31] Johnson had thrust Grant into a role of partisan politician by appointing the general as secretary of war. Grant, who remained on active duty for most of the Johnson presidency, resented the attempts he saw on the part of Johnson to misuse his position as commander in chief—he was the only person in the country to outrank Grant—to partisan advantage.

Again, this feud is subject to interpretation. On the one hand, Johnson may have simply misread Grant's willingness to go along with the replacement of Stanton as secretary of war. But what Johnson got wrong in judging Grant may have illuminated Johnson's inability to read the character of other men. Grant's personality can best be described as linear. As a Union general he was perfect in the role because of his straightforward use of the North's general superiority in men and material to simply grind the

Southern armies down. As a person, he was faithful to his friends, faithful to his country, and faithful to the institutions in which he served, including the army. Johnson failed to read this in Grant's personality, and that was in part Johnson's undoing. Grant, who with the death of Lincoln was the most popular person in the country, was a harmful adversary for Johnson to have if the president was to have any hope of being effective in implementing his policies, much less becoming a candidate for the presidency.

Nevertheless, Johnson's impeachment cannot be attributed to personality flaws or a lack of interpersonal skills alone. As noted above, the period of Reconstruction was charged with an unusual amount of urgency and tension. Only the most consummate of politicians could have pulled Reconstruction off, and Lincoln was gone. Maybe Johnson was just thrust into a role that was beyond his capacity? In his defense, it is hard to imagine given the problems of the time who, if anyone, could have won the peace.

While personal animosity may be a factor that would increase the likelihood of impeachment occurring, it does not exist in the case of Johnson at a level that would have affected the decision to impeach. The lack of personal animosity furthers the idea that the motivation for impeachment was largely political and not personal.

6. CLIMATE OF PUBLIC ANIMOSITY TOWARD THE PRESIDENT

Today, the public's perceptions of the performance of politicians are constantly being measured by sophisticated public opinion polls published in a wide range of media outlets. As noted above, presidents who possess public support are much less likely to be impeached. And, in the modern era, on an almost daily basis we have the luxury of knowing just where the president stands in the public eye. This was not so in Andrew Johnson's day. Where Johnson stood in the public's esteem was anybody's guess and depended on how the electorate was parsed.

According to David Mayhew,[32] the primary motivation of members of Congress is to win reelection. Therefore, the act of impeaching a popular president could have negative ramifications for members seeking reelection. We would expect, then, that members of Congress would be significantly less likely to impeach popular presidents.

It is difficult, however, to accurately assess Andrew Johnson's popularity. Johnson was viciously attacked by some newspapers, but this does not conclusively show that the same views were held by most Americans. The only credible method for determining the level of public support or disapproval of Johnson's performance would be to examine election outcomes during his time in office.

Johnson was never elected to the presidency and the results of the 1864 election with Abraham Lincoln heading the ticket are not a fair barometer of Johnson's popularity with the public. People who voted for Lincoln for president had no choice but to also vote for Johnson. While Lincoln selected Johnson as his running mate for both symbolic and political reasons, there is no way to know whether Johnson's inclusion on the ticket helped Lincoln get votes. An examination of the election results provides, at best, mixed evidence. Only states not in active rebellion were able to cast electoral votes in 1864, and only Kentucky's electoral votes were won by the Democratic ticket. The Lincoln-Johnson slate, however, carried the other border states of West Virginia and Missouri, and also the reenfranchised state of Tennessee. Other than Tennessee, it is not known if having Johnson, a Unionist Southerner, on the ballot helped attract votes. With just the Northern states voting, Lincoln was reelected with 55 percent of the popular vote. Johnson, however, could not legitimately claim that he significantly contributed to the victory, and when he took over the presidency he could not assert that he held a popular mandate. Lincoln had won the election, and even though Johnson tried to be true to Lincoln's policies, he was not the "elected" president.

The outcome of the election of 1866, in which Johnson's presidency was a major issue, is a far better indicator of Johnson's public support.[33] Johnson was not on the ballot in 1866 but the entire House of Representatives was. The House of Representatives, at the time, was the only part of the national government directly elected by the people because senators were still selected by state legislatures. Only the House of Representatives at the time could claim that it was truly the peoples' House (male, nonnative people, that is).

The House of Representatives' election in 1866 is a meaningful measure of the public's approval of President Johnson's performance for several reasons. Johnson was clearly identified as a Democrat and virtually all House Democratic candidates openly opposed impeachment and supported Johnson's Reconstruction policies. In contrast, most Republican candidates espoused anti-Johnson sentiments and favored a punitive Reconstruction policy, and some openly campaigned in favor of impeaching the president. The issue of Johnson's view of Reconstruction and his personal popularity also affected the selection of senators, but voters could only directly express their opinions in their vote for House candidates. Some House races were undoubtedly affected by other local issues and the qualifications and skills of the particular candidates involved, but the conflict between Congress and Johnson was so visible that it dominated the election. The election of 1866, therefore, could be accurately considered a referendum on Johnson's performance. Voters who opposed Johnson voted for the Republican candidate and those who supported him voted for the Democrat.

The election of 1866 was disastrous for Johnson. Prior to the election, the Republicans held 134 seats in the House, but after the election their number increased to 174 seats, a net pickup of forty seats. That result is actually understated as, with the exception of Tennessee, congressmen elected from the former Confederate states who could have helped Johnson were challenged by the House leadership and prevented from taking their seats. After the election, the Republicans held a massive 77 percent majority in the House of Representatives. It was clear to anyone from these election returns that, outside of the former Confederacy, Johnson's public popularity was very low.

Johnson's low level of popularity paved the way for members of Congress to impeach him as there would be few electoral consequences for such a vote—in fact, quite the opposite. Thus, beyond a legal calculation was a political calculation by members of Congress who would be seeking election that the political climate was favorable to impeachment when the president is unpopular. Therefore, Johnson's unpopularity in most of the country played a significant role in his impeachment in 1868.[34]

7. Accused of Criminal Behavior—Actual

Chapter 1 outlined the constitutional provisions that refer to actual criminal behavior as "high crimes and misdemeanors." While the definition of what actions constitute a high crime and what actions constitute a misdemeanor is not clear, these actions can be said to have general, though not exclusive, application to actions by a president that are criminal in nature. In other words, this involves some criminal wrongdoing by the president and something that is clearly legal in nature.

Andrew Johnson was never accused of committing a real crime at any time during his presidency, with the dubious exception of the Tenure of Office Act. Additionally, during his long public career he was never tarnished by any legal scandal and there was never a hint of criminal activity in his public or private life. His personal life was exemplary. He had a reputation for being trustworthy and honest. His loyalty to the United States was beyond reproach. His steadfast refusal to support the secessionist movement in Tennessee and his firm commitment to preserving the Union demonstrated his unwavering allegiance to his country.[35] In fact, during the trial, his defense attorneys went to great lengths to extoll Johnson's patriotism and to recount how he put his own life in danger during the early days of the war by staying loyal to the Union.

Ironically, there was an unscrupulous conspiracy by a couple of congressmen early in his presidency to falsely implicate Johnson in the assassination of Abraham Lincoln. Johnson was also the victim of false accusations during the first attempt to impeach him when it was rumored that he blocked the confiscation of a Southern railroad for personal gain. In fact, Johnson took steps to prevent the railroad from being seized from its rightful owner who Johnson personally knew was pro-Union. Johnson acted because taking the railroad owner's property after the war was completely unjustified.

Johnson, therefore, was not a criminal or a traitor. He did not take bribes and had a reputation as an honest, principled man. The worst offense he was ever accused of was being intoxicated in public, including at his own inauguration, but that was hardly an impeachable offense. Since Johnson was certainly not a criminal, an interpretation of a "high crime and misdemeanor" that went far beyond the normal legal definition had to be found to justify his impeachment.

In fact, Johnson was impeached and brought to trial for committing what can be considered a procedural crime. As discussed earlier, Johnson's supposed impeachable offense was to disobey a law passed by Congress that Johnson believed was unconstitutional. Because the law was passed over the president's veto, Johnson believed he had no choice but to assert his authority in disagreement with the law. The proper course of action then would have been for Congress to go to the Supreme Court to compel Johnson to comply. If Johnson then refused to comply, an impeachment might have been appropriate. But that never happened.[36]

In the aftermath of the Johnson impeachment, it became clear that a policy disagreement between the branches does not rise to the level of a high crime or misdemeanor in the meaning of the Constitution. Policy disagreements are not just the consequence of, but the reason for, the separation of powers. But is it possible that differences between the branches can rise to the level of an impeachable offense?

One can imagine a situation in which all of the procedural steps in the relationship between the branches of government have been exhausted and the only remaining option for Congress is to impeach. For example,

Congress might well be justified to impeach if a president defies a court order (as Nixon may have done in producing a set of Oval Office tapes with an eighteen-minute gap in the recording) or possibly when the president misuses the power to pardon, a power not subject to any reversal or review, to obstruct justice. That is more than a theoretical possibility.

In other words, it is possible that our Constitution can lead us into a structural cul-de-sac, a point at which both the president and Congress are conducting themselves properly but cannot find a solution that is in the public interest. But that sort of thing happens all the time. In this case, Johnson thought the Tenure of Office Act was unconstitutional and that it certainly didn't apply to the position held by Edwin Stanton, an official he didn't even appoint. So, he ignored it.

Congress saw that they were relying on a law that had been legally adopted (over Johnson's veto). When Johnson disobeyed, they should have gone to the courts. So maybe the procedural violation in this case was on the part of Congress for deciding to impeach rather than sue.

8. Accused of Criminal Behavior—Political

While Andrew Johnson violated an act of Congress, he was never accused of crimes that could be considered *political* in nature. These kinds of crimes violate accepted standards of behavior while seeking or serving in office. They usually consist of informal principles of ethical behavior that are sometimes labeled "the rules of the game." In other words, these actions might be considered political crimes in the sense that they undermine the democratic process. As Hamilton wrote in the Federalist Papers, political crimes are "those offences which proceed from the misconduct of public men, or in other words from the abuse or violation of some public trust. They are of a nature which may with peculiar propriety be denominated *political*, as they relate chiefly to injuries done immediately to the society itself."[37]

Considering the purposes of impeachment, Johnson was never accused of engaging in unethical behavior to promote his election. He was a hard campaigner who made long and robust speeches, but he never had a reputation for dirty politics or for breaking the rules of accepted campaigning. He surely attacked his opponents and their positions, but he never was accused of blatant dishonesty, even though his opponents sometimes charged that he exaggerated and created his own interpretation of facts. He was never blamed for creating false stories to damage a rival. Considering the malicious effort to implicate him in the Lincoln assassination, one could conclude, rather, that he was the victim rather than the perpetrator of political crimes. On the contrary, congressional Republicans wanted him out of the White House for policy reasons. Thus, political crime in Johnson's case should not be considered a contributing factor to his impeachment.

Why Was Johnson Impeached?

It is our contention that Johnson was impeached as the result of a combination of factors. First, he was from the opposite party that held a majority in Congress (and then, after 1866, a supermajority), and the ideological differences between the president and Congress were profound. Second, the fact that the Republicans held such a large majority in the Senate led the leaders of the impeachment movement to believe that Johnson could be removed (to be replaced by a reliable Republican). Third, Johnson was never elected president and was, in fact, brought in from the other party, and from the South, as a unity candidate. Thus, the Republicans in Congress had no reservoir of loyalty to even the vice president chosen by Abraham Lincoln. Fourth, Johnson courted disagreements with some of the most important and powerful political figures of his time, including Secretary of War Stanton, the Republican congressional leadership, and Ulysses S. Grant. Fifth, based on the election returns of the 1866 midterm election, Johnson did not have public support as president. Finally, Johnson stood in the way of a policy goal, Reconstruction, that had a limited window of opportunity and was so important to the Republicans in Congress that they simply couldn't wait until the next election for Johnson to be out of office. Given the limited effectiveness of Reconstruction in the South, it turns out they were right.

Thus, in retrospect, the Johnson impeachment was predictable, as all these conditions coincided to increase the likelihood of impeachment. Generally, in other similar situations, it would be easier for members of Congress to just wait the president out. By 1868, it was clear that Johnson wasn't going to get either party's nomination and that he wouldn't be president by April 1869 (the inauguration of a new president was in March in those days). However, the success of Reconstruction hung in the balance and Johnson was doing everything he could to sabotage the plans of congressional Republicans. Congressional Republicans had the motive, means, and opportunity, so they acted. The fact that they didn't succeed highlighted the difficulty of ending even the most compromised presidency.

Thus, the impeachment of Andrew Johnson was largely political in nature. While the Constitution provides the procedural and legal standards for impeachment, we observe that the impeachment of Johnson was due to partisan, ideological, and policy differences, a lack of public support, and the unsettled issues left behind at the end of the Civil War. We note that there was an absence of criminal or political crimes that might have constituted the necessary requirements of a "high crime or misdemeanor" under the Constitution. Thus, the Johnson impeachment supports our contention that impeachment is largely a political matter.

In chapter 4, we continue our discussion of the politics of impeachment via the impeachment of President Richard Nixon.

CHAPTER FOUR

The Impeachment and Resignation of Richard Nixon

The presidency of Richard M. Nixon is one of the most complex and contradictory in American history. Nixon is the only president to resign from office under the threat of an impeachment. Yet he was never impeached by the House of Representatives nor convicted by the Senate. Unlike impeachment efforts in the nineteenth century that were mounted against unelected presidents, Nixon was elected by a slim margin to a first term and then reelected by lopsided majorities in both the popular and electoral vote. And yet what was most striking about the Nixon presidency was that the Watergate scandal produced a cascading series of events that led to Nixon's resignation. And that resignation occurred despite the fact that there wasn't a hint of question about the legitimacy of the Nixon presidency. Thus, the Nixon impeachment was not so much a constitutional as a political crisis.

Presidential impeachment, which had been dormant for over a century, reemerged during Nixon's second term in office. While on the surface the Nixon case bore little resemblance to any previous presidential impeachment efforts, a thorough review of the conditions that characterized Nixon's time in office shows that there are some interesting commonalities. Nixon's presidency at first seemed very unlike that of Andrew Johnson, but a careful look reveals some remarkable parallels.

Some of the same factors present in the Johnson impeachment resurfaced during Nixon's tenure. Both Nixon and Johnson served during intensely emotional times when extreme governmental actions seemed justifiable. The Vietnam War's level of carnage was devastating, and even though the number of Americans killed in it never approached that of the Civil War, Vietnam divided the country more than any other conflict in over a century. During Nixon's years in office, the country was still shaken by the assassinations of President John Kennedy, Senator Robert Kennedy, and the Reverend

Martin Luther King Jr., just as the country was in mourning for Abraham Lincoln during Johnson's presidency. And, most critically, both Nixon and Johnson were confronted by a Congress in which the overwhelming number of members were from the opposite party. This was up to this time not the norm in American politics. These and other factors suggest that a thorough analysis will help us understand why presidential impeachment so abruptly reappeared during Nixon's presidency.

Why Impeachment Resurfaced

In 1973, after Richard Nixon's impressive reelection triumph, the mere thought of a presidential impeachment seemed inconceivable. Gradually, as revelations unfolded related to what became known as the Watergate Affair, momentum built that led to the first serious attempt to remove a president from office in over a hundred years. The proximate cause of the Nixon impeachment emerged from a seemingly unrelated burglary of a Democratic Party office. The break-in attempt of the national Democratic Party headquarters in the Watergate office complex in Washington, DC, during the 1972 election eventually evolved into a national scandal.[1]

While the Watergate break-in was initially treated as an ordinary criminal case, it led to an inquiry by the FBI and a Senate committee that uncovered startling information about the possible involvement in a cover-up of the burglary by the president's Committee for the Re-election of the President (CRP). Over the course of the next few months an investigation by a special prosecutor (and a couple of intrepid reporters at the *Washington Post*) documented additional connections between the Watergate burglars and the White House itself. Furthermore, it appeared that the White House, including the president, had engaged in a separate conspiracy to obstruct justice and hide the extent of the president's involvement in the initial conspiracy to silence the Watergate burglars. Ultimately, substantial and mounting evidence of both the original cover-up and an attempt to obstruct justice was capped off and confirmed by the revelation that the president had taped his conversations in the Oval Office concerning these matters in their entirety.

The president responded by firing and thereby distancing himself from his most senior aides in the White House, H. R. Haldeman, John Ehrlichman, and John Dean. But when Special Prosecutor Archibald Cox continued to press the White House to release the actual (not redacted) recordings of Nixon's conversations, the president ordered that Cox be fired as well. Both

Attorney General Elliot Richardson and Deputy Attorney General William Ruckelshaus refused Nixon's order and resigned. Eventually Solicitor General Robert Bork carried out Nixon's orders. The act of firing Cox led to a backlash that set the formal impeachment of Richard Nixon in motion.

The "straw," as it were, that broke the camel's back was the president's firing of Archibald Cox. Nixon's interference in an investigation that was authorized by Congress has some parallels to Andrew Johnson's firing of Secretary of War Stanton in defiance of the Tenure of Office Act in 1867. In both instances, the president interfered in what was a normal and ostensibly legal process of government for no other reason than the benefit of his presidency. In Johnson's case, however, the firing took place over what was a legitimate and deeply held disagreement over the policies of Reconstruction. But in the Nixon case it was not difficult to conclude that the firing had nothing more than to do with the protection of the president from criminal prosecution and impeachment.

The House Judiciary Committee was then charged with investigating the case and ultimately recommended that the House of Representatives vote on articles of impeachment. Finally, after months of building tension between Nixon and Congress concerning the president's right to withhold information, a decision by the United States Supreme Court siding with Congress prompted President Nixon to resign.[2] By the conclusion of these events, the public's attitude toward impeachment had been unmistakably altered as a new political reality took hold.

The Watergate break-in and its subsequent cover-up were undisputedly the reasons why Nixon faced an impending impeachment vote, but there were several other contributing factors. Cultural and societal conditions that characterized the nation at the time seemed ripe for this type of controversy. The makeup of the political institutions also created an environment where impeachment was more likely. Furthermore, the fact that Richard Nixon himself had a long and often controversial political career that generated a significant amount of ill will certainly played a role in the impeachment as well. All these factors combined suggest that the impeachment effort directed against Richard Nixon was a result of more than just a simple crime.

Early Life and Career

Richard Milhous Nixon was elected the thirty-seventh president in 1968 after a long political career that included a previous presidential run in 1960 and eight years as vice president from 1952 to 1960. He had earlier served in both the House of Representatives and the Senate. His campaign in 1968 dubbed him the "New Nixon," but his long political career and experiences shaped and molded not only his policies and worldview but also his future.[3]

Richard Nixon was born in Yorba Linda, California, in 1913, into a Quaker family of modest means. He developed a strong work ethic during his childhood, which he described as stern but with a loving family.[4] Yorba Linda was a small agricultural town about thirty miles east of Los Angeles. The Nixon family eventually moved to neighboring Whittier where Nixon's father opened a small store. Tragedy struck his family when first his younger brother and then, some years later, his older brother died. His older brother succumbed to a lingering case of tuberculosis, which drained the family both emotionally and financially. Young Richard Nixon was always an excellent student and won a scholarship to attend Harvard University, but his family could not afford the related expenses, so he chose to remain at home and attend nearby Whittier College. While in college, he continued to excel in his studies, but also found time to become active in student politics and participate in the drama club and football. After graduation he attended Duke University Law School where he graduated third in his class.

After receiving his law degree, he returned home and joined a small local law firm. He continued his interest in drama with community theaters, and while in a local play, he met his future wife, Thelma "Pat" Ryan. They married in 1940 and eventually had two daughters, Julie and Tricia. In 1942 he took a position with the federal Office of Price Administration and moved with his wife to Washington, DC, but later enlisted in the Navy. He served as a naval officer in the Pacific and returned to Whittier after the end of the Second World War. It was at this time that his political career began.

Nixon's early political career was marked by an uninterrupted string of successes. He entered political life in 1946 as the Republican nominee for the Whittier area congressional seat. He challenged incumbent Democrat Jerry Voorhis, who had represented the Republican-leaning 12th Congressional District for five terms. Nixon conducted a tenacious campaign in which he presented himself as a strong anticommunist and suggested that Voorhis had connections to communist-leaning organizations. In a series of debates Nixon consistently outperformed Voorhis. Nixon rode the strong Republican wave of 1946 to an upset victory. He was reelected unopposed in 1948.

While in the House of Representatives, Nixon developed a reputation as a vehement anticommunist. During this time of heightened national concern about the Soviet Union's aggression in Eastern Europe and the spread of international communism, Nixon was selected to serve on the House

Un-American Activities Committee (HUAC). This committee, which had authority to investigate cases of treasonous breaches of national security, gave Nixon national visibility. The committee's most notable case was an investigation of Alger Hiss, a former State Department official and president of the Carnegie Endowment for International Peace. Hiss was accused of being a Communist and of giving national security information to agents of the Soviet Union. Whittaker Chambers, a former Communist Party member, testified before the committee that Hiss had been a Communist Party member, a charge that Hiss denied. Nixon, however, had been given incriminating evidence in secret from the FBI that convinced him that Hiss was lying, so he doggedly pursued the investigation. Nixon was appointed the chairman of a subcommittee that questioned Hiss and Chambers about their association. Chambers eventually admitted to espionage and implicated Hiss in his plot to give secret State Department information to the Soviet Union. Hiss admitted that he may have had contact with Chambers, but he continued to vehemently deny any involvement in Communist activity or espionage. Hiss was eventually convicted of perjury, but he continued to proclaim his innocence throughout his life.[5]

The Hiss case was highly controversial, and many thought it a witch hunt in an era that became known as the Red Scare. The case was headline news and Nixon was constantly portrayed as an anticommunist crusader. Nixon, however, felt that he was also unfairly labeled as a witch hunter and that this adversely affected his later political career. Nixon's aggressive pursuit of Hiss antagonized many liberals who related to Hiss as one of their own. Nixon also felt, with some justification, that his role in the case alienated many members of the eastern-based media who believed Hiss was innocent. Regardless of the political fallout, the Hiss case certainly affected Nixon's understanding of news leaks, the role of the media, and the internal operation of the Justice Department and FBI. The Hiss case was a double-edged sword for Nixon. While it may have branded him as a red baiter and earned him the resentment of eastern liberals, the publicity from the case gave Nixon a respected national reputation.

In 1950, Nixon decided to forego reelection to the House to instead seek California's open U.S. Senate seat. The reputation Nixon had earned during the Hiss case gave him a distinct advantage in this race. Nixon was the only major Republican candidate to seek the seat as other potential Republican candidates felt they could not match his public appeal. His Democratic rival in the general election was Congresswoman Helen Gahagan Douglas, the wife of the well-known actor Melvyn Douglas. She had prevailed in a contentious primary in which her opponent accused her of being too left wing even within the confines of the Democratic Party. The election took place just as the Korean War broke out, and Nixon was able to take advantage of the situation by accentuating Douglas's weakened position in her own party and her far left liberal credentials. The campaign was bitter and polarizing and soon became very personal, with both candidates vigorously assaulting each other's character. It was at this time that the derogatory name "Tricky Dick" first appeared in a newspaper story. Again, Nixon was able to successfully question the anticommunist commitment of his rival and portray himself as a staunch defender of American values. This strategy again helped him win a substantial victory. After the bruising campaign, Nixon was victorious, earning 59 percent of the vote.

Presidential Election of 1960

By 1960, it was assumed that Richard Nixon would run for the Republican presidential nomination. After two full terms as vice president, Nixon had amassed a significant amount of executive experience that far exceeded that of any other Republican rival. It was assumed also that Nixon would get the incumbent president's endorsement. At times during the preceding eight years it appeared to many American voters that Nixon was already president. Because of his expanded duties due to President Dwight Eisenhower's health problems, Nixon had in some sense already been entrusted with the powers of the presidency.

The outcome of the 1960 presidential election was one of the closest in history. In the popular vote Kennedy prevailed by the incredibly narrow margin of 49.7 percent to 49.6 percent, with only a little more than a hundred thousand votes separating the two candidates out of over sixty-eight million votes cast. Kennedy's victory margin, however, was greater in the electoral college where he won by 303 to 219 votes by carrying large eastern states plus Texas and Illinois. Nixon carried the West and the Midwest, but that was insufficient to offset Kennedy's advantage in traditionally Democratic states. Kennedy's selection of Lyndon Johnson as his running mate secured Texas's votes and results from the Chicago Democratic political machine helped place Illinois in the Democratic column. There were some reports of voter fraud in both these states, but Nixon resisted the urging of some of his supporters to request a recount. Nixon felt that demanding a recount would portray him as a spoilsport and could only serve to delegitimize America's democratic institutions.[6]

As Kennedy settled into the presidency, Nixon and his family returned to California and took up residence in Los Angeles where he resumed the practice of law. Nixon believed that his political career was far from over and when California Republican Party leaders suggested that he consider running for governor in 1962, he accepted. Being governor of California would give him a strong base of support from which he could run against Kennedy again in 1964. Even though California had a popular Democratic incumbent governor, Edmond G. "Pat" Brown, running for reelection, the state had been a Republican stronghold that had elected Nixon to the Senate twelve years earlier and supported him in the 1960 presidential election. Unfortunately for Nixon, several unexpected obstacles blocked his path back to elected office.

On election night, Brown received 52 percent of the vote, dashing Nixon's hopes for a political comeback. In the aftermath of the campaign, Nixon held what seemed like his last news conference in which he was quoted as bitterly warning the press that it would not have Nixon "to kick around anymore."

Road Back to the Presidency

After the gubernatorial election defeat, Nixon left California to practice law in New York, and it seemed for a time that he had retired from politics. Nixon, however, felt that his destiny had not yet been fulfilled, so he gradually started to reenter politics. After all, even though he had already held the second highest office in American government, he was only fifty years old with ample time to try again for the White House. While working at a prestigious New York law firm, he met several people who would be influential in his eventual return to political life. John Mitchell, another attorney in his firm, had a strong and controlling personality that impressed Nixon, and they developed a bond that would later make Mitchell an important player in Nixon's renewed efforts to seek the presidency. During this time, Nixon also wrote articles in newspapers and magazines expressing his views on a wide range of important issues. These articles enabled him to remain in the public view even though he held no office. His most important political activity during his hiatus from office, however, was his extensive involvement in campaigning on behalf of other Republican candidates.

Nixon believed that the 1964 presidential election was too soon to attempt a political comeback.[7] His gubernatorial defeat was too recent, and he thought it best to avoid the infighting that was engulfing the Republicans. The Republican Party in 1964 was badly split between the eastern business establishment and the more culturally conservative voters in the West. The West won and Barry Goldwater, the outspoken libertarian senator from Arizona, became the party's presidential nominee.

The Democrats nominated Lyndon Johnson, the now incumbent president who pledged to continue and expand the agenda of the late President Kennedy. This approach had widespread appeal. In the November election Goldwater and a large number of Republicans in Congress suffered a massive defeat. With the Democratic ticket's landslide election, Johnson was now president in his own right; with large Democratic majorities in both the House and Senate, he undertook an ambitious agenda.

The 1964 election, however, showed there was a growing fracture in the Democratic Party that a united Republican Party could exploit.[8] As the Democratic Party began to increasingly embrace civil rights, its regional coalition began to weaken. The South had consistently voted Democratic since the Civil War, and while elements of the southern vote had deserted the Democrats as early as 1948 and again in 1960 over its support for civil rights, the region had remained solidly Democratic in both the 1952 and 1956 elections.

Along with other moderate Republicans, Nixon avoided endorsing Goldwater's bid for the Republican nomination, but once Goldwater became the party's standard-bearer, Nixon actively supported the ticket. Nixon traveled the country giving speeches in support of Goldwater and other Republican candidates. Two years later, in the midterm election of 1966, Nixon became even more involved in campaigning for other Republican candidates. He frequently appeared at campaign events sponsored by Republican congressional office seekers to lend them his notoriety and to help with their fundraising. It soon became clear, however, that Nixon was more than just a not-so-elder statesman mentoring younger Republicans. Nixon was reconstructing a network of supporters who could pave his way back to the White House.

His renewed ambition started to become even more visible when Nixon hired Pat Buchanan, a conservative journalist, as a speech writer. In the following years Nixon expanded his paid staff by hiring several others who would become the core of his election campaign in 1968. Maurice Stans and Charles Colson soon joined Nixon's staff as he began preparations to seek the Republican nomination in 1968.

The 1968 Election

By 1968, the country was confronted by several intractable issues that would shape the upcoming election. The Vietnam War had taken a new and more disturbing turn in January. The Tet Offensive, in which Communist forces laid siege to the South Vietnamese capital, Saigon, made it clear to the American people that the war would not end soon. Americans now realized that the limited conflict in Southeast Asia had grown into a major war with no possibility of an easy or quick resolution. Even though the Tet Offensive was a military disaster for the Communists, it irrevocably contradicted the American government's claim that the war was progressing well and would soon be over. Antiwar protests on college campuses across the country became more common as opposition to the government's war policy grew. The national situation worsened in April when race riots broke out in several big cities in the wake of the assassination of Reverend Martin Luther King. These and other similarly disturbing events shook the nation and made the 1968 election anything but routine.

Turbulence also became increasingly evident inside the Democratic Party. Alabama governor George Wallace, disenchanted with the pro–civil rights stance of his party, left the Democrats to form a third party in order to run for president. The remainder of the party was increasingly split over the conduct of the Vietnam War with a growing antiwar faction demanding a change of course. Senator Eugene McCarthy mounted a primary challenge to President Johnson's reelection bid, and when McCarthy performed above expectations in the New Hampshire primary, Senator Robert Kennedy threw his hat in the ring, offering himself as a pro–civil rights and antiwar candidate. At the end of March, President Johnson announced his intention not to seek renomination and Vice President Hubert Humphrey entered the race to claim the support that would have gone to Johnson. Kennedy and McCarthy battled though several primaries, but after Kennedy won the California primary, he appeared to have clinched the nomination, but then catastrophe struck. After giving his victory speech in Los Angeles, Kennedy was gunned down by an assassin and died within hours. The nation was again in shock after Kennedy's assassination. Confusion reigned as the Democrats prepared for their convention in Chicago later that summer.

The Republican nomination at first was equally unsettled as some of the same divisiveness from 1964 still lingered. At first, elements of the eastern business establishment favored Michigan governor George Romney until he made some politically ill-advised remarks about Vietnam, advocating a rapid American withdrawal from the war. It soon became clear that this was not a popular position with most Republican voters, and he dropped out of the race at the end of February. New York governor Nelson Rockefeller again made it known that he wanted the nomination and attracted some support from eastern moderates while western conservatives began backing California governor Ronald Reagan. Many party loyalists, however, sensed that the Republicans could capitalize on the mood of the country and the dissension within the Democratic Party and recapture the White House. They sought a candidate who could unite the party, and gradually Richard Nixon reemerged as a serious contender. Nixon first won the New Hampshire primary with 78 percent of the vote and then went on to win eight more primaries across the county. He lost only three of the twelve primaries he entered, losing in states with native son candidates such as Governor Reagan in California and Governor Jim Rhodes in Ohio. As the Republican Convention in Miami neared, more and more delegates came to the conclusion that Nixon was the only candidate acceptable to the entire party, and his nomination became increasingly certain.

On the other side, Democrats held one of the most chaotic political conventions in modern history, with widespread demonstrations outside in the streets of Chicago and open hostility inside the convention hall. Vice President Humphrey was the overwhelming choice of the Democratic convention delegates if not of the party rank and file. Street demonstrations outside the convention became increasingly chaotic as the Chicago police used extraordinarily aggressive tactics in response, all on live television. The demonstrations only highlighted the disharmony within the Democratic Party, which would prove disastrous for the Democratic candidate in the subsequent campaign. Despite strong opposition from the McCarthy antiwar delegates, Humphrey was nominated and became the party's nominee with Senator Ed Muskie of Maine as his vice-presidential running mate.

On the Republican side, Nixon, with a unified Republican Party behind him, had to reach out to swing voters who could provide him with a margin of victory. The Republican campaign aggressively attacked the Democrats for being out of touch with mainstream Americans and for being responsible for the chaotic conditions plaguing the country. Nixon talked about representing the "silent majority" and of being able to restore law and order and often spoke in positive statesmanlike tones while letting his running mate Spiro Agnew attack the Democrats for weak leadership.

The election was close with Nixon getting 43.4 percent of the popular vote to Humphrey's 42.7 percent and with Wallace collecting 13.5 percent. Nixon's electoral college vote, however, was more convincing as he received 301 votes to Humphrey's 191 votes with Wallace getting 45. As expected

Wallace received all his electoral votes from deep southern states, but Nixon's southern strategy paid off as he carried all the southern border states except Texas, where support for Lyndon Johnson's legacy was still strong. Nixon also carried vote-rich California, Ohio, and Illinois, but ironically not Maryland, Agnew's home state. Among others, Humphrey won the traditionally Democratic states of New York, Pennsylvania, Michigan, West Virginia, and Massachusetts.

Nixon had come full circle since the razor-thin loss in 1960 and was now returning to Washington as the thirty-seventh president of the United States. However, he would have to deal with a Congress that was still firmly in Democratic hands. While the Republicans made some congressional gains in the election, the Democrats still held fifty-seven seats in the Senate and had a comfortable margin of 248 to 187 in the House of Representatives. The southern states were still overwhelmingly sending Democrats to Congress. While southern congressmen may have been more conservative than their northern Democratic colleagues, they still viewed Nixon as the president from the rival party. Nixon realized that this divided government would be difficult to navigate and would require him to devise new ways to govern in order to enact his agenda.

The Presidency

Nixon entered office handicapped by conditions that many preceding presidents did not have to endure. Most presidents before Nixon, even when they won by small margins, began their term in office with a supportive Congress. Nixon was confronted by a Congress dominated by the opposition party that viewed his election as an aberration. Nixon's election victory in a three-way race deprived him of the majority of the popular vote needed to claim a clear mandate. Nixon also inherited an unpopular war in Southeast Asia and a nation with a multitude of domestic problems. Nixon, however, believed that he could expand the president's traditional executive powers and find solutions to the nation's ills despite being a president without a congressional majority. To do that, he would have to rely more heavily on his executive powers not only to circumvent Congress but also to get around the bureaucracy itself. But as he did so, he sowed the seeds of dissension as the other branches of government protected their prerogatives.[9]

He had made several promises during the campaign that he planned to honor, and he adopted a philosophy that he would work with Congress when possible but confront it or go around it when necessary. This often meant that he had to take an adversarial role in his relationship with Congress, which ultimately set the stage for impeachment.

Prior to Nixon's election and beginning in the 1930s, the power of the presidency had been consistently expanding in both domestic and foreign policy.[10] Franklin Roosevelt exercised unprecedented executive power in his effort to deal with the harsh economic challenges of the Great Depression. Harry Truman committed the American military to a full-scale war in Korea without asking for a declaration of war from Congress. And Lyndon Johnson continued the tradition of an active, strong president who used his powers to the fullest to promote his Great Society programs and expand the American military presence in Vietnam. But the difference between Johnson and the presidency to come was that throughout all of Johnson's presidency, he held a majority in both houses of Congress. This was true even after 1966, when the Democrats lost forty-seven seats in the House.

In the emerging tradition of a strong presidency, Nixon believed that he could also enact an ambitious agenda, but he probably overreached. In the absence of congressional support, Nixon tried to advance much of his agenda through executive action. Not only did the president conduct a secret war in Cambodia and impound appropriated funds, he also sought increased White House control over the federal bureaucracy and to reduce the size of the federal government.[11] These actions put Nixon at loggerheads with the Democratic majority in Congress. This, despite the fact that Nixon and the Democrats in Congress did find common ground on several important domestic issues, such as the National Environmental Policy Act, the Clean Air Act, the Occupational Safety and Health Act, the Consumer Product Safety Act, and the Equal Employment Opportunity Act of 1972.

In fact, in a legislative sense, given the fact of divided government, the Nixon administration was remarkably successful in Congress. For example, the Nixon administration, with the cooperation of Congress, established Amtrak, revised revenue sharing with the states, initiated a major anticancer program, increased federal support for the arts, and authorized an extension of the Voting Rights Act. But, despite these landmark laws and programs, Nixon also frequently found it necessary to confront Congress on many policies that he opposed.

Foreign Policy Conflicts

While Nixon found himself frequently at odds with Congress over domestic issues, foreign policy dominated the Nixon agenda and was the source of some of the most ferocious conflicts with Congress. In his conduct of the war, Nixon often took actions that were condemned by congressional Democrats who opposed his policies in Vietnam. During his campaign, Nixon promised to bring "peace with honor" in Vietnam, but once in office this pledge required him to further escalate America's combat role. This antagonized those who wanted a quick American withdrawal.

Antiwar demonstrations expanded across the nation during Nixon's first term in office, and his critics in Congress became more vocal in their opposition. Nixon, however, was steadfast in his desire not to be the first American president to lose a war. Early in his first term, without consulting or informing Congress, Nixon ordered military incursions into Vietnam's neutral neighbors Laos and Cambodia and stepped up aerial bombing of North Vietnamese supply routes in both these countries. While Nixon hoped to deflect both public and congressional criticism by proclaiming a policy of "Vietnamization" of the war, in which the South Vietnamese Army would gradually take over ground combat, his decisions to, in the short run, increase American military operations generated intense opposition from Democrats both inside and outside of Congress.

Domestic Conflicts

In domestic affairs Nixon engaged in several major areas of conflict with Congress. Two of the most prominent points of contention were the battle for the Supreme Court and the impoundment of legally appropriated funds. Conflict in these and other areas of domestic policy were ideological as well as partisan and illustrated the difficulties Nixon had with the majority of members in Congress. At times, these disputes overshadowed foreign policy disagreements and created a combative atmosphere in which members of Congress, even from his own party, viewed the president more as a rival than as a participant in shared governance. These confrontations provided tinder to the spark that was ignited over Watergate.

The Battle over the Supreme Court

When Nixon came to office in 1969 there were immediate opportunities to change the makeup of the court. He would eventually appoint a new chief justice and three other associate justices. Many of these appointments were tinged with controversy.[12]

Chief Justice Earl Warren, an Eisenhower appointee, had already announced his intention to retire before Nixon was elected. Despite being appointed by a Republican president, Warren during his time as chief justice developed a reputation as an activist justice who made decisions on civil and criminal rights that were applauded by liberals. Warren announced his retirement during the last year of Lyndon Johnson's presidency, but with the unusual proviso that his replacement would have to be confirmed before Warren's resignation was made final. Sitting Associate Justice Abe Fortas was nominated by Johnson to replace the chief justice (with Judge Homer Thornberry to fill the vacancy). In the Senate confirmation process, however, information surfaced that Fortas had received speaking fees from interested parties in lawsuits. Strictly speaking, this was not illegal, but it did undermine his support in the Senate. But what really destroyed Fortas's nomination was opposition from powerful conservative Democratic senators from the South like Richard Russell from Georgia. Fortas's promotion to chief justice was eventually blocked by a Republican filibuster and he returned to his position as associate justice. When additional information came to light about Fortas receiving money from a foundation, which appeared to create another conflict of interest, he resigned from the court. Warren, then, stayed on through the end of the Johnson presidency.

After the election, in 1969 Warren retired from the court. Along with the Fortas resignation, this created two Supreme Court vacancies for the new president to fill.

For the position of chief justice Nixon selected appeals court justice Warren Burger from Minnesota who was known as a critic of Earl Warren's judicial approach. Burger favored a Supreme Court that adhered to a strict literal interpretation of the Constitution. After an uneventful Senate confirmation, Burger was confirmed in June 1969 with only a handful for dissenting votes. Nixon's next appointee, however, had a different experience.

The effort to fill the other Supreme Court vacancy created by Fortas's resignation encountered intense opposition. Nixon had considered appeals court justice Lewis Powell of Virginia for the position, but Powell deferred because of the negative circumstances surrounding the Fortas affair. He later accepted a nomination to fill a different Supreme Court vacancy. Nixon again selected an appeals court justice who could help reverse the path of the Warren Court. Clement Haynsworth from South Carolina, Nixon's nominee to fill the vacancy, encountered opposition not only from Democrats but also from liberal Republicans. Haynsworth was accused of taking racially segregationist stands and being hostile to labor unions. After a rancorous confirmation hearing, the Senate rejected his appointment by a

55–45 vote; he became the first presidential nominee to the Supreme Court to be turned down in forty years.

The battle to fill the vacancy did not end with the Haynsworth rejection, and Nixon's next nominee met with similar resistance.[13] In January 1970, Nixon selected G. Harrold Carswell of Georgia to fill the lingering Supreme Court vacancy. Carswell had been a federal district judge, but had only recently been elevated to the court of appeals. It was uncovered during the Senate confirmation that Carswell had made racist remarks in a speech when he was a candidate for the Georgia legislature in 1948. His defenders argued that he could not be held accountable for remarks made decades earlier. But he had said what he was reputed to have said. Furthermore, his brief tenure on the court of appeals was referenced by critics who claimed he was not qualified to sit on the highest court in the land. Ultimately, fifty-one senators voted against his confirmation with forty-five in support.

The newly elected president had encountered two stinging defeats in his effort to alter the course of the Supreme Court. Nixon complained publicly that the Senate was preventing him from exercising his constitutional authority to make appointments to the judicial branch. Not wanting another battle, Nixon relented in nominating a relatively nonactivist judge who was not from the South. His appointment of appellate court justice Harry Blackmun from Minnesota was much better received. Blackmun was a colleague and personal friend of Warren Burger and was rated by the American Bar Association as exceptionally well qualified. The Senate approved the nomination 94–0. While Blackmun was a reliable conservative vote during his first years on the court, he gradually became moved to the left over time.

Nixon had two additional opportunities to change the Supreme Court in his first term when both Hugo Black and John Harlan experienced ill health. Both retired. In their place, Nixon considered nominating Congressman Richard Poff of Virginia for Black's seat, but Poff took himself out of consideration before being officially nominated. Nixon then made known his intention to nominate Herschel Friday, an Arkansas attorney, for Black's position and California appeals court judge Mildred Lillie for Harlan's seat. Nixon pulled both out of the running, however, after the American Bar Association rated both as unqualified. Nixon then returned to his earlier choice and convinced Lewis Powell to accept his nomination for Black's seat. Powell did not produce the animosity of the earlier nominations, and he was confirmed by an 89–1 vote.

Nixon's other choice to fill Harlan's seat with William Rehnquist of Arizona did not go as smoothly. Nixon had originally appointed Rehnquist as assistant attorney general under John Mitchell in 1969. No problem. But a major controversy erupted during his Senate confirmation concerning a memorandum he wrote for Justice Robert Jackson defending the separate-but-equal doctrine used to justify racial segregation.[14] When questioned in the Senate hearings about the memorandum, Rehnquist insisted that he was only reflecting Justice Jackson's perceptions in the memorandum and that it did not represent his own view on the issue. Regardless, the NAACP opposed his confirmation as did many labor unions. Despite this controversy, Rehnquist was approved by a 68–26 vote, fairly easily obtaining the three-fifths vote necessary to avoid a filibuster. All the votes against his confirmation came from Democratic senators.

IMPOUNDMENT CONTROVERSY

The battle between President Nixon and Congress over withholding (impounding) appropriated federal funds was almost as contentious as the conflict over his Supreme Court appointees.[15] The impoundment struggle, however, occurred primarily during Nixon's second term when he became increasingly concerned about the stability of the American economy. Jumps in the prices of consumer goods (inflation) threated to undermine the prosperity that Americans had enjoyed since the end of World War Two. Nixon had tried several techniques to control inflation, such as wage and price controls, but they had proved ineffective. He became convinced that the growing federal debt produced by massive federal spending was the underlying cause of inflation, and he believed that the best solution was to reduce government spending. During the 1972 election campaign, Nixon had called on Congress to grant him authority to withhold the expenditure of, or "impound," appropriated funds. Particularly after his landslide reelection in 1972, Nixon believed that the American electorate had given him a mandate to cut excessive governmental spending, and he proposed in the 1973 federal budget to cut $18 billion from federal programs. By and large, Congress refused to comply. Even though these funds had been appropriated by Congress and the president had signed the legislation, Nixon ordered the federal agencies not to spend a significant amount of the disputed money.

The effect of President Nixon's impoundment was that many programs favored by congressional Democrats were cut. This created an immediate outcry from members of Congress who believed that impoundment was an unconstitutional expansion of presidential power. Many members of both the House and Senate reacted sharply to what they perceived as an executive power grab, but Nixon claimed that as chief executive he had discretion over how funds were distributed. Nixon noted that many presidents, beginning with Thomas Jefferson, had occasionally withheld funds from expenditure.[16]

Many members of Congress were not satisfied, however, by this argument and clamored for legislation that would unambiguously prevent presidents from taking this type of action. The struggle between the president and Congress over the impoundment of funds at first pitted liberals against fiscal conservatives, but it soon expanded because many members of Congress felt uneasy with the growth of presidential budgetary power. Congressional leaders, realizing under current interpretations of presidential power that Nixon had the authority to take this action, drafted the Congressional Budget and Impoundment Control Act of 1974. The act had widespread support in both the House and Senate and passed easily. Even when Nixon vetoed it, enough votes were mustered in both chambers to override the veto. The Congressional Budget and Impoundment Control Act became law in July 1974.

The impoundment confrontation created a bitterness that extended beyond partisanship. It inflamed hard feelings between the president and Congress that had been simmering throughout Nixon's entire presidency. There was a sense in Congress that Nixon was usurping power from Congress and creating what his critics termed an "imperial presidency." Despite impressive cooperation between Nixon and the Democratically controlled Congress on a wide range of domestic issues, ranging from environmental policy to civil rights, Nixon's conduct of the Vietnam War and the conflicts over judicial appointments and the impoundment of appropriated funds antagonized many members of Congress.

REELECTION

The 1972 election was the pinnacle of Richard Nixon's political career, but in a strange irony it also led to a series of events that would ultimately contribute to his downfall. In 1972, it was a foregone conclusion that Nixon would be renominated as the Republican presidential candidate. The only suspense was whether Spiro Agno would continue as vice president. Agnew remained on the ticket only to resign under a cloud shortly after Nixon's reelection.

The Democrats went through a long and often rancorous primary to select their nominee, but it seemed almost tame compared with the upheaval of 1968. Ed Muskie of Maine, the vice-presidential candidate under Humphrey in 1968, was the early front runner, but after suffering several political mishaps, he suspended his campaign. Senator George McGovern of South Dakota, an outspoken critic of Nixon's war policy, surged to the lead. With Muskie out of the race, Hubert Humphrey belatedly reentered the contest and the nomination remained uncertain, at least until the influential California primary in June. McGovern soundly defeated Humphrey in California and his nomination was all but assured.

On election night, Nixon coasted to a landslide victory with 60.7 percent of the popular vote and a margin of 520 to 17 in the electoral college. McGovern carried only one state, Massachusetts, plus the District of Columbia. This truly was the zenith of Richard Nixon's career. Unlike the narrow victory in 1968, this overwhelming victory seemed to give him the popular mandate he was denied four years earlier. Nixon could now claim that the public approved of his policies and that his critics lacked popular support.

Almost lost in the election night celebration, however, was that Nixon's landslide did not have congressional coattails. Despite the strong Republican presidential results, the Democrats lost only thirteen seats in the House of Representatives and maintained a substantial 242 to 192 seat majority. The results of the Senate election were even more startling. The Democrats actually picked up two additional seats and now held a 56–42 majority. The Democrats were well short of the two-thirds vote need to override Nixon's vetoes, so they could not dominate the government, but they could block any legislative proposals of which they disapproved. This absence of coattails meant that under any circumstances, Nixon was likely to face a difficult second term.

Origins of the Watergate Scandal

There has been a vast amount of scholarly and journalistic attention paid to the Watergate Affair, and books written about it are still being published more than fifty years after the fact.[17] It is far beyond the scope of this book to provide a comprehensive and complete examination of all the facets of this unique episode in American history. The analysis below summarizes the episode and illustrates the fact that the Watergate break-in and its subsequent cover-up were the most important but not the only factors affecting the impeachment process.

On June 17, 1972, an odd crime occurred that at first seemed unrelated to the Nixon presidency. Five burglars were arrested breaking in to the national Democratic Party headquarters in the Watergate office complex in Washington, DC. Since the burglars had wiretapping equipment in their possession, political motives were immediately suspected. However, the break-in was treated as a simple criminal case and the suspects were brought before the federal district court in Washington, DC. While Democrats attempted in vain to use the crime to raise suspicions about possible ties to the Republican White House, those efforts had little traction with the voting public and had no impact on the 1972 election. While the break-in attracted some national attention, the *Washington Post* was the only news organization to thoroughly investigate the matter.[18] But it wasn't until well after the presidential inauguration in 1973 that the importance of that event was fully realized.

The Watergate scandal had its origins in President Nixon's concern about news leaks. In 1971, President Nixon was infuriated by the leak of a secret Defense Department report that became known as the Pentagon Papers. Nixon believed that the publication of this report greatly compromised his war effort and was an unacceptable breach of national security. He lost confidence in the ability of traditional government agencies to prevent these types of news leaks and ordered the White House staff to take its own steps to prevent a recurrence. The result was the creation of a secret Special Investigations Unit working out of the White House. This unit became known as the "White House Plumbers" because its objective was to fix news leaks. This unit engaged in covert activities including a break-in at the office of the psychiatrist who had treated Daniel Ellsberg, the former government official who had leaked the Pentagon Papers. They also investigated CBS reporter Daniel Schorr and even the Kennedy administration's involvement in the assassination of South Vietnamese president Ngo Dinh Diem. The unit eventually proved ineffective and was more or less deactivated. Elements of the unit, however, were resurrected during the presidential campaign of 1972.[19]

In January 1972, G. Gordon Liddy, a former FBI agent and member of the Plumbers, proposed an elaborate plan to assist the Committee for the Re-election of the President (CRP) gather information that could be useful to the campaign. Many of the methods proposed were illegal. Liddy met with Attorney General John Mitchell, who would soon be appointed CRP director, and Jeb Magruder, a special assistant to the president serving as the CRP deputy director, and White House counsel John Dean. They discussed the various features of Liddy's proposal, much of which they rejected. A key part of the plan, however, was retained.[20]

The decision was made to covertly gather information from the Democratic National Committee by wiretapping its headquarters in the Watergate office complex. The wiretapping operation was to be carried out by breaking in to the Democratic National Committee office and installing telephone bugging devices. A break-in in March 1972 was successful, but the bugging device malfunctioned, so another break-in was scheduled in June to fix the broken wiretap. This time, however, the break-in was detected by a security guard. Five burglars were arrested. Three were Cubans, all of whom had previously been associated with the Plumbers or Central Intelligence Agency—sponsored surveillance activities. The five burglars were also linked to Liddy and E. Howard Hunt, a former CIA agent who worked for the White House as a security consultant. The burglars along with Liddy and Hunt were indicted and tried in federal district court.

President Nixon evidently learned of the arrest from a newspaper story while on vacation. When he returned to Washington he held several meetings in the White House to develop a strategy to minimize political damage to his reelection campaign. Nixon met with his top aides John Ehrlichman and H. R. (Bob) Haldeman and others to discuss how to handle the matter. Nixon said in his memoirs that at this point he was not sure if there was any connection between the break-in and his campaign, but he was concerned about adverse publicity hurting his reelection bid.[21] It is not clear exactly what information Nixon had at this time, but it is certain that a decision was made at these meetings that the CRP and the White House would deny any connection with or knowledge of the Watergate burglary. It was also decided that steps would be taken to keep the burglars from confessing any association with the Nixon campaign. Unfortunately for the Nixon presidency, a decision was also made to ask the CIA to request that the FBI back off the investigation because of national security concerns. These decisions in the late summer of 1972 to conceal the Watergate burglary's association with the CRP became known as the "cover-up" and were eventually the basis for the obstruction of justice charges related to impeachment.[22]

The plan to conceal the Watergate burglars' connection with the CRP soon began to unravel because of pressure from presiding Judge John Sirica. The five burglars' link to Liddy and Hunt was quickly uncovered and those two were also indicted. Hunt had a close association with Charles Colson, a member of President Nixon's inner circle, which greatly increased suspicions about a possible White House connection.

The cover-up plan included a scheme to buy the burglars' silence with laundered campaign funds. But the trail of funds from the campaign to the burglars became increasingly difficult to hide. When the trial of the apprehended burglars concluded on January 30, 1973 with conviction, Judge Sirica still believed that there was far more to the case. He handed down an extremely harsh forty-year sentence to the convicted burglars in order to force them to reveal additional information about the crime. In March 1973, Judge Sirica made public a letter written by Watergate burglar James McCord in which it was claimed that the break-in was linked to high government officials. Eventually, all the burglars received much reduced sentences after agreeing to cooperate with prosecutors.

During this time, news stories appearing in the *Washington Post* provided new, provocative information inferring that the Watergate burglars were linked to the Nixon campaign. Two reporters, Bob Woodward and Carl Bernstein, had been receiving information from a confidential source known only as "Deep Throat." Years later it was finally revealed that the source was the second highest-ranking official in the FBI, Associate Director Mark Felt, who had access to information about the break-in and the Committee for the Re-election of the President. Felt also let it be known to the *Post* reporters that the White House was orchestrating the cover-up.[23]

In March 1973, President Nixon asked White House counsel John Dean to prepare a report about the Watergate break-in. While writing the report, Dean realized that he would actually incriminate himself by documenting his involvement in the original plan calling for the break-in. As White House counsel, he was the president's legal representative at that meeting and had approved a burglary. Dean believed that the president could claim then that he, Nixon, was completely unaware of the illegal plan, and it had gone forward only because of Dean's unauthorized approval.[24] It is unknown if Nixon intended to use Dean as a scapegoat, but Dean feared that he was being set up to take the blame. Dean, therefore, contacted the FBI and began providing information about the White House complicity in the cover-up.

During a subsequent conversation in April 1973, Dean told President Nixon that he suspected that Haldeman, Ehrlichman, and John Mitchell were all involved in covering up the CRP connection to the Watergate incident. Dean also told the president that he had been cooperating with the U.S. Attorneys' office. Dean did not know that the president was already aware of this situation. Nixon at that point realized that the cover-up had failed and on April 30 he announced that he was accepting the resignations of Bob Haldeman and John Ehrlichman and asking for the resignation of Robert Kleindienst,

Mitchell's replacement as attorney general. Also, Nixon, now aware of Dean's secret cooperation with the investigation, fired the White House counsel as well. Dean later would become a star witness in the Senate hearings.

Senate Watergate Actions

With the Watergate Affair simmering, the Senate in February 1973 approved the creation of a select committee to investigate the burglary. The Senate Select Committee for the Investigation of Campaign Practices (the Watergate Committee), which began hearings in May 1973, was chaired by North Carolina senator Sam Ervin. The opening of the Senate hearings was filled with drama as the media anticipated the testimony from Dean, whom Nixon had fired a month earlier.

Even before it met, the Senate adopted an unusual approach during the confirmation of Elliot Richardson to replace Robert Kleindienst as attorney general. As a condition of its confirmation, the Senate required the Justice Department to appoint a special prosecutor to investigate the Watergate case. Once in office, Richardson appointed Archibald Cox, a Harvard law professor and former solicitor general during the Kennedy administration, to fill this position. The Senate committee and the special prosecutor were both charged with investigating the Watergate break-in far beyond the district court's criminal inquiry.

Furthermore, in April 1973, a month before the Senate Watergate Committee was to convene, during the confirmation hearing of L. Patrick Gray for FBI director, the Senate Judiciary Committee accidentally stumbled across incriminating information about a potential tie between the Watergate break-in and the White House. While suspicion was growing about the Nixon campaign's involvement with the burglary, it wasn't until the Senate hearing to confirm Nixon's appointment to replace J. Edgar Hoover that evidence of a cover-up was revealed.[25]

Gray, the acting FBI director, admitted in testimony that he had received and destroyed documents in June 1972 about the CRP's possible ties with the Watergate burglars. This shocking admission added even more urgency to the upcoming Senate hearings and prompted the Senate Judiciary Committee to vote not to confirm Gray.

During the May through July 1973 Senate Judiciary Committee hearings, most of the key White House and CRP participants testified with the sole exception of the president. The hearings were broadcast live on all major television networks and attracted a massive audience. While John Dean's testimony about his role in the scandal was riveting, the most startling moment in the hearings was a revelation by Alexander Butterfield. Butterfield had been a special assistant to the president during his first term and had played no part in either the burglary or the cover-up. However, under questioning, he revealed that every conversation in which the president participated within the Oval Office had been recorded.

Immediately, the Senate Watergate Committee, the special prosecutor, and Judge Sirica sought to obtain the tapes of the president's conversations. The consensus was that the tapes would conclusively show, in the words of the Judiciary Committee's vice-chairman, Republican Howard Baker, "what the President knew and when did he know it."

The Watergate Tapes

The battle for control of the White House tapes became the central feature in the subsequent Watergate investigation. Archibald Cox and many others believed that the tapes contained evidence that could show the extent of President Nixon's knowledge and involvement in the Watergate burglary and its subsequent cover-up. Cox asked Judge Sirica to subpoena the tapes directly relevant to the Watergate Affair.

President Nixon, however, resisted any attempt to turn over the tapes, which he believed would make the tapes public. He contended that he was under no obligation to give the tapes to Congress, the courts, or the special prosecutor. His view was that the tapes were exclusively presidential property and that his right of executive privilege put them completely under his control. He also asserted that the tapes contained sensitive material that could compromise national security if made public.[26]

President Nixon's unwillingness to turn over the tapes, however, had the unanticipated consequence of magnifying their importance. Because Nixon was so hesitant to give up the tapes, many began to suspect that they contained incriminating evidence that would implicate the president in criminal activity. The media began to increasingly speculate about what was in the tapes that Nixon wanted to hide. Nixon's withholding of the tapes only exacerbated the feeling in Congress that Nixon had committed a crime and that impeachment might be necessary.

Eventually, under pressure, Nixon sought a compromise with Archibald Cox, offering to have Mississippi Democratic senator John Stennis, a Nixon ally, read the transcripts of the tapes and report his findings. Cox found this offer to be completely unacceptable and continued to demand access to the actual tapes. Cox's refusal to accept Nixon's offer created a confrontation that once again produced a wave of negative publicity for the president. Nixon was so enraged by Cox's refusal to compromise that he came to the conclusion that Cox was hopelessly biased. Nixon, therefore, felt he had no alternative but to remove Cox.

In October 1973, Nixon ordered Attorney General Richardson to fire Cox. Richardson, who was Nixon's appointee, nevertheless refused to fire Cox and instead resigned. Deputy Attorney General William Ruckelshaus similarly refused to carry out the order and also resigned. Robert Bork, the solicitor general, said he disagreed with the action, but that the president had the right to fire Cox, and he carried out the order. Leon Jaworski was then appointed to replace Cox as Watergate special prosecutor. Even with Cox no longer on the case, Jaworski continued to take aggressive steps to obtain the tapes. The media dubbed this episode the "Saturday Night Massacre," which only added to the perception that President Nixon must be guilty of something and added more momentum toward his impeachment.

Vice President Agnew's Resignation

The intensified suspicions surrounding the Watergate Affair coincided with an unrelated but extremely damaging scandal involving Vice President Spiro Agnew. While this scandal had absolutely no connection to either the Watergate burglary or the cover-up, the Watergate investigation created an atmosphere of heightened awareness of wrongdoing by the Nixon administration. The result was that in the fall of 1973, the U.S. attorney for Maryland brought forth evidence that indicated Vice President Agnew had accepted bribes as an elected official. The charges dated back to when Agnew was a county executive and extended through his time as governor of Maryland. When Agnew was confronted with the prospect of being indicted by a federal grand jury on counts of bribery and extortion, he instead accepted a plea bargain. In order to avoid a trial, Agnew agreed to plead guilty to one count of tax evasion and to resign from office. In October 1973, Spiro Agnew, the thirty-ninth vice president of the United States, left office in disgrace.

The hostile political conditions that accompanied Agnew's resignation had enormously negative consequences not only for Agnew but also for

President Nixon. During the early Watergate investigation, the possibility of presidential impeachment was seldom mentioned, but Agnew's demise added fuel to the impeachment fire. After the Agnew resignation, presidential impeachment began to be seen as a real possibility (as well as a political advantage for the Democrats). If Agnew could be pushed out of office, it was no longer impossible to imagine that Nixon could be forced from office as well.

Agnew's resignation created a more immediate problem for President Nixon. In the midst of the Watergate investigation, Nixon had to appoint a new vice president. This was a predicament with many potential pitfalls. First, Nixon needed to select a replacement who could be confirmed without further antagonizing Congress, but who was not apparently eager to succeed him as president.

Furthermore, Nixon had to act quickly so as not to run the risk of being impeached at a time when the vice presidency was vacant. If that were to happen, he would be succeeded by the Speaker of the House, Carl Albert, who was a Democrat.[27] Consequently, Nixon had to weigh many delicate factors in his effort to pacify Congress, select a nominee and have him confirmed quickly, and all without exacerbating the nascent movement to impeach.

Nixon carefully considered his options and decided that Congressman Gerald Ford (R-MI), the House Minority Leader, was the best choice. Nixon nominated Ford on October 12, 1973. Fortunately for Nixon and the Republican Party, Ford's confirmation encountered little resistance even as the president set off a firestorm on October 20 by firing Cox. At that point, the Saturday Night Massacre, as the Cox firing became known, made impeachment a very real possibility. Nevertheless, Ford was so well liked in Congress and his behavior in office and in his personal life was so above reproach that he had an easy road to confirmation.

Path to Impeachment

The events of 1973 foretold a very difficult year ahead for President Nixon. The Senate hearings generated new suspicions that Nixon had been deeply involved in the Watergate cover-up, and the continuing battle over possession of the White House tapes raged on with little hope of an amicable resolution. The resignation of Vice President Agnew and the preemptive firing of Special Prosecutor Cox generated more pressure on Nixon and paved the way for further congressional action. In February 1974, the House of Representatives authorized the House Judiciary Committee to schedule deliberations on the possibility of impeachment. The committee chaired by New Jersey Democrat Peter Rodino would meet later in the year as impeachment now seemed a real possibility.

In March 1974, a Washington federal grand jury indicted seven close associates of President Nixon on charges of conspiracy related to Watergate including White House staffers H. R. Haldeman, John Ehrlichman, Charles Colson, and former attorney general John Mitchell. The grand jury also mentioned an unnamed "unindicted coconspirator," who was, in fact, President Nixon. This action indicated that the grand jury had wanted to indict the president, but was reluctant to do so while he was serving in office. Despite the exclusion of the president's name, these indictments made it abundantly clear that illegal behavior had probably occurred in the White House. And with that, momentum continued to build to impeach the president.

As the House Judiciary Committee prepared for its deliberations in July, the fight over control of the White House tapes intensified. In April 1974, newly appointed Special Prosecutor Jaworski asked Judge Sirica to subpoena the tapes. Sirica complied and Nixon attempted to appease the court by turning over edited written transcripts of forty-three of the requested tapes. Portions were blacked out with the phrase "expletive deleted" in their place. Among other things, these redactions revealed that President Nixon often used profanity in private conversations, along with racial and anti-Semitic slurs, which further eroded his public image. Judge Sirica ultimately rejected the offer of partial compliance and ordered all the actual tapes turned over by the end of May. Nixon refused, and both he and Jaworski appealed directly to the U.S. Supreme Court. The Supreme Court heard arguments in July in the landmark case, *United States v. Nixon.*[28] On July 24, 1974, the court ordered that the White House tapes be turned over to the special prosecutor. On those tapes was a conversation President Nixon had with aides on June 23, 1972. This became known as the "smoking gun" tape because it made it clear that Nixon was a full participant in the Watergate cover-up.[29]

Even before the tapes were released, but after the firing of Cox, the House Judiciary Committee began its consideration of impeachment. By the end of 1973, two dozen impeachment resolutions had been introduced in the House and referred to the Judiciary Committee. As the articles of impeachment were debated in the committee, the proceedings were broadcast live on national network television. The deliberations generated even more public excitement than the Senate hearings the year before. The Democratic majority of the committee seemed ready to vote for impeachment. But there was a feeling on the committee that a vote along party lines would not be enough.

The committee, therefore, hired a special investigations unit that was charged with investigating the Watergate Affair and, above all else, with doing so in a nonpartisan manner. Eventually, based on the findings of the special investigatory staff, the committee did vote out several articles of impeachment, a vote that was supported by a number of the committee's Republican minority.[30]

A rapid secession of events in late summer 1974 ended the Nixon presidency as the last attempts to salvage it finally collapsed. The Supreme Court ruled against Nixon on July 24 by an 8–0 vote. The court found that even a president did not have the authority to withhold evidence in a criminal investigation. This decision forced Nixon to turn over all the tapes to the special prosecutor. Just a few days later, on July 30, the House Judiciary Committee approved three articles of impeachment on the charges of obstruction of justice, conspiracy, and contempt of Congress and then sent its recommendation for impeachment to the entire House for its vote. Even though some Republicans on the committee defended Nixon and voted against the articles, there was bipartisan support for each of the approved articles of impeachment.

Before the full House had the opportunity to vote on the articles, the previously unreleased tapes were made public. They contained incontrovertible evidence that Nixon had lied to the public when he said that he was not involved in planning the Watergate cover-up. This evidence eroded much of the remaining support Nixon may have had in Congress. Several of the Republicans on the House Judiciary Committee who had defended Nixon before the release of the incriminating tapes said that they felt betrayed and would now support impeachment. On August 7, Republican senators Barry Goldwater and Hugh Scott held a painful meeting with Nixon in the White House. They told him that only about fifteen senators would consider voting against his conviction, far less than the thirty-four votes needed to prevent a vote for removal. Faced with this bleak reality, Nixon made the wrenching decision to resign from office. He appeared on television on August 8 to announce his decision, and the next day, as the resignation became official, Nixon and his family left the White House for the last time.

What Did the President Know
and When Did He Know It?

There have been several accounts of who approved the break-in and wire-tapping of the national Democratic Party headquarters.[31] There have also been disagreements about who knew about and participated in planning the cover-up of the burglary. The exact role of President Nixon has been a thorny subject in this continuing debate. While the White House tapes answered some questions, others still linger. It is clear that the Watergate scandal created illegalities that sent many people to prison and forced a president from office, but were all the accused perpetrators guilty, and, if so, were they properly punished? Incredibly, even after four decades, the evidence surrounding Watergate is still being scrutinized.

But what we do know is that John Dean, the White House counsel, was a participant in the meeting that approved the Watergate break-in. He may not have initially planned its cover-up, but he soon became aware of it. Dean worried that because of his prior knowledge of the break-in he would be blamed for the entire incident. Fearing that he would be a scapegoat, he cooperated with the FBI and became an informer. Later, he was an important cooperative witness in the Senate investigation. Dean was eventually convicted of one felony count and sentenced by Judge Sirica to one to four years in a minimum-security facility, but because of his cooperation, the four months he was held in a witness protection facility was substituted for his sentence and he served no further time in jail.

Most of the other members of President Nixon's inner circle were also caught up in the Watergate scandal and were convicted and served time in prison. Attorney General John Mitchell was involved in the planning and approval of the break-in as well as the cover-up of its connection to the Nixon reelection campaign. The evidence shows that after the burglars were arrested he was aware of the use of campaign funds to pay for their silence. He was convicted of obstruction of justice, conspiracy, and perjury in 1975 and served nineteen months in a minimum-security federal prison. H. R. Haldeman, the White House chief of staff, originally oversaw the creation of the Special Investigations Unit (the Plumbers) and knew about their activities to stop news leaks. Despite this early involvement, he evidently became aware of the Watergate break-in only after the burglars were arrested. Haldeman, however, was complicit in planning and carrying out the cover-up of the crime's links to the Nixon campaign. He was convicted in 1975 of conspiracy and obstruction of justice and served thirteen months in a minimum-security prison. John Ehrlichman, special assistant and counsel to the president, helped create the original Plumbers, but he became aware of the Watergate break-in only after it occurred. He, like Haldeman, was intricately involved in planning its cover-up. He was first convicted of conspiracy and making false statements to the grand jury about the original Plumber's activities, and then found guilty of conspiracy and making false statements to the grand jury related to the Watergate break-in. He eventually served eighteen months in a minimum-security prison. Charles Colson, special counsel, who was in contact with Howard Hunt during the Watergate break-in, also had conversations with Nixon, showing that he was at least aware of the cover-up. He pleaded guilty and was convicted of obstruction of justice related to the Pentagon Papers case.

What is clear from most of the evidence is that President Nixon did not approve or have prior knowledge of the break-in of the national Democratic Party headquarters. While members of his campaign staff planned the break-in, Nixon only found out about it after the arrest of the Watergate burglars. He originally referred to the break-in as "stupid" and demanded to know whose idea it was.[32] It is also not clear exactly how much he initially was told about the Plumbers' unit and its connection with the Committee for the Re-election of the President. There is an eighteen and one-half minute erased gap on a critically important tape of Nixon speaking with Haldeman soon after the arrest of the burglars. There has been a great deal of speculation about how this gap occurred, with many voicing suspicions that it was intentional. Rosemary Wood, Nixon's secretary, always contended that it was accidental. What is certain is that this part of the evidence has been lost forever, and the different recollections of this conversation that have emerged have only obfuscated the truth.

Regardless of when Nixon learned about the burglary, it is certain that he soon realized that there was a connection between the illegal act and his campaign that would produce publicity that could hurt his reelection chances. There is abundant evidence that Nixon's involvement in the scandal started when, in consultation with his aides, he began to devise what became known as the cover-up. He was aware of and agreed to plans to minimize the potential political damage from the burglary by hiding all links between it and his campaign committee. He also agreed with the proposal to ask the CIA to falsely tell the FBI that national security issues were involved so that the investigation into the burglary would be impeded. His knowledge and involvement in this "cover-up" was an illegal action to "obstruct justice" and was appropriately the basis for the House committee approved articles of impeachment.

Analysis

1. Opposite Party Control of the House

Throughout his presidency, Nixon had to contend with a majority in Congress belonging to the opposition party. In the House, even though there was a contingent of conservative southern Democrats who supported much of the president's policy objectives, they never felt any allegiance to a Republican president.[33] After the 1972 election, in which the Democrats lost thirteen seats in the House, they still held a 242 seat to 192 seat advantage over the Republicans. Nevertheless, in the House, a simple majority being needed to impeach, the Democrats fifty-seat majority probably had an impact on President Nixon's decision to stonewall, particularly on the issue of the Oval Office tapes.

Despite the wide Democratic margin in the House, it is remarkable how many important, even landmark, pieces of legislation were passed under these circumstances. Nixon found ways to cooperate with the Democratic majority to pass numerous laws including far-reaching environmental and civil rights legislation. He was also able to forge a Democratic and Republican coalition that worked together surprisingly well given the contentious problems facing the nation at the time.

Nevertheless, House Democrats tangled with the president over a number of perceived executive excesses including the impoundment of appropriated funds. Democrats were angered by the president's refusal to spend the money they had appropriated and saw impoundments as an example of Nixon's desire to grab power. That specific issue, however, was settled in the courts. The courts ruled in every circumstance, when challenged, that the president could not for policy reasons refuse to spend funds appropriated pursuant to statute.[34]

In the wake of this dispute, many Democrats were in a confrontational mood and seemed eager to rid themselves of the Republican in the White House. In the House Judiciary Committee's proceedings, every Democrat, liberal and conservative, voted to approve the three articles of impeachment.

It is reasonable to assume that had the partisan makeup of the House of Representatives been dramatically different, with the Republicans in control, the entire atmosphere surrounding Nixon's second term would have been much different. In the chapters to follow, we will address the issue of partisan division and the likelihood of impeachment.

In a Republican House, congressional outrage might have been far more muted. House Democrats would still have been angered, but it is highly unlikely that a Republican-dominated House would have been so ready to consider impeachment.

It is also conceivable that President Nixon, feeling far more secure with a Republican majority in the House, might have adopted an alternative course of action in response to the Watergate break-in, being far more cooperative. Events still may have forced the House to hold impeachment hearings, but in a Republican House the majority on the committee would have been much more sympathetic to the president, who was the leader of their party.

2. OPPOSITE PARTY CONTROL OF THE SENATE

Like the House of Representatives, Nixon as president had always had to contend with a Senate controlled by the Democrats. On the Senate side, despite a landslide victory for Nixon in 1972, the Democrats actually picked up two seats for a 56–42 majority. Were Nixon impeached, the vote to convict and remove in the Senate would now require at least eleven Republican votes.[35] By that standard, Nixon seemed safe.

It is possible to speculate that if the Republicans had been in firm control of the Senate, there might never have been a special prosecutor and there might never have been the initial Senate hearings to investigate the practices of the presidential campaign. Certainly, there would have been intense pressure from Senate Democrats after the Watergate break-in, even if they were in the minority, to take some action as the trial of the burglars preceded and their stories came out. However, it is safe to assume that a Republican-dominated Senate would have treated the Watergate Affair differently and been much more reluctant to take decisive action.

An investigative committee may have been formed with witnesses brought in to testify, but the creation of a special prosecutor outside of the Justice Department was an unprecedented act that probably would have been resisted by a Republican-dominated Senate. And let us not forget that if the Senate hearings had taken a different path, the existence of the Oval Office tapes might never have come to light. Furthermore, with a Republican majority it would have been that much more difficult to even hold the trial itself.

According to Rule XI of *Senate Procedures and Guidelines for Impeachment Trials in the United States Senate*, articles of impeachment adopted in the House and sent to the Senate can be referred to a special committee of the Senate appointed for the purpose of hearing evidence and examining witnesses on the impeachment charges. The committee is invested with all the investigatory powers of the Senate and can issue a report making recommendations to the full Senate, which is the only body that can convict.

Presumably with the Senate in control of the president's party, impeachment recommendations can get bottled up in this committee. The original intent of this rule was to keep the House from voting articles of impeachment that would then constitute a dilatory expenditure of the Senate's time as it tried an impeachment at the expense of consideration of other matters. But the net result is that, in the modern era, according to the Senate rules, the crimes charged in articles of impeachment must rise to a high level, indeed, to get even a trial in a Senate controlled by the president's party.[36]

Thus if the Republicans had controlled the Senate, President Nixon might have decided not to resign but to take his chances with a trial in the Senate (and such a trial may have long delayed). Or, as an alternative, a Republican Senate could have taken up impeachment and voted quickly to dismiss.

3. Important Policy Differences between the President and Congressional Leaders

As noted above, there were some policy differences between President Nixon and the majority party in Congress, but there was also a substantial amount of cooperation on a number of issues. In fact, the sharpest substantive differences between the president and Congress in the Nixon era were more in the nature of disagreements over the proper distribution of authorities under the separation of powers. The policy disagreements were more typical partisan disagreements.

As president, Nixon was more a pragmatist than an ideologue. He often demonstrated that he was willing to try different approaches to solving the country's problems regardless of their ideological label. When inflation emerged and damaged the economy, he was willing to implement wage and price controls, which are abhorrent to conservative free market true believers. Also, often overlooked is that the Republican president and the Democratically controlled Congress enacted a surprisingly wide range of important legislation. Some of that legislation, including the National Environmental Policy Act and a proposed negative income tax that eventually became the Earned Income Tax Credit, can even be properly considered landmark progressive and bipartisan legislation.

But where Congress and the president really differed was in Nixon's prosecution of the Vietnam War, which generated harsh criticism from most congressional Democrats. But by 1974, with the policy of Vietnamization, the war became less of an issue.

Nixon's two major points of domestic conflict with Congress were over judicial appointments and the impoundment of appropriated funds. Furthermore, in order to avoid battles with Congress over control of the bureaucracy, the Executive Office of the President was expanded enormously under Nixon to circumvent congressional interference.[37] In addition, the president used the White House and federal law enforcement to surveil and harass political enemies.

These separation of powers disputes created conflict between the president and congressional Democrats and were seen at the time as a harbinger of the creation of an imperial presidency.[38] But they were not to the point where the president would have been seen as an actual threat to the Republic who had to be removed. The policy conflicts between Nixon and Congress, therefore, never rose to the level of the stark disagreements over Reconstruction that affected President Andrew Johnson's relations with the Radical Republicans a century earlier. But what was most alarming to Congress was President Nixon's use of the offices of the federal government to pursue his personal political agenda.

4. TIME OF NATIONAL CRISIS OR SOCIAL UNREST

Nixon's presidency took place in a time of great social upheaval that was almost unique in American history. The national climate in the late 1960s was turbulent, as demonstrations and protests were commonplace. President Nixon inherited an unpopular and divisive war in Vietnam that had no quick and easy resolution. Nixon's decision to "not lose the war" and thereby continue it resulted in massive street demonstrations and protests that attracted extensive media coverage.

Civil rights remained a serious concern. It had been less than a decade since the passage of the Civil Rights and Voting Rights Acts. The nation had experienced widespread race riots just prior to Nixon's election in the wake of the assassination of Martin Luther King.

The national situation became even more unsettled in the early 1970s as a seemingly unrelated war in the Middle East produced an oil embargo in the fall of 1973 that severely hampered the economy and impinged on the lives of millions of ordinary American citizens who had to wait in long lines just to buy gas for their car.

Thus, during the time of the Watergate Affair, the national economy was the most unstable since the end of the Great Depression of the 1930s. Unemployment went up, as did prices on many consumer goods. Inflation gripped the nation. The 1973 gas shortages and the subsequent economic recession all contributed to a sense of public unease. All these factors contributed to the general feeling that Watergate, and by association the Nixon presidency, was destabilizing the nation in some undefined way.

5. PERSONAL ANIMOSITY BETWEEN THE PRESIDENT AND CONGRESSIONAL LEADERS

Richard Nixon's long political career highlighted numerous confrontations with various members of Congress that could have produced harsh feelings and grudges.[39] Some of these were undoubtedly shaped by normal partisan animosities, but some certainly resulted from personal antagonisms. Nixon had a strong personality that could rub some people the wrong way, and he also held grudges toward some of his political opponents. It would be inaccurate, however, to conclude that the pressure to force Nixon out of office was motivated primarily by personal strife between him and congressional leaders.

There is no evidence of an extensive feud between President Nixon and any congressional leader that would have driven an impeachment effort. Carl Albert, the Democratic Speaker of the House during the Watergate Affair, certainly disagreed with many of Nixon's polices, but he never exhibited any behavior that would indicate that he had personal motives to remove Nixon from office. When Agnew resigned from office, Albert, as Speaker of the House, was next in line for the presidency until the vice presidential vacancy was filled. Albert controlled the House agenda and could have prevented any confirmation vote of a new vice-presidential appointment; however, he chose not to interfere. When President Nixon picked House Minority Leader Gerald Ford as the next vice president, Albert expedited the confirmation. Albert was well aware that he could have blocked Ford's confirmation, but he felt that the people had elected a Republican to be president and that any effort by him to gain the presidency would have been viewed as grossly self-serving and borderline unethical.[40]

Nixon had even better relations with Mike Mansfield, the Democratic Senate Majority Leader. Mansfield appointed the chairman and members of the original Senate Watergate Committee and supported the creation of a special prosecutor, but these actions were not motivated by any personal dislike for Nixon. Nixon conferred with Mansfield on numerous occasions and their relationship was professional and cooperative. Nixon seemed to respect Mansfield and thought that he could find common ground with the Democratic senator. Mansfield even had kind things to say about Nixon early in his term of office.

While Nixon's critics often accused him of being detached and distant, Nixon could be sociable and often attempted to reach out in a personal way to others both in and outside government. He had formed lasting friendships and was not the bitter recluse sometimes depicted in the popular media of the time. Clearly, some in Congress did not like Nixon and some may have even hated him, but there is no reason to conclude that congressional leaders wanted Nixon out of office solely on the basis of any personal vendetta.

6. CLIMATE OF PUBLIC ANIMOSITY TOWARD THE PRESIDENT

There was a growing underlying sense among the American people that something was seriously wrong in the nation during the later years of the Nixon presidency. War in the Middle East had created a worldwide oil embargo that produced gasoline shortages in America, which severely shocked the economy. The resulting recession increased unemployment and ended the prosperity that Americans had become accustomed to. This occurred after years characterized by widespread antiwar feelings and anxiety about the future of the Vietnam War. This all led to a national climate of ill at ease, which, while not directly related to Watergate, occurred at the same time. In the minds of many Americans, it was not difficult to think that Nixon's troubles were in some undefined way contaminating the nation.

President Nixon's popularity declined precipitously almost immediately after his inauguration for a second term. By the time he resigned, Nixon was burdened by the lowest presidential popularity rating in history (at only 24%).[41]

Even decades after his death, books are still being written about Richard Nixon that attack his character and political style.[42] Books of this nature make a case that Nixon's harsh and aggressive manner, which helped him win elections, ultimately created a climate that made a scandal like Watergate not only possible but inevitable.[43] There is little doubt that Nixon during his long career gave rise to hostility from opponents who readily attacked him when it appeared that he had been caught in some type of wrongdoing. When the Watergate scandal emerged, venomous assaults by Nixon distractors became more visible.

Prior to the Nixon presidency, the media typically followed an unwritten code that the president of the country deserved a great deal of respect and should be treated with deference. As the Watergate scandal deepened, and perhaps as evidence of nascent polarization of the body politic, this attitude gradually changed.[44] Thus, by 1974, Nixon's popularity ratings had dropped to historic lows and much of the American people seemed willing to accept and in fact supported his removal from office before the conclusion of his term.

7. THE PRESIDENT ACCUSED OF CRIMINAL BEHAVIOR—ACTUAL

President Nixon did not plan, oversee, or approve of the Watergate burglary. The evidence is clear that he did not even know it was happening until the burglars were caught. The eighteen and a half minute gap on one of the White House tapes has long allowed for speculation about the president's knowledge of the burglary. Despite numerous attempts using the latest technology to retrieve the conversation it appears to be lost forever. The lost conversation apparently was between Nixon and H. R. Haldeman, but it took place three days after the burglars were arrested. The gap therefore is unlikely to have shown that Nixon had prior knowledge of the break-in, and no other evidence has ever surfaced that Nixon had been involved. Additionally, virtually all the other participants in the Watergate Affair have consistently denied that the president had prior knowledge of the burglary.

The Constitution states that impeachable crimes are "treason, bribery, and other high crimes and misdemeanors." Nixon made false public statements, but he never lied under oath, and therefore never committed perjury. He never accepted a bribe nor in any way was he suspected of any treasonous act.

President Nixon's impeachable "high crime" was obstruction of justice, failure to comply with Congress, and conspiracy. While, initially, he wasn't even sure that the Watergate burglary was connected to his campaign, there is ample evidence that he was aware of efforts and even directed efforts by his staff to hinder the criminal investigation of the burglary. He was also at least aware that his office had attempted to have the CIA intervene in the FBI investigation on grounds that national security issues were involved when, in fact, they were not.

Therefore, it is clear that President Nixon engaged in actions that were beyond the law. The question that needs to be asked, however, is were these actions sufficient to warrant an impeachment? Was involvement in this type of criminal behavior of sufficient magnitude to be considered a "high crime" and would Nixon have been judged differently under entirely different circumstances?

8. The President Accused of Criminal Behavior—Political

The three charges approved by the House Judiciary committee can mostly be properly classified as procedural in nature.[45] Obstruction of justice is based on withholding evidence. Contempt of Congress is based on not complying with congressional orders to turn over the White House tapes. Nixon contended that withholding of the tapes was justifiable because he was president and that they contained personal information that was his private property. The U.S. Supreme Court, however, ruled that even though there was a justifiable principle of executive privilege, because the tapes contained potentially criminal evidence even the president must comply with the courts and hand them over. Nixon then complied (but there was still that eighteen-minute gap). Congress then found Nixon's unwillingness to cooperate with their subpoenas an impeachable offense, even though Nixon finally relented after the court made its ruling and gave over the tapes.

Nixon made disingenuous public statements about his involvement in covering up the Watergate burglary. These statements were not made under oath and do not constitute a criminal act and were not the bases for any of the approved articles of impeachment.

Nixon's campaign staff did not even at first consider the Watergate break-in to be a criminal act, but just a normal tactic in a high-stakes political campaign. They felt that wiretapping was widespread in political campaigns and that they were just engaging in normal political practice. After all, in 1968, the Johnson White House had engaged in wiretapping albeit arguably in the cause of national security.[46]

While the use of bugging in a campaign may have been debatable before Watergate, the events of the Nixon presidency clearly redefined what is and is not an acceptable campaign tactic. Breaking into an office is a criminal action, and planning and approving it is also illegal. It cannot be disputed that John Mitchell, Jeb Magruder, and John Dean along with E. Howard Hunt, G. Gordon Libby, and the five burglars all committed a crime.

Nixon, however, was never guilty of these offenses. His major misdeed was making false statements about the involvement of his campaign in these actions to avoid political embarrassment. These statements, however, were never made in court nor to a police authority. He withheld evidence related to the crime, but he always was able to make the legal argument that he was under no constitutional obligation to turn it over to Congress or the special prosecutor, or even to the federal district court. When the U.S. Supreme Court rendered its judgment that a president had no special privilege to withhold evidence, Nixon complied with the ruling.

Nixon's impeachable actions were originally motivated by political objectives. He wanted to avoid damage to his reelection bid that could result from embarrassment related to the criminal acts of members of his reelection campaign. Unfortunately for Nixon, his attempt to contain a political crime led to committing other offenses that provided Congress with sufficient grounds to consider articles of impeachment.

Was the Watergate Cover-up an Impeachable Offense?

On August 7, 1974, at five o'clock in the afternoon, a delegation of Republican congressmen led by Senator Barry Goldwater, a former presidential candidate, met with President Nixon to inform him that there was enough support in the House to adopt articles of impeachment and, more ominously, there were enough votes in the Senate to convict. Senator Goldwater, himself, informed the president that he was ready to vote to convict. Nixon resigned the next day.

In the emotional climate of the time, there was an overwhelming belief that President Nixon's involvement in the Watergate burglary cover-up was sufficiently serious to justify impeachment and conviction. In cool hindsight, however, one needs to ask whether the Watergate Affair truly rose to the level of a "high crime" that justified the removal of a president from office.

President Nixon made a series of errors, which only intensified the perception of his guilt. The battle over the White House tapes greatly exacerbated the public's false perception that the president ordered the break-in. Members of Congress were outraged by the president's use of executive privilege to limit their rights to obtain subpoenaed evidence, including the White House tapes. This, even though the Supreme Court eventually supported the executive privilege claim, at least in principle. The eagerness of many congressmen and senators to support impeachment and removal was undoubtedly a by-product of this struggle between the branches.

Once the tapes were released, however, Nixon's "goose was cooked." The tapes provided incontrovertible evidence that Nixon approved of a plan to raise money to buy the silence of the Watergate burglars. That act alone constitutes a textbook case of obstruction of justice.

However, had Nixon had the luxury of a Republican majority in Congress, he would have handled the situation differently (as would have Congress), and, thus, he probably would not have been close to impeachment in the first place. But this was not the case, and Nixon chose his actions with the realization that the majority of both chambers would have preferred that he was not reelected in the first place.

The Constitution gives Congress the sole authority to determine what is and what is not an impeachable offense. The circumstances surrounding the Watergate Affair all lead up to the judgment that President Nixon's actions had been sufficiently criminal in nature to warrant impeachment and removal. If the make-up of Congress had been different then the outcome of the Nixon presidency might have been different, but once history happens, it does not change. The House Judiciary Committee judged, and probably both the House of Representatives and the Senate would have judged, President Nixon's behavior as a "high crime," and therefore it was.

The operative conditions that produced an impeachment were divided government, an inept and some would say paranoid management of the scandal, and, above all, demonstrable criminal behavior. The fact that Nixon was unpopular both in the public and in Congress didn't help either. Thus, the move to impeach Nixon was by and large a political act. Presidents before and since have engaged in demonstrably criminal behavior, Clinton's perjury, for example, and have gotten away with it. That is not to say that Nixon shouldn't have been impeached and, if necessary, removed. But if Nixon's probable impeachment demonstrates anything, it demonstrates that the impeachment process is under most circumstances political, and, for Nixon, the political context was not in his favor.

CHAPTER FIVE

Ronald Reagan and the Iran-Contra Affair

The Nixon case breached the century-old aversion to presidential impeachment and created an entirely new mind-set about its use. Once an unthinkable possibility, removing an elected president from office, gained new legitimacy, the use of impeachment as a political weapon was rediscovered. The Nixon impeachment effort, while never producing a Senate trial, had nevertheless forced a sitting president to resign from office, and members of the political establishment began to realize that they had a new, powerful weapon. The Watergate Affair that brought down Nixon had many unique qualities, but it demonstrated how, under the right circumstances, the threat of impeachment could credibly be used to attack a president.

The nineteenth-century presidential impeachments had been used exclusively against presidents who had never been elected to the office and had only obtained their high position through the death of an incumbent. Nixon, however, had not only been elected but reelected by a large margin. It became clear that impeachment could be used even if the president had gained office through the vote. Impeachment was no longer reserved for the removal of an "accidental" president. This realization created an entirely new arena for partisan combat.

But there are limits to the tactic. Nixon was wildly unpopular and faced a divided government. His crimes were not even arguably within his responsibilities as chief executive. Therefore, the Nixon case for impeachment was easy to make. Not so much for President Ronald Reagan.

Ronald Wilson Reagan was born in 1911 in Tampico, a small town in rural Illinois. His father, Jack Reagan, was a salesman and his mother, Nelle Wilson Reagan, had strong religious feelings. "We were damn poor," Reagan liked to say as he talked about being a young man during the Great

Depression. He was a well-liked young man who worked as a lifeguard at a local lake. He then earned an athletic scholarship at nearby Eureka College. In college he majored in economics and sociology and listened to his favorite professor push social reform and lament the plight of exploited workers in factories such as those owned by Henry Ford.

He was not a good student and only paid attention long enough to narrowly pass his classes so that he could pursue his true passions, acting in school plays and playing varsity football. In combining the two he followed his love of sports to become a sportscaster. He then rejoined the acting profession and went on to act in over fifty films, some memorable, others in the B category. In Hollywood, he defended the New Deal, and even became the member of organizations that were later to be labeled subversive. He then went on to become president of the Screen Actors Guild. During the McCarthy era, Reagan avoided the blacklist by becoming an informer for the FBI, although it is apparent that his anticommunist stance was largely principled.

Reagan's hostility toward communism had its roots in the Alger Hiss affair. Becoming disillusioned with Josef Stalin's totalitarian regime and communism, he began to view some Hollywood activists in support of the USSR as Soviet agents. He would soon discover that liberal organizations that he belonged to, such as the Hollywood Independent Citizens Committee of the Arts, Sciences and Professions, along with the American Veterans Committee, had members who were "communist sympathizers." His increasingly conservative views caused him to have a falling out with his colleagues. When a series of actors' strikes crippled the film industry in the 1940s, Reagan came to the conclusion that the strikes were "tangled in a plot by communists to take over Hollywood."[1]

Reagan's aversion to communism compelled him to act as an informant for the FBI. Later, Reagan testified as a friendly witness before the House Committee on Un-American Activities. In testimony, Reagan favored the barring of communists from the Screen Actors Guild but was reluctant to "name names" in the investigations (at least in public).

Governor of the Golden State

In California, where the film industry is a major part of the economy, actors are elected as governors, as mayors, and to Congress on a fairly regular basis. Reagan, though a transplant to the state, began to enter politics just as his movie star began to fade. Reagan's impressive speech "A Time for Choosing," in support of presidential candidate Barry Goldwater in 1964, brought Reagan to the attention of the California Republican Party, and he was later approached by a group of wealthy Republican donors who convinced him to run for governor in 1966.

The incumbent governor, Pat Brown, took this ambitious conservative actor lightly. However, inner-city riots in Los Angeles, anti–Vietnam War demonstrations in Berkeley, a reneged promise not to seek a third term, and a harsh primary challenge from Los Angeles mayor Sam Yorty weakened Brown going into the general election. Reagan easily beat the incumbent by fifteen points.

Reagan would win all but three counties in the state, and except for San Francisco, he barely lost the other two. So, Reagan, the well-liked political outsider, inherited a state with a higher education system that was the envy of the world, but also with growing student radicalism, farm worker exploitation, and urban unrest. Reagan was a quick study and in short order he learned the intricacies of the office and how to work with a recalcitrant Democratic legislature.

Under Reagan, California became the seventh largest economy in the world and America's most populous state. California also became somewhat of a curiosity. It became home to large numbers of people seeking a counterculture lifestyle even as Southern California continued to be the symbol of urban sprawl. But Reagan made no apologies for the freeways and the corporate state. While liberals such as Jerry Brown and other progressives derided excess development and a lack of social consciousness, Reagan embraced the pursuit of personal and material gain.

Reagan's attractiveness to the GOP led to his bid to become president in 1968. An anti-Nixon Republican movement and Reagan's conservatism made him increasingly popular in the South, and thus a formidable candidate. But Nixon's considerable establishment party strength pushed him over the top with Nelson Rockefeller in second place in front of Reagan who garnered about 15 percent of the delegates. This result probably understated Reagan's strength in part as he was running against a fellow Californian.[2]

Reagan's gubernatorial policies ranged between sometimes unexpected liberalism and bedrock conservatism. He supported a fair housing bill that assisted minorities; signed, albeit reluctantly, a pre-*Roe* bill that allowed abortion in the case of rape or incest and in cases where the mother's life was in danger. Previously, he had signed the Mulford Act, which repealed a law allowing "open carry" of a loaded firearm. Reagan also signed a Family Law Act that was the first no-fault-divorce legislation in the country. (As an example of his liberal positions, after Reagan was no longer governor, he opposed and helped defeat a 1978 ballot initiative that would have prohibited gays and lesbians from teaching in public schools.)

On the other hand, he drastically cut the budget for the Department of Mental Hygiene. This resulted in the release on to the street of thousands of mentally ill patients. He was also a strong supporter of capital punishment, but California Supreme Court decisions allowed for only one execution during his two terms.

One of the more entertaining aspects of Reagan's leadership in the state was the skirmishes he engaged in with the University of California's radical students. Colleges across the country were in turmoil over the Vietnam War and California was one of the leading battlegrounds. Reagan detested the long-haired extremists. Nonetheless, he did side with them when he declared that campuses run by bureaucrats and "punch-card" functionaries could stifle learning and the spirit of inquiry. Ironically, therefore, both the radicals and the governor saw the state as the enemy of freedom, a monstrous bureaucracy demanding higher taxes from the people.

For the most part, however, the governor made few friends in California's academic community. Cuts to higher education led to increases in tuition, further enraging students. As Reagan tightened the financial screws, confrontations between police and demonstrators reached an ugly climax in 1969 when students tried to create a "People's Park" in Berkeley at a construction site for a new University of California building. Reagan ordered the National Guard, the California Highway Patrol, and the Oakland Tactical Squad to disperse those who refused to leave the area. Helicopters dropped tear gas for days, bystanders were hit with stray bullets, and one person was killed.[3]

But the governor had few regrets about the use of force and continued to follow the hardline platform he had touted in his gubernatorial campaign.

Reagan's second term as governor was devoted to welfare reform, and to "cut," "squeeze" and "trim" the cost of government. The governor campaigned against "welfare bums." In particular, the federal Aid to Families with Dependent Children was in his crosshairs, gaining the governor a reputation for having little compassion for the poor. Reagan considered such programs a plague on future generations. He chided welfare recipients for spending their checks at the liquor store or at the racetrack. His California Welfare Reform Act of 1971 created so many stipulations that the welfare rolls dropped by some 300,000 recipients. On the other hand, Reagan funded the University of California system at a much more generous rate than his progressive successor, Jerry Brown.[4]

The Politics of the Presidency: The First Two Years

In 1976, Reagan challenged the incumbent but nonelected president, Gerald Ford, touting himself as the true conservative Republican candidate. Reagan, however, may have felt the pressure of an impending Ford victory when he promised to choose Richard Schweiker, a centrist senator from Pennsylvania, as his running mate should he win the nomination. The selection probably hurt more than helped with his base. Primary victories in North Carolina, Texas, and California bolstered his hopes, but defeats in New Hampshire, Florida, and his childhood home state of Illinois helped lead to Ford's victory. Reagan campaigned on the threat of the Soviet empire and the dangers of nuclear war. In the end, Ford would lose the general election to Jimmy Carter.[5]

The October Surprise and the 1980 Campaign

Reagan's showing in 1976 made him the frontrunner for the 1980 Republican nomination. This time he beat the moderate, George H. W. Bush. In the general election it was Reagan who asked the nation, "Are you better off than you were four years ago?" Americans had little trouble answering that one. Inflation and interest rates peaked during the Carter administration and the economy was slowing.

In addition, for President Jimmy Carter, the Iranian hostage crisis and a failed rescue attempt that left eight American servicemen dead was an ongoing foreign policy disaster—as was Carter's massively unpopular "giveaway" of the Panama Canal.

Consequently, Reagan carried forty-four states and 489 electoral college votes to Carter's forty-one. In what was a "wave" election, Republicans gained control of the Senate and added thirty-four seats in the Democratic-controlled House. This would provide President Reagan an avenue for early legislative success.

During the campaign, there may have been back-channel contacts between the Reagan campaign and the Iranian government to prevent the release of the U.S. hostages held by Iran until after Reagan was elected president. Certainly, the motive was there. If the hostages had been released during the campaign that "October surprise" would have delivered a massive boost to the Carter campaign.[6]

According to the *New York Times*, a foreign policy advisor to the Reagan campaign and the eventual CIA director, William Casey, is supposed to have met with representatives of the Iranian government to arrange a deal for the release of the hostages when Reagan became president. To the extent that these meetings took place *before* the November election, they were in violation of U.S. law.[7] The first two meetings were alleged to have occurred in July 1980 in Madrid. A second round of meetings, at which a deal was consummated, supposedly took place in October of that year in Paris. At least three witnesses placed vice-presidential candidate George H. W. Bush at some or all of those meetings. To this day there is tremendous controversy as to whether these meetings or any meetings at all took place between the Iranians and the Reagan campaign prior to the election and during the transition.[8]

While a rumored surprise release of the hostages did not materialize, it is clear that there were numerous attempts by the Iranians or persons representing themselves as Iranian emissaries to contact the Reagan campaign both before and after the election. Most of these inquiries were attempted by expatriate Iranians who hoped to parlay their contacts back in the old country into some kind of financial return. Many in fact were scams. But the Iranian government had good reason to want to contact the United States, even if it wasn't all that interested in dealing with President Carter (who had provided asylum to the hated shah).

On September 22, 1980, Iraq, trying to take advantage of the chaos created by the Iranian Revolution, launched a full-scale invasion of Iran. The Iraqis were supplied by the Soviets and the Iranians were or at least had been supplied by the Americans under the shah. As the Iraqis advanced, the Iranians were desperate for replacement parts for their American-made weapons. They were so desperate, in fact, that they approached the Israelis who, for their own part, hoped to curry favor with the new Iranian regime. But the problem for the Iranians, as noted above, was that they were determined not to deal with the Carter administration. All that was left for them was Reagan. Consequently, the Iranians had every incentive to contact the Reagan campaign. They needed the weapons that they could only get from the United States, but they would not deal with President Carter and, in fact, had an interest in humiliating him. Finally, and most convincingly, Reagan himself in a postpresidency interview as much as admitted that his campaign was in contact with the Iranians. In a 1991 interview Reagan said,

Reagan: "I did some things actually the other way, to try to be of help in getting those hostages . . . out of there. . . . The only efforts on my part were directed at getting them home."

Question: "Did that mean contacts with the Iranian government?"

Reagan: "Not by me. No."

Question: "By your campaign, perhaps?"

Reagan: "I can't get into the details. Some of these things are still classified."[9]

In 1992 the House of Representatives, then under Democratic control, convened a task force to investigate Reagan campaign collusion with the Iranian government. But the committee found no credible evidence to link the Reagan campaign with the timing of the release of the hostages. The campaign *had* been contacted by persons claiming to be representatives of the Iranian government, but there was no way to know whether the contacts were legitimate or not. Furthermore, there is still no conclusive evidence to prove that William Casey met with Iranian representatives on behalf of the campaign.[10] However, whether he did or didn't, the Iranians had plenty of incentive on their own to schedule the release of the hostages as they did at the moment President Carter left office in order to both influence the election and humiliate President Carter. All the Reagan campaign needed to do was stay out of the way. In fact, just as Reagan was sworn in, the Iranian hostages were set free.

Later on, with Reagan as president, Casey and Oliver North did entertain overtures from the Iranians, probably in contravention to the law, but that was in the course of the conduct of foreign policy by a sitting president. Whether those contacts predated the Iran-Contra Affair, maybe even back to the campaign of 1980, we'll probably never know.

The Reagan Presidency

At sixty-nine Reagan was the oldest president to be sworn in for his first term. But for his age, Reagan brought a new style of governing. He was what presidential scholar Stephen Skowronek would call a "reconstructive president."[11] Because reconstructive presidents challenge the status quo in fundamental ways, they attract fierce opposition, opposition that can include efforts toward impeachment. In Reagan's case, what angered his opponents was not so much that he was dealing with divided government, although he was, it was that he was attempting to do something different, not in concert with the existing order.

A reconstructive president disrupts the existing order, or what Skowronek calls the prevailing regime, in three ways. First, the reconstructive president builds a new political coalition. Reagan transformed the Republican Party by recruiting evangelicals and southern Democrats, thereby creating a Republican lock on southern politics that exists to this day. Second, a reconstructive president reforms the office. Reagan brought Roger Ailes, a television producer, into the White House as communications director and the Reagan presidency was conducted according to entertainment values with an actor at the helm. But there was more to it than that. The Reagan administration was exceptionally careful in vetting the ideological purity of judicial and bureaucratic appointments. To work in the Reagan administration was not just to be a Republican but also to be a Reagan acolyte. Finally, a reconstructive president reorders policy norms. In policy terms, the Reagan presidency was revolutionary but not in a progressive way. Reagan's politics can more accurately be described as the politics of retrenchment. In many ways, the policy proposals of the Reagan administration conformed to those of President Reagan's most admired chief executive, Calvin Coolidge.

Because a reconstructive president challenges the conventional wisdom, he is also likely to arouse opposition beyond the norm. Not only are his policies perceived to be wrong, they can also be perceived to be crazy or even illegal. Reagan was regarded by his opponents as a political lightweight and not particularly bright. And, because of his advanced age, he was also suspected to be past his prime. All of this was important, because in combination with divided government, the Reagan victory in 1980 laid the political groundwork for an impeachment.

In 1981 Reagan's termination of 11,345 striking air traffic controllers set the philosophical tone for his presidency. In this one decision, he firmly indicated that these government employees could not strike due to stipulations in their contracts. And with this act, he indicated that would stand tough against an entrenched federal bureaucracy, while at the same time signaling support for corporate interests against those of the unions.[12]

The president's judicial appointments also reflected his push toward a "new conservatism," the basis of his campaign platform. He had a litmus test for his appointments, putting an emphasis on judges supporting smaller government, including a revived federalism, and he reversed the trend to get religion and moral issues out of politics. Those policies were so old, they were new. His lower court appointees tended to be younger, ensuring longer terms for those supporting his policies. He appointed the first woman to sit on the Supreme Court, the moderately activist (but in the Reagan mold) Sandra Day O'Connor. He did receive a setback in his second term with the rejection of his conservative Supreme Court nominee, Robert Bork. A subsequent nominee, Douglas Ginsburg, withdrew his nomination after revelations of his marijuana use. In his place, Anthony Kennedy would be confirmed.

Civil rights advocates and feminists were angered by the nomination of Clarence Pendleton Jr. as chair of the U.S. Commission on Civil Rights. The conservative African American director broke with the Carter administration's previous civil rights programs including opposition to busing and comparable worth.[13]

The economy was the central theme of Reagan's candidate platform. The new president was a fan of supply side economics, or the belief that the most successful intervention by the government in the economy was no intervention. The fact that as an actor he received most of his income through salary, which was taxable at relatively high rates (above investments, for example), meant that he had a lifelong aversion to income taxes. Thus, he sought to reduce taxes on personal income, estates, and corporations dramatically.

With support from a Republican majority in the Senate and party gains in the House, along with the support of some conservative "Blue Dog" Democrats, Reagan skillfully forged legislative victories, particularly on taxes. Apocryphally, Arthur Laffer, Reagan's favorite economist, fashioned the Reagan tax plan on a napkin at his favorite hamburger restaurant. And based upon that plan, Reagan successfully passed the Economic Recovery Tax Act of 1981.

Reagan's bill reduced the top marginal tax rate of 70 percent to 50 percent while the lowest rate fell from 14 percent to 11 percent. The president hoped that lower taxes and reduced regulation would produce enough tax revenue to reduce the national debt. This never materialized, in part because of Reagan's long-standing aversion to communism and his view of the Soviet Union as the "evil empire" that compelled him to convince Congress to increase military spending by some 40 percent.

Heavy borrowing by the federal government and the consequences of the "savings and loan crisis" would also increase the debt throughout his term. As a result, the president in 1982 had to call for a $98.2 billion tax hike, a move he had previously promised never to make. The gross national product did grow, however, at an average annual rate of close to 7.91 percent.[14]

One of the most important reversals of his predecessor's policies came in the form of rejecting détente and escalating the Cold War. Reagan detested communism and viewed the Soviet sphere as an evil empire. The president called for increases in the development of high-tech weapons such as the neutron bomb (the people killer but building saver) and the Trident nuclear submarine, which President Carter had halted. The president also proposed a controversial and costly Strategic Defense Initiative, known as "Star Wars," to counter the Soviet strategic nuclear weapons threat. Reagan's proposals represented no less than a rejection of mainstream deterrence theory, which was based on the principle of mutually assured destruction.

The 1982 Midterm Election

The 1982 midterm election resulted in a loss for the Republicans of twenty-seven seats in the House. Democratic membership went from a majority of 56 percent to 62 percent after the election. The Senate Republican majority of fifty-four remained unchanged.

Prior to 1982, along with the Republican Senate, the president had managed to forge a coalition of Republicans and conservative Democrats in the House in order to pass the lion's share of his legislative program, but after the midterm elections building that coalition became all the more difficult. There were some amendments to Social Security in 1983. But as is common with the recent advent of partisan polarization, once the honeymoon is over, it's over, especially when the president is dealing with divided government.[15]

When a president faces resistance in the domestic arena, he will begin to focus on foreign affairs. It is in that arena that the president has more unchallenged authority. And Reagan was no different from other presidents in that regard.

In 1983 a U.S. Marine barracks in Beirut, Lebanon, was destroyed by a terrorist bomb and 241 servicemen and women were killed. The troops were stationed there as peacekeepers in the Lebanese Civil War, but they had increasingly been caught in the crossfire as they were stationed at one of the most contested locations in the country, the Beirut Airport. In the aftermath of the bombing it was clear that there was no role for the United

States in what had become a full-scale civil war. In the face of opposition at home—Congress had tried to invoke the War Powers Act to limit the deployment—Reagan withdrew the troops.

Concurrently with the withdrawal from Lebanon, citing threats from a communist takeover in Grenada, and appeals from the Organization of Eastern Caribbean States, the president sent in troops to help install a new government on the island of Grenada. The Cubans, and presumably their Soviet sponsors, had established an increasingly large presence on the island. This included the construction of a landing strip that was ostensibly meant to accommodate larger commercial jets, but could also, in fact, accommodate long-range military bombers. In addition to the Cuban presence, President Reagan also cited the dangers faced by American citizens on the island who were attending a local medical school.[16]

The Grenada invasion was part of the "Reagan Doctrine" aimed at creating a network of assistance to opponents of Soviet influence around the world. Mujahidin forces in Afghanistan as well as "freedom fighters" in Africa would receive military training and equipment. Ultimately, this doctrine would lead to the largest scandal the administration faced and potential charges of impeachment.

Reelection

Reagan was returned for a second term after a resounding reelection victory. The president captured forty-nine states and a record 525 electoral votes with 58.8 percent of the popular vote compared to 40.6 percent for the Democratic candidate, former vice president Walter Mondale. The Republicans also made modest gains in the House with the Democrats still in the majority and left the Senate unchanged with a three-vote Republican majority. The president, therefore, was still facing a divided government.[17]

During the campaign, to quell fears that the United States sought a military confrontation, Reagan argued that the United States should at all costs avoid war with the Soviets. Furthermore, Reagan stressed that the United States posed no threat to the Soviet Union. The president outlined a strategy for cooperation, normal and regular dialogue with the Soviets, and a focus on arms reductions, including the resumption of START nuclear weapons negotiations in 1985. For his part, the glasnost and perestroika reforms of Soviet leader Mikhail Gorbachev opened the door for constructive dialogue between the superpowers. A series of peace talks ensued and helped to reduce tensions. Subsequent talks in Reykjavik resulted in an agreement with a goal to eliminate intermediate and short-range nuclear missiles in Europe, reducing the number of Soviet and U.S. nuclear weapons on the continent.[18]

But just as Reagan was negotiating with Gorbachev, the United States was supporting clients in counterinsurgency operations in Afghanistan and Nicaragua against Soviet clients. The problem for Reagan was that Congress had passed a law that specifically forbade the arming of either side in the Nicaraguan civil war. It was Reagan's resistance to that restriction that laid the groundwork for the biggest scandal in the Reagan administration, the Iran-Contra Affair.

The 1986 Midterm Election: Threats to the Nation and the Origins of Iran-Contra

Midterm elections rarely bolster presidencies and 1986 was no exception. Democrats regained control of the Senate and added five seats to their majority in the House. These results would be a factor in the politics of the upcoming Iran-Contra controversy.

The Soviet Union wasn't the only adversary of the Reagan administration. Relations between the United States and Libya were contentious as were relations between the United States and Cuban dictator Fidel Castro. In 1986, Reagan called Libyan strongman Muammar Gaddafi the "Mad Dog of the Middle East." The administration had even claimed that the dictator had dispatched agents to the United States to assassinate Reagan. This tension came to a head in April 1986, when a bomb exploded in a Berlin discotheque, injuring sixty-three American service personnel and killing one. Reagan's response was to launch a series of air strikes against Libya. Reagan justified the strikes as self-defense on the part of the United States under the United Nations Charter. However, a large majority of the UN General Assembly condemned the attack.

But going back to his ideological roots, the president was continuously preoccupied with the presence of a communist threat in the Americas. He criticized President Carter for a weak response to a civil war in Nicaragua in which American ally and dictator Anastasio Somoza was overthrown by the left-leaning Sandinista National Liberation Front, headed by Daniel Ortega. Reagan also had long asserted that the Farabundo Martí Front for National Liberation in El Salvador was a communist insurgency backed by Russia and Cuba. The president claimed that for no good reason (due to human rights abuses), Carter had abandoned the conservative El Salvador regime.

In the White House, the president was caught up in a debate on what to do in Central America between hard liners, such as Secretary of State Alexander Haig, UN ambassador Jeanne Kirkpatrick, and CIA director William Casey, and pragmatists, such as Chief of Staff James Baker and White House deputy chief of staff Michael Deaver. How would the administration respond to the communist threat in Central America? Would the administration risk direct intervention and send troops to Central America or just send arms and economic aid?

In Nicaragua, Reagan publicly called for Congress to provide military aid for the anticommunist opponents of the Sandinista regime, the Contras. Because it was apparent that the public (along with a congressional majority) was in no mood to send more troops to fight new communist governments, wanting to avoid another Vietnam, the administration settled on military and economic aid. The administration proposed that covert logistical and training assistance would go to the Contras. The problem was that the Contras did not have much support in their own country. They were largely composed of Somoza's former National Guard who, along with the despot they protected, had raided the nation's treasury and brutally repressed opposition for decades. Consequently, they were wildly unpopular, including among the democratic liberal opposition to Ortega.

Anticipating the administration's covert activities, Congress adopted three amendments between 1982 and 1984 designed to prevent the president from delivering covert assistance to the Contras. These amendments, sponsored by Edward P. Boland and subsequently by Joseph P. Addabbo, came to be collectively known as the Boland Amendment, and were attached to military appropriations bills. President Reagan was forced to sign into law all three amendments as parts of larger, more complex legislation. But the intent of these amendments was unambiguous. They stipulated that no military aid whatsoever could go to Nicaragua or the Contras.[19]

Origins of Iran-Contra: An Impeachable Offense?

The controversy that sparked the major scandal of the Reagan administration began on October 6, 1986 when Eugene Hasenfus and his C-123 cargo plane was shot down over Nicaragua. The plane was loaded with U.S.-supplied illegal weapons intended for the Contras. Hasenfus was wearing a parachute and was the only member of the four-man crew to survive the crash. He was captured and put on trial by the Nicaraguan government. In a public statement made while he was in custody, Hasenfus admitted to having run guns for the CIA in Southeast Asia and now in Central America. While he claimed to have no direct knowledge of CIA involvement in the Nicaraguan operation, the contacts he identified who were involved in the operation were clearly associated with the CIA. Hasenfus received a thirty-year sentence from the Nicaraguan court but was later pardoned and sent back to the United States. He subsequently recanted his statement as being made under duress. Nevertheless, the incident did prompt Democrats in the U.S. House to launch an investigation.[20]

The downing of the plane provided strong evidence to the effect that someone, almost certainly the U.S. government, was supplying arms to the Contras. As the administration was forbidden by law to use public funds to supply the Contras, it was not clear how these weapons shipments were being financed. But upon examination, congressional investigators made a bizarre discovery. It appeared that proceeds from covert arms sales to Iran (another country that was restricted by law from receiving U.S. arms) were being used to fund shipments of weapons to the Contras in Nicaragua.

As noted above, the Iraqis had invaded Iran in the fall of 1980. Even then the Iranians were desperate to resupply their American-made weapons, which had been purchased under the shah. Consequently, they had made contracts with the Reagan campaign, which may or may not have amounted to anything. By 1985 the war had dragged on for five long years and the Iranians were, if anything, even more desperate for resupply. The problem was that Iran had been designated a "State Sponsor of Terrorism" under U.S. law in January 1984. Pursuant to that designation, it was illegal for the United States to supply weapons to Iran without a direct waiver voted by Congress and signed by the president. It appeared that along with the Boland Amendment, the Reagan administration had been violating that prohibition as well.

The Iran-Contra initiative actually had its origins in July 1985 when President Reagan was recovering from colon cancer surgery. While Reagan was recuperating in the hospital, National Security Advisor Robert McFarlane and presidential aide Michael Deaver approached the president with a plan suggested by the Israeli government to open a dialogue with Iran. It was possible that if the United States would agree to allow Israel to transship arms to Iran, the Iranians would facilitate the release of six U.S. citizens held hostage in Beirut by radical Islamists aligned with Iran. Israel would then be replenished with more arms by the United States soon thereafter.

Secretary of State George Shultz and Secretary of Defense Caspar Weinberger got wind of the plan and were opposed. Declassified documents reveal that Weinberger commented to an aide, "This is almost too absurd to comment on . . . like asking Gaddafi to Washington for a cozy chat." The president did not approve the plan at that time but was open to the idea.[21] This is a matter of some contention. It is not clear what Reagan explicitly approved or whether he even knew about the plan.

However, as Reagan had always delegated extraordinary amounts of authority to his staff, with or without the president's specific authorization, the Iran part of Iran-Contra was put into motion. The responsibility for implementing the project was put in the hands of Lieutenant Colonel Oliver North, a member of the National Security Council staff.

With the transshipment plan approved, in August 1985 the Israelis shipped a quantity of U.S. manufactured shoulder-launched antitank missiles to Iran. The Iranians had been desperately trying to procure these weapons to counter Iraq's military advantage in tanks supplied by the Soviet Union. In exchange, the Iranians were supposed to provide assistance in securing the release of American hostages held in Lebanon.[22]

The Americans were particularly concerned about the fate of one of the hostages, William Francis Buckley, the CIA's Beirut bureau chief who had been kidnapped by Hezbollah in March 1984. Buckley had subsequently been sent to Iran for interrogation and then returned to Lebanon where he probably died as the result of the abuse of his captors, sometime between June and October 1985. Therefore, even as the Americans began to negotiate for his release, Buckley was possibly already dead.

It was Buckley's kidnapping that prompted President Reagan to sign National Security Directive 138 authorizing the creation of a secret counterterrorism task force headed up by General Joseph Secord and his assistant Oliver North. The purpose of this task force was to conduct covert operations against the state sponsors of terrorism including Iran. It was through this task force that the Iran-Contra weapons exchange was orchestrated.

Even after it became clear that Buckley was already dead, the United States continued to negotiate for the release of four other hostages held by Hezbollah in Beirut. For a go-between they relied on two shadowy Iranian businessman, Albert Hakim and Manocher Ghorbanifar, who had initially declared that they would facilitate the release of the kidnapped CIA bureau chief and later the other hostages as well.

The legal and practical consequences of the operation began to mount. President Reagan claimed that the arms sale was intended to open up dialogue with Iran. But, in fact, the trade was what it appeared, an attempt to pay ransom to obtain the release of hostages. This was an embarrassment to the administration as the president had stated many times that he would never negotiate with terrorists. In fact, since 1983, the administration had been engaged in something called Operation Staunch, a program to discourage other nations from sending military supplies to Iran.

Even so, a second shipment of TOW missiles occurred in September 1985 and this worked out better than the first. A hostage was finally released, but it was not Buckley. The Iranians now began to explicitly state how many weapons it would take to buy the release of a hostage and other problems began to arise. The HAWK missiles that were delivered were faulty, and Portugal no longer wanted to serve as a staging delivery area for the weapons. Then there were the legal difficulties as well. The Arms Export Control Act stated that Congress had to be notified in advance of any arms sales in excess of $25 million (even if a third party, Israel, was being used as an intermediary). Congress had never been notified. Furthermore, it appears that the administration had never planned to let Congress know that the arms exchanges were taking place.[23]

In addition, under the National Security Act, a president could not send or sell arms as part of an intelligence covert action. A presidential finding would first have to be supplied to Congress around the time of the action. Since these activities were never reported to the legislative branch, the question arose as to whether, in acting against the law, the president had committed an impeachable offense.

Unknown to Congress, the administration had sent a number of negotiators to Tehran including National Security Advisor McFarlane. The Iranians did not take the meetings seriously and sent low-level officials to meet with the national security advisor who eventually wanted to scrap the whole plan. In fact, probably in order to avoid blowback for an operation that was bound to become public, McFarlane resigned in December 1985 to "spend more time with his family."

But the president did not want to quit. Shortly after the second shipment, another hostage was released. McFarlane had wanted all the hostages released at once, but the Iranians would never give up all their bargaining chips at once. So, in some sense, the administration was playing into the Iranians' hands. Secretary of State Shultz would go on later to state in testimony before Congress that "our guys got taken to the cleaners."[24]

Colonel North, encouraged by the release, convinced John Poindexter, the new national security advisor, to expand the operation. North saw bigger and better things ahead. He wanted prisoners in Kuwait released and, even with the cooperation of the Iranians, a new regime installed in Baghdad. High-stakes meetings were going on between the United States and Iran. However, with more missiles supplied to Iran, along with intelligence information on Iraq, only three more hostages were released. Meanwhile, the cause for which this program was instigated, CIA station chief William F. Buckley, was already dead.

But the shipment of arms wasn't only for the exchange of hostages. While the weapons were ostensibly transshipped by the Israelis, they were sold for a price. The Israelis were to be compensated both in cash by the Iranians and in military supplies by the United States to replace the weapons they sold to the Iranians. But the Israelis were only superficially in control of the sales to the Iranians. The actual sales of weapons, in fact, were brokered by Ghorbanifar and North, both of whom charged the Iranians a substantial markup, which the Iranians in their desperation had no choice but to pay. Ghorbanifar was in it for his own personal profit, but North was in it for a cause that was entirely unrelated to the Middle East, the Contra rebels in Nicaragua.

North knew that American financial aid to the Contras was forbidden under the Boland Amendment. However, because weapons sold to Iran had been shipped to the Israelis as military assistance and because the transaction generated excess revenue, there were no actual appropriations taking place. Thus, by North's estimation, the surplus funds could legally be used to purchase weapons for the Contras. Furthermore, the administration had begun to solicit funds for the Contras from third parties including the governments of Argentina, Saudi Arabia, and Taiwan, as well as the assistance of Panamanian dictator Manuel Noriega and the conservative government of Honduras to provide staging grounds and training for the Contras. There is some suggestion that drug money was involved as well. At the very least, North and Poindexter overlooked the drug connections of some their Central American contacts. In order to hide the provenance of those arms transfers, the Contras were supplied with Russian-made weapons purchased from the Israelis that had been captured during the Yom Kippur War in 1973.[25]

The sale of arms to Iran was indeed a significant intelligence activity in the legal sense, not to mention the funding of and sales of weapons to the Contra rebels. There is no question the administration went to great lengths to keep Congress from knowing about these transactions. The CIA general counsel, when rendering an opinion on the legality of these activities, stated in 1986, "The key issue in this entire matter revolves around whether or not there will be reports made to Congress."[26]

The arms shipments were purposely structured to avoid the preshipment reporting requirements of the Arms Export Control Act. The leadership in Congress, as noted above, did not know about the military supplies being sent to the Contras until the Hasenfus plane was shot down on October 5, 1986. At that point, the connection had still not been made between aid to the Contras and military sales to Iran.

But when the Contra operation became known to the public, the whole operation began to unravel. On November 3, 1986 a newspaper in Lebanon published a story outlining the sales of U.S. weapons to Iran. The Iranian government then confirmed the accuracy of the story. That same day, President Reagan, who had at first denied the existence of any sales of arms to the Iranians, admitted in a nationally televised speech that the sales had taken place but said he did not inform Congress as he did not want to jeopardize any timely release of the hostages. Congressional investigations discovered that the president and his top advisors helped to plan the sales of arms to Iran from the beginning with no intention of informing Congress. Furthermore, it eventually was revealed that North had actually falsified National Security Council chronologies to make it look as if the sales to Iran consisted of oil drilling equipment and not arms.

In November 1986 the FBI initiated Operation Front Door, which began securing and analyzing documents related to arms sales to Iran. At the same time, North was frantically destroying documents related to the affair and smuggling other records out of the White House. In December 1986, an independent counsel, Lawrence Walsh, was appointed. The president also created his own investigatory panel, the Tower Commission, chaired by Texas senator John Tower, including former national security advisor Brent Scowcroft and Edmund Muskie, a former Democratic governor of Maine, U.S. senator, and U.S. secretary of state. The Tower Commission report found fault with National Security Advisor Poindexter and the president's Chief of Staff Don Regan but not with the president himself.[27]

Investigation by Independent Counsel

At first, many of the key figures in the Iran-Contra transaction, such as North, Secord, Hakim, and North's secretary, Fawn Hall, refused to appear before the independent counsel, invoking their constitutional right to not incriminate themselves. The problem for the independent counsel was that if there were to be hearings before Congress, the committee in charge would probably grant immunity to some or all of the prime suspects in exchange for their testimony. Certainly, immunity minimized the chances of prosecutions of North, Poindexter, and Hakim, who all claimed their privileges against self-incrimination.

Treatment of the defendants as conspirators further complicated the problem. The prosecutor could not use hearing testimony, and subsequently Judge Gerhard Gesell ruled that defendants could not be tried together so as to not have one defendant's testimony incriminate another. And, if defendants were tried separately, then other trials would have to be in the dark about the others' work. Restricting the use of coerced testimony honored the Constitution's pledge not to force individuals to convict themselves.[28]

The president would give written testimony for the grand jury later in 1987. Many other executive officials, advisors, and cabinet officers willingly testified and professed little knowledge of the operation. After a series of personal interviews, Fawn Hall, Oliver North's secretary, admitted that she had smuggled documents out of National Security Council offices and shredded papers for her boss. After much political wrangling with the government of Switzerland, the Swiss bank account where the proceeds of the arms sales to Iran were deposited revealed enough proof for a conspiracy indictment. Criminal charges were filed against North, Secord, Poindexter, and Hakim. Notes obtained from White House chief of staff Donald Regan also indicated that he knew of the arms for hostages operation. Walsh believed that William Casey, the CIA director, knew of the diversion of funds as well.

But the chain of proof had not yet extended to President Reagan. The question as always in these sorts of affairs was "what did the president know and when did he know it?" The independent counsel reported that Chief of Staff Regan didn't believe that the president knew of at least the first round of sales.[29] That makes sense as Reagan was in the hospital at the time of his first briefing, but after that it is hard to believe that Reagan didn't know.

Congressional Investigations of Iran-Contra

The model for what was about to repeatedly happen was in the testimony of Robert McFarlane who was one of the few players to willingly testify before Congress. At first, he lied to the committee about his knowledge and involvement with the affair. Only after documentary evidence appeared that contradicted his testimony, and after plea negotiations, did he testify truthfully, emphasizing that while he had known about the transactions, he resigned as national security advisor rather than continue. He was eventually found guilty of four misdemeanor counts of lying to Congress and sentenced to two years of probation and a $20,000 fine. He was pardoned by President H. W. Bush in 1992.[30]

In the aftermath of the 1986 midterm elections, with a Democratic majority now in both houses of Congress, investigations of the Iran-Contra Affair commenced on both sides of the Capitol. In 1987 the House Select Committee to Investigate Covert Arms Transactions with Iran began its investigations in tandem with the Senate Select Committee on Secret Military Assistance to Iran and the Nicaraguan Opposition. Investigations also commenced in the House Foreign Affairs Committee, the House Permanent Select Committee on Intelligence, and the Senate Committee on Intelligence.

John Poindexter, McFarlane's successor as national security advisor, testified in multiple hearings before Congress that the administration had disapproved any shipments and that Reagan knew nothing of the deal. However, it soon became clear that he was lying. A plan had been set in place that would make Oliver North the "fall guy" and thereby insulate the president from any responsibility. The problem was that emails between Poindexter and North were not secure. North and Poindexter communicated through an email channel labeled "private blank check" that could theoretically not be breached, even by government investigators. Furthermore, North and Hall had carefully shredded documents relating to the plot. However, a Justice Department official found a "diversion memorandum" that had missed the shredder indicating profits from sales to Iran were to go to the Contras. Furthermore, "private blank check" was breached by the White House Technology Office and parts of the electronic exchange orchestrating the cover-up between North and Poindexter were revealed. Poindexter was eventually convicted of five counts of lying to Congress, but his convictions were reversed on appeal. Poindexter eventually returned to government in the administration of President George W. Bush.[31]

Were McFarlane's lies and the obvious cover-up plotted by North and Poindexter proof that the president was involved? With the destruction of so many documents and the death of CIA director William Casey in January 1987, all the facts of this operation will probably never be known. Caspar Weinberger, who as secretary of defense almost certainly knew about the arms transfers to Iran (even though he opposed them in principle), was indicted on charges of perjury and obstruction of justice, but he was pardoned before he was convicted by lame-duck President George H. W. Bush on Christmas Eve 1992. Bush took what was then the unusual step of pardoning Weinberger before he even went to trial.[32] Weinberger died in

2006 without ever revealing the extent of his involvement and knowledge of the Iran-Contra Affair.

What did the president know and when did he know it? It appears that the arms for hostages plan existed on a couple of different levels. The U.S. Congress and even the secretary of state were not notified, and some elements of the plan were intentionally withheld from the president as well. Consequently, there was evidence to the effect that the president did not know the exact details of the plan, but he still did have a hand in setting the plot in motion and the crimes that occurred, such as they were, took place on his watch. That being the case, were presidential powers overreached? Or was the president negligent and perhaps even betrayed by his wayward staff?

Investigations reveal that just as Reagan was about to leave for an October 1985 summit with Gorbachev in Geneva, National Security Advisor McFarlane briefed the president about the plan to sell missiles to the Iranians in exchange for the hostages. Declassified documents reveal that the president replied with the rather cryptic response, "keep your fingers crossed or hope for the best."[33] Thus, it is clear that in the fall of 1985 the president knew about the transshipped sale of weapons to Iran. He did not inform Congress. Whether he knew about the use of the proceeds of that sale and others to support the Contras is another matter.

Before McFarlane resigned from the White House, he had a conversation with Secretary of Defense Weinberger concerning the sale of weapons to Iran. Weinberger learned more about the transaction on his own through a series of highly classified electronic intercepts and transcripts of intercepted telephone conversations. According to information released during the trial of North, the transcripts were quite explicit about the operation, though the secretary of defense reported that the conversations were garbled, and that code words were often employed. More declassified documents revealed that the plan to ship the HAWK missiles to Iran from Israel in conjunction with hostage recovery efforts were definitely in place. Such information was distributed from North, McFarlane, and Poindexter to Weinberger, Casey, National Security Agency chief William Olden, and CIA deputy director John McMahon.

Later, on December 7, 1985, a series of top-level advisors met with the president in the White House. At the meeting Weinberger explained to the president that sending missiles to Iran was against the law. He told Reagan that there was an embargo against Iran that made arms sales illegal and that the president couldn't violate that law, and that "washing" the transactions through Israel would not make it legal. Shultz and the chief of staff agreed. Weinberger's notes report that the president's response was that "he could answer the charges of illegality," but could not answer the charge that big, strong President Reagan passed up on a chance to free hostages.[34]

Weinberger's answer (according to his notes) was that "visiting hours are on Thursday," implying that proceeding with the operation could result in a prison term.[35] But Reagan did give verbal approval to go ahead with the deal. CIA director McMahon then asked for a written authorization of the exchange so as to provide "cover" for the CIA's involvement. He was provided with a written authorization. The original copy of this authorization was destroyed, but a copy was found. Weinberger's daily notes also indicate that the president decided to go with the Israeli-Iranian offer to release five hostages in return for four thousand TOW missiles to Iran by way of Israel. Nevertheless, the president continued to maintain in public that "the administration does not deal with terrorists, no bargaining."[36]

North also brought Vice President Bush into the operation. Bush's job was to go to Tel Aviv and find out from an Israeli intermediary, Amiram Nir, how the strategy was going. Bush would later go on national television on January 5, 1988 and, in a famous squabble with journalist Dan Rather, angrily deny knowing anything about an arms for hostages deal.[37] But Bush's diary reveals that he knew of North taking money from Iran and placing it in a Swiss bank account to be used for the Contras.[38]

As the scandal grew and became more sensationalized, on November 26, 1986 President Reagan and Attorney General Edwin Meese held a press conference to "expose" the diversion of funds and blame Israel for the operation. Meese insisted that there was no need for a criminal investigation. He and North had hoped that the Israelis would become implicated by admitting that they knew the proceeds of the sales of arms to Iran would be diverted to a Swiss bank account and ultimately to the Contras. But the Israelis refused to confess.

Then came the second line of defense. North was to become the fall guy. The Iran-Contra operation was to be framed by the administration as a rogue operation conducted by overzealous members of the president's staff. The president intimated as much when he announced at that same news conference, because he had not been apprised of the details of the operation, that North was to be "relieved of his duty." And Poindexter, although supposedly not directly involved, had been relieved of his job as well.

Attorney General Meese made statements at congressional hearings that were also inaccurate, misleading, and false. He had stated that the United States played no role in the first shipment of arms to Iran via Israel and that the president knew nothing of the shipment until a year later. Both statements were demonstrably false. McFarlane had testified to the committees in December 1986 that the president had approved in advance the first shipment of missiles. Chief of Staff Donald Regan also testified that the president was told "after" the shipment. Indeed, the president had told the Tower Commission that he did not recall authorizing the shipment and was surprised to hear of it. However, during a later hearing he said that he thought that he might have approved it in advance.[39]

The president then changed his story. On March 4, 1987, he went on national television to address the furor surrounding the scandal. He stated that the operation complied with the law and that few arms were delivered to Iran, about one plane's capacity, and, as he told Congress, no arms were traded for hostages. The public didn't buy it: 56 percent believed that the weapons sales were an arms for hostages deal and 76 percent opposed any transactions with Iran altogether.[40]

Aiding the Contras

Despite very little public support for aid to the Contras, Reagan pressed to keep the rebel forces viable. As early as 1984 reports of covert CIA operations aiding the Contras in their military operations, such as mining harbors in Nicaragua without congressional notification or authorization, prompted Congress to exercise its constitutional powers and use the occasion of the passage of an omnibus appropriations bill to cut off all funds to the movement. Inasmuch as provisions of the bill were essential to the operations of government, the president had been forced to sign the bill into law. But Reagan would not be deterred. He told his national security advisor to keep the Contras' "body and soul together." Since Congress denied funding, the president looked to other countries to raise money. And they did. A total of $37 million came from other nations and some even from private contributors.[41]

Despite the Boland Amendment's prohibition against financing or soliciting funds for the Contras, the enterprise to aid the Contras had its own airplanes, operatives, and landing strips. The CIA had a thriving operation in transporting arms and equipment to the Contras, an operation that was prohibited by Congress. Defense Department and Foreign Service personnel in Central America provided additional assistance in these dangerous activities. In hearings, Assistant Secretary of State Elliott Abrams, in charge of the region, professed ignorance of the operations but added that he "was careful not to ask North lots of questions."[42] In later hearings, however, Abrams would admit that he had been lying.

The White House even sponsored a nonprofit organization where funds were allocated for propaganda activities on behalf of the Contras. North and advertising executive Richard Miller raised $10 million for a private organization called the National Endowment for the Preservation of Liberty (NEPL). The White House then assisted in creating pro-Contra advertisements under the auspices of the NEPL to be aired in the television markets of "swing" congressmen. NEPL personnel boasted that during the elections they would help defeat many anti-Contra members of Congress. Of the $10 million raised, some of the money went to advertising and the rest went to Swiss and Miami bank accounts set up for support of the Contras.

NEPL's charter did not include raising funds for a covert war in Nicaragua, and the IRS never would have approved such activity under the auspices of an organization that was granted tax-exempt status. As a result, in May 1987, Miller and NEPL's chief executive officer, Carl Channel, pleaded guilty to defrauding the Department of the Treasury by subverting the purposes of a tax-exempt organization.[43]

In March 1988 the independent counsel returned a twenty-three-count indictment against Poindexter, North, Secord, and Hakim. The defendants were then convicted on a number of charges including the withholding of evidence, destruction of documents, accepting illegal gratuities, obstruction of justice, perjury, and conspiracy. Oliver North was convicted on three counts of the indictment and sentenced to a suspended sentence and community service. That conviction was later overturned on appeal. Poindexter was convicted on five counts and his conviction was later overturned on appeal.[44] Hakim and Secord received probation and Hakim was fined. On his way out of office in 1992, President George H. W. Bush pardoned or granted clemency to six other officials who were convicted or charged with crimes related to Iran-Contra. Most prominent of the pardons was the one for Caspar Weinberger. The Bush pardons effectively ended the investigation.

In the final analysis, Special Prosecutor Walsh revealed that false testimony was given by many members of the administration and conscious efforts were made to conceal the president's involvement. Additionally, the vice president, secretary of state, and secretary of defense had been informed of the details of the operation, which made them complicit.[45]

On the congressional side, Senator Daniel Inouye and Congressman Lee Hamilton's investigative report indicated that, at the operational level,

North, who coordinated all the activities, was indeed the central figure, but that he was not acting alone. Poindexter, as national security advisor, gave express approval of the operations and was supported by his predecessor, McFarlane. CIA director Casey also gave North instructions and guided him in many of the covert operations associated with the plan. Attorney General Meese also had a cloud over his head. His activities as attorney general indicated he had little interest in proceeding with an investigation into the plot. Inouye and Hamilton stated that Vice President Bush knew of the arms for hostages, but probably did not know of the diversion of funds to the Contras.[46]

Still, what did the president know and when did he know it? Much of the information lies in the shredded documents. Poindexter testified that he shielded the president, not from the arms for hostages plan, but from the diversion of funds from the weapons sales. North said he never told the president about the diversion, but assumed he knew. But Secord stated that North had told him that he (North) had discussed it with the president. However, North would later testify that he fabricated that story to bolster Secord's morale. Either way, responsibility lies with the president. If he was not aware of what his national security advisors were doing, which is questionable, then at least, as the committees declared, the president *should* have known it. The president should not have been so disengaged from his staff that they felt justified in the diversion of funds and other elements of the scandal.[47] Furthermore, congressional hearings determined that most of the president's staff believed that their actions were consistent with the president's wishes. Finally, at least in regard to the arms for hostages, the president knew and lied about that to the public.

The Stillborn Impeachment of President Reagan

On March 5, 1987, Congressman Henry B. Gonzalez of Texas, along with six cosponsors, filed a resolution in the House to impeach President Reagan.[48] This is the second time Gonzalez had attempted to impeach Reagan; the first was related to the invasion of Grenada. On both occasions the resolutions were referred to the House Judiciary Committee where they died for lack of action. Even with the emerging evidence of Reagan's possible initiation, knowledge of, or even a criminal lack of knowledge of all or parts of the Iran-Contra Affair, there was no support for actually impeaching the president. While there were clear violations of the law, including charges and eventual convictions of members of the administration all the way up to the cabinet, for some reason Iran-Contra never rose to the level of an impeachable offense.

Democrats in the committees' reports indicate that if the president did not know what his security advisors were doing, he should have, and that in the loop or not, the president was ultimately responsible for the affair. Reagan, however, did seem contrite, and took responsibility for the activities of the Iran-Contra actors, adding that he should have known about all of the undertakings and that he was truly disappointed that he was shielded from all the information. This show of honesty played well with the public, contrasting to the appearance of a cover-up the public perceived with Watergate. But the full extent of Reagan's involvement in the scandal will never be known.

Analysis—Why No Impeachment?

1. OPPOSITE PARTY CONTROL OF THE HOUSE

About the time that the Iran-Contra scandal broke, in January 1985, the Democrats held a firm majority in the House of Representatives, albeit one that was somewhat reduced on the coattails of the Reagan landslide of 1984. They lost sixteen seats that year and only won back five seats in what was otherwise a groundswell election in 1986 (see discussion of the Senate below). After 1986, the Democrats enjoyed a 258–177 majority. It would appear, then, that there was no barrier to the adoption of articles of impeachment. However, because the Senate was controlled by the Republicans, the chances for conviction were basically nil. Even after the 1986 midterm elections, when the Senate flipped to the Democrats, there was still little enthusiasm for Reagan's removal.

Despite the numbers, the partisan landscape was not as unfavorable to Reagan as it seemed. Reagan had done a remarkable job of building a majority coalition in the House that transcended political parties. In fact, he was in the process of transforming the American party system. So much so, in fact, that the House was Democratic in name only. The Reagan victory in 1980 against a southerner, Jimmy Carter, in the South had highlighted the vulnerability of conservatives who still claimed to be Democrats. Consequently, a large number of southern Democrats had begun by the mid-1980s to defect from the party. These Reagan Democrats, who also lived in other parts of the country, were hardly reliable voting members of the majority.[49]

Thus, given the de facto conservative coalition in the House, it was going to be very difficult for the House to adopt articles of impeachment. The Gonzalez resolution to impeach had only six cosponsors and went nowhere. And of course there was no chance of the Senate voting to convict. Furthermore, by March 1987, when the Gonzalez motion was introduced, Reagan had less than two years to go in his presidency. The Iran-Contra scandal, while quite broad ranging, did not appear to be part of a larger, endemic corruption of the Reagan presidency. Consequently, the House let the incident be a cause for embarrassment and a few indictments of administration officials at all levels but not a cause for impeachment.[50]

2. Opposite Party Control of the Senate

The 1986 midterm election was a disaster for Senate Republicans. They lost eight seats and the majority. Even so, the Democrats had only a 55–45 edge, not nearly enough Democratic votes to convict. And there was no prospect that there were any Republican votes to be had. Reagan was still very popular in the Republican Party. Furthermore, the partisan environment that existed in the Senate in 1987 was in the process of changing to the highly polarized political environment of today, meaning that partisanship was more likely to trump policy, especially on primarily political issues such as impeachment.

There was some tension between outgoing Majority Leader Bob Dole and incoming Majority Leader Robert Byrd over the scope of the Iran-Contra investigation in the Senate. Dole wanted it to be narrow and Byrd more wide ranging. However, eventually, they appeared at a joint news conference to announce the formation of a special joint investigating committee chaired by Senator Daniel K. Inouye on the Senate side and Representative Lee Hamilton for the House. The leaders also agreed on a limited duration of the investigation, which was to end with the August recess. A committee report would be issued a few months after.

Nothing about this arrangement gave any indication that the end point would be impeachment. In fact, the joint committee approach circumvented the impeachment process, which according to the Constitution is supposed to originate in the House.

The distinctive feature of the joint committee approach and its leadership was its high degree of bipartisanship. It is important to remember that Hamilton, a Democrat, had chaired the investigation of the "October Surprise" and the possible collusion of the 1980 Reagan campaign with Iran in the release of the American hostages. Hamilton had found no credible evidence to support the charge of collusion, much to the chagrin of some of the more extreme members of his own party. Senator Inouye was a well-respected legislator on both sides of the aisle in the Senate. His leadership of the committee was self-consciously nonpartisan. Finally, unlike the congressional Watergate investigation, there was no majority or minority committee staff on the joint committee.

The committee did eventually issue a majority and minority report. But neither recommended impeachment or removal. Instead, the harshest criticism leveled at the president by the Democrats was that while it wasn't clear what Reagan knew and when he knew it, if he didn't know it, he should have known it. Thus, with the formation of the joint committee investigating Iran-Contra, the chances of impeachment were practically zero.[51]

In a 1990 *New York Times* article, Seymour Hersh wrote that top congressional leaders in the investigating committees had agreed not to impeach the president. They argued that an act of "commission" was needed to warrant such undertakings. No amount of negligence or nonfeasance, they decided, would justify a potential impeachment proceeding.

There was also support for leaving the president alone because he was negotiating an arms-control treaty with the Soviets, and Republicans were pushing for the investigation to be over in no more than three months. Yes, there was the lying to the public, trade with Iran, and the disregarding of congressional policy, yet "we didn't want to go after the president," leaders in the Senate investigating committee concurred, "he was too old, with little time left in office." Lee Hamilton stated, "If you want to go after the king, then you have to kill the king."

Furthermore, there still was no proof that the president had hidden documents from the committees. There was also the consensus that the "President didn't have the mental capacity to fully understand what happened. Pamela Naughton, a lawyer who worked for the House committee told Hersh, 'once you decide the obvious target is not the target, and you give everyone else immunity, who's left to investigate?" Peter Rodino Jr., an investigating committee member and chair of the House Judiciary Committee, added, "We couldn't even get all the documents we needed to prosecute."[52] Even House Speaker Jim Wright stated that he hoped that "there wouldn't be the discovery of an impeachable offense, which would be very divisive for the country, as in the case of Watergate."

Interestingly, in 1993 Wright indicated that notes from Reagan's top advisors were discovered that detailed the president's involvement in the scandal, thus it had been a mistake to end the investigation in little more than six months. Wright added that fear of impeachment and haste in the investigation hurt Congress's inquiry into the affair.[53]

3. Important Policy Differences between the President and Congressional Leaders

The Boland Amendment was a clear expression by Congress of its desire to keep the United States out of the Nicaraguan civil war. Just as clear are the legal prohibitions on the sale of weapons to foreign governments and particularly states that have acquired the designation "terrorist states." There is very little ambiguity in these laws.

However, President Reagan was clearly concerned that the election of the Sandinistas in Nicaragua would be used as a toehold for expanded Soviet influence in Central America. Furthermore, the whole idea of arms for hostages got its start with the kidnapping of CIA Beirut station chief Christopher Buckley by the Iranian-backed terrorist group Hezbollah. There are plenty of reasons besides the simple humanitarian cause that the administration would want to move heaven and earth to get Buckley back. Then, even though Buckley was never returned (and was, in fact, already dead), the administration saw a plausible route for funding the Contras without going to Congress to ask for the money, which would violate the Boland Amendment.

Using funds from foreign sources, private sources, or unappropriated U.S. Treasury funds to facilitate foreign policy, especially policy that violated Congress's Boland Amendment, could certainly be construed as illegal. So, the operation had two illegitimate components, the sale of arms to Iran, where no trade or diplomatic relations existed between the two nations, and the use of those proceeds to fund the Contras. Even Baker warned the president that aid to the Contras could be seen as an impeachable offense. While it is almost certainly the case that this transfer of funds was no more than a fig leaf for U.S. government financing of the Contras, the administration had cause to be alarmed about what they believed was a communist takeover of Nicaragua.

There is an argument to be made that contained in the oath of office, specifically to "protect and defend the Constitution of the United States," presidents vow to do what is necessary in times of emergency to protect the Constitution. And the courts have recognized numerous times that in times of war the president may have to adopt extraordinary measures to protect and defend the country.[54] Furthermore, the courts have often found that in order for the government to adopt extraordinary measures, merely the conditions of war, not an actual declaration of war, are all that is necessary for the president to act, even in contravention of the law.

It could be argued that such conditions existed during the Cold War. However, the administration's actions were never formally challenged in the courts. Instead, the special prosecutor focused on individual behavior and a situation in which a number of individuals decided to lie under oath. The same thing happened in Congress. But Reagan was never asked to testify, and he would have plausibly feigned ignorance anyhow.

The only course then would be for Congress to go to the courts and ask them to put a halt to what was clearly an illegal set of activities. The problem is that the courts rarely intervene in these kinds of disputes between the branches, preferring to demur based on the doctrine of political questions.[55] Furthermore, the full expanse of the plot did not come out until 1987, a year and a half before Reagan was to leave office and after the administration had pledged to cease its activities, especially in respect to the Iranians.

Beyond politics, the Iran-Contra Affair did not rise to the level of an impeachable offense because *even if it was illegal, it was not a high crime nor misdemeanor.* It is not a crime for the president and Congress to disagree on the interpretation of the law and the Constitution. Some members of Congress clearly believed that the president was breaking the law and over-seeing a sleazy operation, yet the president believed he was carrying out his constitutional responsibilities. The president may have been wrong. But it is not a crime to be wrong. Thus, like many policy disagreements between the branches, disagreeing with the other side, and even being found to have erred, is not an impeachable offense.

Furthermore, there is no indication that Reagan and his staff had any intent of benefiting personally or politically from Iran-Contra activities. It is the essential definition of malfeasance for a public official to commit an act for personal benefit at the expense of the national interest. Reagan had a visceral aversion to communism and that may have extended to excess. But there was never any question that the president was in it for personal gain. After all, he wasn't running for reelection and he didn't need the money.

4. TIME OF NATIONAL CRISIS OR SOCIAL UNREST

The last couple of years of the Reagan administration was relatively quiescent by historical standards. The most important development of the period, in retrospect, appears to be the winding down of the Cold War. In international affairs, the signature event of the end of the Reagan term was an agreement between the Soviet Union and the United States to dismantle all 1,752 U.S. and 859 Soviet missiles in the 3,000–3,400-mile range.[56]

On the domestic front, the economy grew at a rate of 3.8 percent with an unemployment rate of 5.3 percent, the lowest in fourteen years. At the end of the Reagan presidency, it *was* morning in America. It is politically difficult to take on a president under such conditions.[57]

Finally, under the pressure of investigations, the sales to the Iranians stopped. Additionally, the war against the Sandinista regime began to wind down. In August 1987, the united opposition, UNO (Unión Nacional Opositora), agreed to enter into peace talks with the Sandinista regime. At the same time, the war wound down in the expectation that the Contras would participate in the next round of national elections, which they did.[58] The opposition coalition won. It's hard to argue with success.

5. PERSONAL ANIMOSITY BETWEEN THE PRESIDENT AND CONGRESSIONAL LEADERS

President Reagan actually had quite a good relationship with congressional leaders. Tip O'Neill, Speaker of the House, came out of the "old school" of American politics where politics was a game and not a blood sport with the prize being a larger portion of the spoils. For all of his ideological bombast, Reagan was surprisingly adept at brokering compromises. After all, he had cut his teeth in politics in a state, California, that was hardly fertile ground for hard-right conservatism. While Reagan was, as we have seen, uncompromising when it came to his anticommunism (until toward the end of his administration when many of his detractors on the right thought he went soft), on other issues he was willing to compromise to get what he wanted.

This played well with O'Neill who if anything was more frustrated with Jimmy Carter's pontification and absolutism. For O'Neill in some sense, Reagan was a breath of fresh air, a politician who was predictable and practical, while in public O'Neill called Reagan "the most ignorant man in American politics" and "Hoover with a smile." According to Reagan, "after 6 p.m." they got along quite well.[59] On a personal level, the two men had a lot in common and they enjoyed a cordial relationship. But that was the tenor of the times. O'Neill got on well with the minority party in the House as well, sharing drinks and earmarks with the opposition as long as they behaved.[60]

When O'Neill retired in January 1987, he was replaced by Jim Wright, another old-school politician who had apprenticed under Speaker Sam Rayburn and Lyndon Johnson.

On the Senate side, Reagan had even fewer problems. Upon his election in 1980, the Republicans took a majority in the Senate with Howard Baker as the Majority Leader until 1985 and Bob Dole after that. Only after January 1987 did the president have to face a Democratic majority in the Senate and his relations with Majority Leader Robert Byrd were cordial. By that time, the Iran-Contra Affair was pretty much over.

6. CLIMATE OF PUBLIC ANIMOSITY TOWARD THE PRESIDENT

President Reagan, on average, was one of the most popular presidents (after John Kennedy) in recent history. His approval ratings did take a dip after the Iran-Contra Affair, but the public always maintained an affection toward the Gipper (Reagan's nickname). By the middle of 1987 Reagan's job approval ratings had stabilized at about 50 percent (from a high in the 60s), and for the rest of his presidency he rarely fell below that mark. In his last full month in office, December 1988, Reagan's ratings again rose beyond 60 percent.[61]

7. THE PRESIDENT ACCUSED OF CRIMINAL BEHAVIOR—ACTUAL

As noted above, violation of the Boland Amendment by the president was not a criminal act. In fact, because the funds that went to the Contras were not appropriated, at least directly, by the U.S. government, it is not even clear that the president was circumventing the will of Congress. The same can be said for the sale of weapons to the Iranians, ostensibly by the Israelis. There was an arms embargo against the Iranians regarding U.S. sales. But the prohibition did not apply to the Israelis. Furthermore, the law generally applies to the sale and transshipment of weapons by U.S. companies, but it is not clear that the law applies to the U.S. government itself.[62] The transshipment of American weapons by the Israelis to the Iranians was authorized by the White House. The fact that Congress didn't know, and maybe even the president didn't know, might be reflective of a policy disagreement but it is not necessarily a criminal act. The law does require that the president report to Congress on the sale of weapons to a foreign military, but in this case that law may not have applied.[63] The United States wasn't selling the weapons, hence there was no need for a report.

While these excuses for ignoring the law may seem inane, they also reflect a difference of opinion between the branches on the interpretation of the law. Policy disagreements cannot as a matter of principle be criminalized. The whole concept of the separation of powers is based on the principle that the branches will likely have policy disagreements that stem from their differing constituencies and responsibilities. The Andrew Johnson impeachment, while ostensibly based on the Tenure of Office Act, was really at its most basic level a policy disagreement. And even then, even with a president who hadn't been elected and a supermajority in opposition in the House and Senate, the Congress was unwilling to remove a sitting president from office.

There is a tradition in American law of deference to the president's judgment in matters of national security. The Reagan administration was clearly alarmed by the prospect of another Soviet intrusion into the Caribbean/Central America. Congress was more concerned the human rights abuses by the governments and forces Reagan was supporting and the possibility that the United States would be involved in another Vietnam. What is a president in that situation supposed to do? The president is charged with the responsibility, pursuant to the oath of office, to "protect and defend" the Constitution of the United States. If that means ignoring Congress when, in the opinion of the president, Congress is wrong on a matter of national security, the president is obligated to act. Therefore, even if the president knew of the Iran-Contra transaction, it is not a stretch to suggest that he acted properly and certainly not in an impeachable manner.

Finally, most of the criminal convictions on the American side were related to lying under oath. None of the convictions were based on the Boland Amendment or the Arms Export Control Act. Furthermore, there didn't seem to be any attempt on the part of, at least, the Americans involved to personally profit either financially or politically from the Iran-Contra transactions. Lying under oath is certainly a serious crime, as is obstruction of justice, but in pursuit of a legitimate national security goal, that is where the high crimes and misdemeanors of impeachment diverge from common criminality. And President Reagan never lied under oath.

Thus, there is little reason to believe that President Reagan committed an impeachable offense in the meaning of the Constitution.

8. The President Accused of Criminal Behavior—Political

Here again, there is no evidence that the White House pursued this policy for personal enrichment or in an attempt to gain political advantage. In fact, at the time of the Iran-Contra Affair, military intervention in Central America was not popular with the public.[64] There is little reason to believe that Ronald Reagan was pursuing some kind of political agenda in trying to aid the Contras. This is particularly true after his reelection of 1984 when Reagan wasn't even running for reelection.

Why Wasn't President Reagan Impeached for Iran-Contra?

While the public believed that the president was in fact involved in Iran-Contra, they also believed that the affair was conducted for philosophical and policy reasons, not for personal gain. As Republican Henry Hyde stated in the minority report to the House committee investigating Iran-Contra, "All of us at some time confront conflicts between rights and duties, between choices that are evil and less evil, and one hardly exhausts moral imagination by labeling every untruth and every deception an outrage."[65]

There are many instances of differences in policy interpretation between congressional leadership and the president. In the case of Iran-Contra, while everyone wanted to see the release of the Lebanon hostages, there was the argument that the United States should never deal with terrorists. However, was the government of Iran a terrorist organization? And, in regard to Central America, would the goal of containing communism be seriously harmed if Nicaragua fell under the control of a Soviet puppet? And what if, in the opinion of the president, Congress did not take the threat of Soviet infiltration of Central American seriously enough?

These are matters of policy. They may be subject to a sharp difference of opinion. The president, while bound by the law, is also beholden to the constitutional admonition, written into the president's oath of office, that the president "preserve, protect and defend the Constitution of the United States." Furthermore, on matters of national security, in particular, the president is given quite a bit of leeway in regard to a response to foreign threats. The appropriate response, then, is to define the controversy as a "political question" and rely on the electoral and policy process to adjudicate an outcome. It is important to remember that the controversy in the Iran-Contra matter was a foreign policy issue, not so in the case of the Tenure of Office Act (Johnson) and the Watergate scandal. Furthermore, congressional oversight was successful in halting the administration's activities and bringing some of the principals in the scheme to account.

Procedurally, Regan probably did not appear to stonewall the investigation. He answered to the best of his ability, or so it seemed, the questions posed by the independent counsel and the Tower Commission. He did not lie, at least, when under oath. His testimony to Congress was not given under a grant of immunity. He appeared to be cooperative and did not attempt to "fire" the special prosecutor as Nixon had.

Furthermore, there was very little support for impeachment. The economy was healthy and the nation was not at war. It was politically hard to oppose Reagan. The president was genuinely an amicable fellow. He was no paranoid and secretive President Nixon. Reagan left the dirty work to his subordinates. Despite political differences, Reagan would socialize after hours with members of the opposite party. The rancor between the parties seen during the Barack Obama and Donald Trump administrations did not exist at the time.

Then there was the sympathy factor. Reagan was clearly aging toward the end of his presidency. He seemed tired, drowsy, and confused when answering questions and conducting business. He forgot many of his past undertakings. There were unsubstantiated reports of him sleeping at meetings. In a summit with Japanese prime minister Yasuhiro Nakasone, he kept referring to Vice President H. W. Bush, sitting next to him, as "Mr. Prime Minister."[66] Cabinet members often found him inattentive, "not curious," and disinterested. His hearing loss exacerbated the problem. He began to rarely leave the Oval Office, skipping his usual walks around the White House. Perhaps he was suffering from the onset of the dementia that later affected him. It's hard to impeach anyone under those circumstances. In addition, Reagan would have probably finished out his term before the impeachment process was concluded.

In summary, the Iran-Contra Affair was a classic illustration of the principle that impeachment is primarily a political process. There were clearly wrongdoings by both the president and administrative officials. All made false statements to the public. Subordinates lied to Congress, the independent counsel, and the Tower Commission, under oath. But there was no smoking gun. There were no Watergate secret tapes, even though, as noted above, many documents were destroyed. And with Reagan's well-known propensity to delegate responsibilities, the general perception was that the president's subordinates were primarily responsible for the operations.

Should the president be held responsible for a secret and sleazy operation? Maybe, if one is grading his management style, but not if one is looking for criminal behavior by the commander in chief that rises to the level of an impeachable offense.

Nevertheless, while Reagan may have escaped impeachment by following the letter, if not the spirit, of the law, it is important to observe a salient point made by committee chairs Inouye and Hamilton in the "Report of the Congressional Committees Investigating the Iran-Contra Affair." They reference the words of Chief Justice Louis Brandeis, "Crime is contagious, if the government breaks the law it breeds contempt for the law. It invites anarchy." Inouye and Hamilton stated that "the Iran-Contra affair may have failed to heed this message."[67]

CHAPTER SIX

The Impeachment of Bill Clinton

The second impeachment and trial of a sitting president had nowhere near the import of the trial of Andrew Johnson, the trading of arms for hostages (and the use of the proceeds to support the Contras in contravention to U.S. law), or even a "second-rate" burglary and cover-up of the Democratic Party campaign headquarters in the Watergate office complex. Clinton was impeached for a consensual sexual affair with an intern in the White House and lying about it under oath. That's pretty "small potatoes" when compared to a subversion of Reconstruction.

Or maybe there was more to the Clinton impeachment than meets the eye. What the Clinton impeachment represents is the consequence of what journalist Bill Bishop calls the Big Sort.[1] By the mid–1990s, the U.S. Congress had fallen into a structure of hyperpartisanship so extreme that the parties were willing to play "constitutional hardball" in order to achieve their goals.[2] That included, but was not limited to, the removal of a sitting president, on the flimsiest of grounds, who had just been reelected by a large margin. Furthermore, because of the level of partisanship in Congress, the impeachment never really had much of a chance to result in removal. The point of the whole exercise, then, was to discredit Clinton and delay any substantive policy initiatives until the end of his second term.

The Formative Years

In his book *Presidential Character*, Professor James David Barber suggests that the character of presidents in their outlook on the world and the way they handle political problems are shaped by a series of "formative political experiences," or FIPs as he describes them for short. The life journey of William Jefferson Clinton crafted the management of political attacks on his person into an art.[3] And one of his most singular talents was his ability to compartmentalize his political problems. Perhaps that is why even when his most intimate public affairs were being dragged through the national arena, Clinton was able to maintain public equanimity. He just didn't seem to care and, perhaps, that capacity emboldened him to take substantial risks, risks that ultimately put his presidency at risk.

Clinton's biological father was killed in an automobile accident before William was born. His mother was forced to farm Bill out to her parents while she trained for a job. She also remarried and, as it turned out, Clinton had to endure an unstable household under an abusive stepfather. Nevertheless, his school grades were unaffected. Outwardly, to his classmates, he seemed unperturbed by matters at home. He threw himself into his schoolwork. He participated in every extracurricular activity in his high school with the exception of sports, with a particular affection for the band and music.

On one occasion, preserved on film, Clinton seemed to set a path for his future. This occurred when seventeen-year-old Bill Clinton was selected by the American Legion from his state to travel to Washington, DC, where he was photographed meeting and shaking the hand of President John Kennedy. The look on Clinton's face says it all. He was going to set his sights on the presidency.

After high school, Clinton attended Georgetown University where he was elected class president in his freshman and sophomore years but was defeated for student body presidency in his junior year. His obvious political ambition was something of a turnoff to his fellow students.

Georgetown University was an unusual choice for a Baptist boy from small-town Arkansas. But Clinton wanted to be in Washington, and he landed a job with one of Arkansas' senators and a leading opponent of the Vietnam War, J. William Fulbright. Clinton attended Oxford University on a Rhodes Scholarship after graduating from college. It was on to Yale Law School where he prepared for a political career, and there he met Hillary Rodham. As the first of the baby-boom presidents, Clinton, as had many in his generation, found ways around military service, experimented with marijuana, and engaged in sexual relations outside of marriage, all activities that would haunt him later on in his political career.[4]

Impeachment and the Presidential Character

The theme of Barber's book and our focus on the character and personality of the individuals in office in some ways makes the U.S. presidency unique.

In our system, future presidents rarely come out of political movements. By contrast, in multiparty parliamentary systems leaders emerge at the head of some kind of popular movement, such as a labor union, an environmental movement, or a business coalition that eventually organizes itself into a political party. American parties, by contrast, are broad coalitions and the partisanship of their leaders tends to be tactical, if often not particularly principled. Thus, when examining the motivations of most presidents their actions seem to come from within, not on the basis of some set of strongly held principles. Thus, to glean any meaning from presidential behavior, we must plumb the depths of their subconscious, as did Barber when he famously predicted that Nixon's peccadillos would be the undoing of his presidency. And this dynamic may also have a hidden effect on the politics of impeachment.

As noted in the previous chapter, Reagan seemed to have a genuine, principled aversion to communism and Soviet communism in particular. He and his administration were sincerely alarmed by the prospect of Soviet penetration into Central America and by the cavalier attitude with which Congress seemed to perceive the threat. Whether we agree with the Reaganites or not in their judgment, we can at least appreciate their authenticity. And if the definition of corruption in government is malfeasance for personal gain, then a disagreement over policy is not an impeachable offense. These policy disagreements are what the courts describe as political questions.

In the case of Clinton, his personal ambition to become president bordered on the corrupt. From that fateful on day when he met President Kennedy, Clinton seemed to want to be president not so much to do something as to be something. And if that meant cutting corners, he was willing to try. For example, to delay his induction into the military, Clinton advised his local draft board that in lieu of induction he would attend the ROTC program after he returned from his Rhodes Scholarship in England while he was attending law school at the University of Arkansas. But a high number on the national draft lottery the following year enabled him to avoid military service altogether. He then reneged on his promise to enter the ROTC. He didn't go to law school at Arkansas anyhow. But in this case, the voters had this information in 1992 and still elected him president.[5]

But was this or the other transgressions of which he was later accused corrupt in the meaning of the constitutional provision of impeachment? Thus, while the result of the Whitewater investigation and the Monica Lewinsky scandal might have resulted in his disbarment from the practice of law for lying under oath, that did not properly constitute an impeachable offense.

Bill Clinton Becomes Governor of Arkansas

Clinton first ran for Congress in 1974, and almost won. In the next electoral cycle, he was elected attorney general of Arkansas in 1976 and then governor two years after that. After an unsuccessful bid for reelection in 1980, he won again in 1982 and remained Arkansas' chief executive until his election as president in 1992.[6]

Albeit somewhat liberal for Arkansas, by national standards Clinton was much more conservative than much of the rest of the Democratic Party. Nevertheless, in his first term as governor he signed a modest increase in the motor vehicle tax that proved disastrous in a conservative state. That specific policy and the negative optics of a governor sporting a full beard with a wife who would not share his name cost Clinton his first reelection. Clinton was quick to adapt, and the lesson Clinton learned was that progressive politics could only make trouble. He would rarely stray from the conventional throughout the rest of his career.

As governor of Arkansas, Clinton forged an alliance with large corporations, particularly Arkansas' agribusiness industry, angering labor and the state's small environmental movement. His appeal was widespread, however, and, in particular, he remained very popular with the state's African American community. He campaigned to remove Jim Crow laws in the schools, universities, and public facilities of Arkansas. Setting a pattern for later, his wife (after 1980, Hillary Clinton, no longer Hillary Rodham) would also become an important participant in the Clinton administration. She was the chair of a commission responsible for major reform of the state's educational system.

Ronald Reagan's landslide presidential victory in 1984 convinced Clinton that the Democratic Party's traditional support of big labor and broad-based social programs was hurting the party and was out of touch with the prevailing national political sentiment. He, along with other southern Democrats, such as Georgia senator Sam Nunn and Tennessee senator Al Gore, believed that the party's future lay in tougher stances on crime, in streamlining the bureaucracy, and in reforming welfare. This move to the center Clinton labeled "triangulation."

Helping to form the politically centrist Democratic Leadership Council (DLC), Clinton and others in the party hoped to win back the legion of Democratic voters who jumped onto Reagan's small government and lower tax presidential bandwagon in 1980. By 1988, Clinton himself considered a run for the presidency when frontrunner Gary Hart, a senator from Colorado, withdrew from the race after an extramarital affair came to light. Considering that he had similar skeletons in the closet while governor, Clinton sat out the race, but at the Democratic National Convention in Atlanta that year, as one of the party's rising stars, Clinton nominated Massachusetts governor Michael Dukakis in a laughably lengthy and uninspiring speech. His career in national politics seemed at that point stillborn. But if Clinton can be characterized as anything, it would best be said that he is the "comeback kid."[7]

The First Presidential Election

The presidential election of 1992 cemented Clinton's reputation as a spectacular campaigner. In Little Rock, the previous year, when Clinton first threw his presidential hat in the ring, it was ironically because of the immense popularity of President George H. W. Bush. Having ousted Saddam Hussein from Kuwait in the First Persian Gulf War, Bush was riding an almost unprecedented wave of popularity. Leading Democratic contenders such as House Majority Leader Richard Gephardt and Senator Al Gore decided not to attempt to unseat a president with stratospheric approval ratings.

Clinton seized the opportunity of the absence of other high-profile candidates. But rather than act like a fringe candidate and appeal to a narrow constituency, his top priority was to avoid the mistakes of the Dukakis campaign. As a man of progressive impulses who had polished his political skills in a conservative state, Clinton had perfected the art of centrist politics.

Clinton managed to tie disparate parts of the party together. He was personally popular with both minority groups and moderate Democrats. He knew that the country in the Reagan era was in no mood for a candidate perceived as a supporter of big government. At the same time, Clinton endeared himself to large-city mayors with promises of federal aid and billion-dollar programs to stimulate economic growth and employment in the inner city. In the early New Hampshire primary Clinton skillfully shook off credible rumors of extramarital affairs, cementing his reputation as the "comeback kid" after placing a respectable second. He then followed with an impressive Super Tuesday win in several southern states.

With subsequent wins in New York and Illinois, Clinton had the nomination in hand going into the convention. He brought further harmony and stability to the party with the announcement that Al Gore would be his running mate. Seeking to transcend categories of liberal and conservative, the pair was successful in portraying themselves as the agents of change who would turn people's fortunes around with programs benefiting those who played by the rules, supported their children, and paid their taxes. As the convention played out, Clinton and Gore were able to depict the Democratic ticket as having a combination of solid experience in Congress with long-term service as chief executive (of a state).[8]

During the campaign, President Bush resorted to attacking Clinton's character. Clinton's campaign team, led by the contentious James Carville, responded with a program focused on the principle that "it's the economy, stupid!" Job creation and economic growth were their platform, along with support for a reduction in the federal deficit. Clinton and Gore supported the North American Free Trade Agreement (NAFTA) that Bush had successfully constructed with Canada and Mexico, with added promises of consideration of the concerns of environmentalists and labor.[9]

While Bush was able to oversee the end of the Cold War and the fall of the communist empire, it was Clinton's focus on the problems of the economy, unemployment, and the ruthless corporate downsizing associated with the Republican Party that proved the most successful appeal.

Clinton won the 1992 presidential election with 43 percent of the popular vote (he did not get a majority because of the independent candidacy of Ross Perot), but with a more impressive 370 electoral college votes. He also bolstered Democratic support in the South for the first time since Jimmy Carter's victory in 1976 with victories in Arkansas, Gore's home state of Tennessee, Louisiana, and Georgia.

In the congressional elections there were no coattails. The Democrats lost one seat in the Senate but still had a 56–44 advantage. In the House, the Democrats lost nine seats, but they retained a substantial majority, 258–176.[10]

The Clinton Presidency:
A Centrist in the White House

After the election, Democratic centrists and liberals vied for positions in the new White House staff. How the new president would handle both factions would define how he would govern and work with Congress. His cabinet, he declared, would "look like America," with women and minorities appointed to key positions. Choosing this type of cabinet was priority number one during the transition. Three women, four African Americans, and two Hispanics were selected, along with another woman, Carol Browner, to head the Environmental Protection Agency. The appointees varied between liberal Democrats, moderate members of the DLC, and a Republican, William Cohen, at the Department of Defense. These appointments created some tension when it came to policy decisions regarding national security, economics, health care, and other domestic issues, but they were an attempt to project an aura of bipartisanship.[11]

While creating the White House staff, the divide between "new Democrats" and liberals became more acute. On the president's staff, centrists held key positions. Mack McLarty was named chief of staff. Robert Rubin, a Wall Street banker, headed the National Economic Council. Leon Panetta, former chair of the House Budget Committee, and Alice Rivlin, former director of the Congressional Budget Office, headed the Office of Management and Budget. All were staunchly committed to balancing the budget. Other appointments bolstered the cause of centrism in the White House, including DLC member Bruce Reed as deputy director of the Domestic Policy Council and William Galston of the Progressive Policy Institute as a domestic policy advisor on the White House staff.

Liberals would be represented in the Clinton administration as well, but not, perhaps, as well as the DLC. Those with strong ties to the liberal wing of the party included Communications Director George Stephanopoulos, White House counsel Bernard Nussbaum, Press Secretary Dee Dee Myers, deputy director of the National Economic Council Gene Sperling, and Congressional Liaison Howard Paster.

Clinton's administration reflected the many sides of his ideology: liberal, moderate and centrist. Centrists wanted deep cuts in the budget; liberals countered that campaign promises could not be met with such reductions. McLarty appeared to take control, appointing deputy directors for the day to day operations of the White House and for long-range planning. The White House staff would also be cut by 350 positions and staff members would take a pay reduction of 6 percent to 10 percent compared to their counterparts in the preceding Bush administration. The chief of staff also took on more of the liaison role, meeting in lieu of the president with many interest groups and members of Congress.

However, probably because of McLarty's (and the president's) lack of Washington experience, there was a notable lack of coordination in the first months of the Clinton administration. Clinton squandered his honeymoon, and the White House seemed in chaos. No one knew if the centrists or the liberals were in control. Hierarchy meant nothing in the Clinton White

House. Unpaid advisors such as Dick Morris had direct access to important meetings as well as to the president. Meetings, especially those concerning the budget, were getting increasingly unruly.[12]

Clinton adapted. One of the most significant changes came when David Gergen, top advisor in the Nixon, Ford, and Reagan administrations and former *US News and World Report* editor, became a leading consultant to Clinton. Nevertheless, building bridges between the factions was difficult. As a result, in the early days of the administration, a myriad of executive proposals were sent to Congress without any seeming emphasis or priority. Most notably was the administration's first major battle with Congress over gays in the military, an important matter to be sure but not a central part of the Clinton program nor the policy he needed to lead with.[13]

Even as much as a year later, Clinton's 1994 State of the Union address seemed to reflect this chaos. It contained policies that moved in so many directions and were so uncoordinated, it was inconceivable that his speech could be construed as a blueprint for the future.[14]

A watershed moment occurred for coordination in the White House when, on the advice of Gore, Gergen, and McLarty himself, Leon Panetta left the OMB and was appointed White House chief of staff to replace McLarty in May 1994. Panetta, it seemed, was the perfect fit for chief of staff, having proven to be a strong manager at the Office of Management and Budget and, further, having a former member's working knowledge of Congress. Centrists, it appeared, were now in control with McLarty moved into the role of foreign affairs advisor and Gergen becoming advisor to the secretary of state.

Panetta, besides his organizational expertise, could work with both houses of Congress, particularly since Democrats were still in control. Panetta managed the White House in a systematic manner. All memos had to go through him before they reached the president, all appointments to see the president were to be approved by him, and the daily meetings he chaired became agenda driven. Staff could no longer stroll into the Oval Office at will.

This style of management did not completely integrate the factions, however, as the White House still had its informal coalitions, but liberal influence appeared to diminish as Panetta increasingly became the gatekeeper for Clinton.

With the Republican landslide in the first midterm election in 1994—the first time Republicans had achieved unified control of Congress since 1952—the moderate wing takeover in the White House gained momentum. So, for example, when Surgeon General Joycelyn Elders suggested that children should be taught about masturbation, she could not avoid being purged. Panetta argued that she represented the too liberal wing of the Party. Furthermore, Dick Morris, a sometimes Republican and advisor to, among others, Dixiecrat senator Strom Thurmond, gained back-channel access to the president leading up to the 1996 presidential election. Morris was later caught up in a tabloid scandal involving the use of prostitutes. He eventually had to publicly disassociate himself from the 1996 Clinton reelection campaign.[15]

With the ouster of Morris, Panetta's control over policy and his closeness to the president increased as he geared up the White House for the 1996 reelection campaign. Panetta was successful in moving the administration toward the right with an agenda that focused on programmatic cuts to the budget and limits on welfare.[16]

One of the president's landmark accomplishments, which occurred at the end of his first term, was the controversial and bipartisan Personal Responsibility and Work Opportunity Reconciliation Act, known colloquially as "welfare reform." Although it was a cornerstone of the Republican Contract with America, it also fulfilled Clinton's promise to "end welfare as we know it." While it satisfied both parties, it pleased no one. Liberals viewed the legislation as too harsh in its work requirements, and conservatives lambasted the bill as an inadequate attempt to dismantle the colossal federal welfare state. However, substantial welfare reform was a major accomplishment Clinton could point to going into his reelection campaign along with the Family and Medical Leave Act, the 1993 Deficit Reduction Act, the Brady Bill, AmeriCorps, the capture of the first World Trade Center bombing terrorists, "reinventing government," and the ratification of NAFTA. All of these were components of an impressive list of accomplishments to be added to his first-term resume.[17]

The Second Term: Entrenched in the Center

After successfully spearheading the administration's spending bill in 1996 and after the reelection of Clinton, Panetta stepped down in favor of former deputy chief of staff Erskine Bowles. Bowles was a close friend of the president. Clinton had never truly warmed to Panetta, the single-mined centrist. As conservative congressmen such as Newt Gingrich gained more power as de facto spokesman of the Republican Party, Clinton sought the harmony that had eluded him in the first term between liberals and moderates in the White House.

In the second term Bowles presided over a further shift to the center. There were a number of personnel shifts in the White House as former congressman Rahm Emanuel joined the staff, while liberals such as George Stephanopoulos left for television news and staunch liberal Harold M. Ickes was fired, perhaps in part for his role in undermining Morris.

What all these moves remind us is that the Clinton administration was basically, as presidential expert George Edwards puts it, the ultimate example of the public presidency, one based on a perpetual campaign.[18] This kind of presidency, fed by opinion polls, focus groups, and public relations campaigns, should help the president withstand attacks from either side of the political spectrum. But that was not to be. In its second term, the Clinton administration was beset by a storm of controversy that ultimately resulted in the second presidential impeachment trial in American history.

Taking on Congress

Given the conscious and aggressive intent of the Clinton administration to straddle the middle of the political spectrum, it is surprising that Clinton faced such virulent opposition from conservatives in Congress. In the past, moderation had worked to sow unity. Eisenhower, Johnson, and even Reagan had made successful appeals to moderates from the other party in Congress. But that was a different time. Starting really with the election of Reagan, partisanship began to deepen, so much so that members of Congress became much more reluctant to deal with a president of a different party regardless of the policy.

As noted above, Clinton had been successful in his first two years in negotiating with the Republican majority in Congress that took over after the Democrats' massive defeat in 1994. But with his reelection, Clinton, particularly a successful Clinton, became a threat to Republican chances of winning back the presidency in the 2000 election. What Clinton didn't know, and the Republicans came to realize, was that the greatest threat to their political success was a moderate, successful Democrat. So, in the second term, Republicans in Congress set out to cripple if not destroy the Clinton presidency.[19]

In order to work well with Congress, Clinton studied the strengths and weakness of recent past presidents. First there was Lyndon Johnson, the consummate dealmaker who relied on his experience as Majority Leader in the Senate to set up majority coalitions and deals that included the recruitment of members from the other party.[20] More uncomfortable with interpersonal horse-trading, Nixon relied on his administrative authority, including his foreign policy accomplishments, to move his policies in lieu of congressional support. Gerald Ford also capitalized on his time in Congress, but in the end he became increasingly reliant on the legislative power of last resort, the presidential veto. Carter, on the other hand, naïvely as it turned out, depended on the notion that support for his programs would be rooted in the fact that they were good for America. Reagan focused more on broad policy goals and relied heavily on staff to work out the details while capitalizing on his personal charisma for general support. George H. W. Bush was attentive to his area of expertise, foreign policy. On domestic affairs, he pursued a limited agenda.

Clinton was not predisposed toward any of these models. Unlike Nixon or Bush, he didn't have a lot of foreign policy expertise, and as his campaign mantra "it's the economy, stupid" suggested, his focus was on domestic politics. But he was too much of a policy wonk to do as Reagan had done and turn over the policy details to staff. He was too much of a realist to think, as Carter did, that a president could actually sell a policy to Congress on its merits. And, unlike Ford, he was a popularly elected president and, at least in the beginning, didn't have to deal with a Congress controlled by the opposing party. He could promote an agenda and didn't have any connection, as Ford did, to the previous administration.[21]

The problem for Clinton was that while his decision-making style was largely appropriate for his first term, he managed to pursue his agenda regardless of its cost to his fellow Democrats in Congress and, more to the point, in ignorance of changes that were taking place in the larger political environment. Specifically, in a highly partisan political environment, moderation, "triangulation," or whatever you want to call it, doesn't work very well if the radicalization of both ends of the political spectrum plays against the middle. Under those conditions, Clinton was on occasion able to split the difference but only by sacrificing his own party in Congress (the 1993 budget bill) or caving to the opposition (welfare reform).[22]

Clinton faced a highly polarized Congress, with conservative Democrats leaving the party in droves (and a similar but less pronounced exodus of moderates from the Republican side). Thus, he failed when he relied on Democrats alone to pass a major health care reform. A bipartisan effort on NAFTA and the General Agreement on Tariffs and Trade only succeeded in angering his base because of the concessions he had to give to the other side. And after the Republican landslide in the midterm elections of 1994 and Gingrich's "Contract with America," in his second term Clinton could only employ the bipartisan approach that further irritated Democratic Party liberals, rendering support from that wing of the party at best lukewarm.

Seeds of the Whitewater Scandal

In the spring of 1978, then attorney general of Arkansas and his wife Hillary Rodham, an associate at the Rose Law Firm in Little Rock, joined with personal friends Jim McDougal and his wife, Susan, to invest in a tract of land of the banks of the White River in Arkansas. Together they borrowed $203,000 to purchase the land. Their intent was to subdivide the land into tracts suitable for building vacation homes. In the meantime, between the time the land purchase was consummated and building the development began, interest rates rose to such an extent that the market for vacation homes dried up and the Clintons and McDougals were stuck with an expensive loan, unwanted real estate, and no income for debt service. (Clinton, who was now, as of 1981, governor of Arkansas, earned about $35,000 a year, and Hillary about $50,000 in her job.) They were unable to secure further funding, and what had become the Whitewater Development Corporation went bankrupt. The Clintons are thought to have lost about $50,000 on the deal. The McDougals lost more, and creditors of the corporation lost money as well. What might have been suspicious here was that the Clintons lost less than the McDougals even though they were even partners. This could have represented a benefit of up to $50,000 to the Clintons, and Clinton was governor of Arkansas until his election loss in 1980.[23]

In the meantime, Jim McDougal purchased two savings and loan banks, the Madison Guaranty Savings and Loan and the Madison Savings and Loan, which were collectively known as Madison Guaranty. McDougal looted his banks, making investments in a variety of questionable real estate schemes. Eventually, McDougal's banks went bankrupt, leaving the Federal Savings and Loan Insurance Corporation "holding the bag" with the responsibility of paying the banks' depositors and liquidating the banks' assets. The entire cost to the U.S. taxpayers of the failure of Madison Guaranty was about $70 million. Jim McDougal and his now ex-wife Susan went to prison for a variety of crimes related to the failure of Madison Guaranty (most of these unrelated to Whitewater).

Besides the fact that Jim McDougal was a friend of the Clintons, there were three possible connections between Whitewater and Madison Guaranty. In 1985, a fundraiser was held for Governor Bill Clinton at a branch of Madison Guaranty. Among other monies raised at that event was a $12,000 check made out to the campaign from the bank. In a possibly related event, David Hale, a Little Rock judge and investor, testified that he had been pressured by Governor Clinton to launder a $300,000 loan through Madison Guaranty, with the money to be lent to Susan McDougal's public relations firm.[24] What the money was to be used for is not entirely clear, but the fact that Bill Clinton was involved would make one think that he was one of the beneficiaries (perhaps to cover his loss on Whitewater). The loan was made, the money disappeared, and because its loss was insured by the federal Small Business Administration, the transaction became subject to a federal investigation.

Adding to the cloud of suspicion, in 1993, Vince Foster, a White House attorney and former partner in the Rose Law Firm, committed suicide by shooting himself in the head in Fort Marcy Park in Virginia. Foster had previously acted as an attorney representing the Clintons in the Whitewater land deal. Several hours after his death, Bernard Nussbaum, another White House attorney, cleaned out Foster's filing cabinet, including some documents on Whitewater, and gave those documents to the president's private secretary. There was quite a bit of speculation that the Clintons had in some way been involved in the death of Foster. Rumors in that regard persist to this day even though Special Prosecutor Kenneth Starr, in his final report on the Whitewater investigation, unequivocally exonerated the Clintons from any involvement in the death.

All these suspicions taken together prompted Attorney General Janet Reno in January 1994 to appoint Robert B. Fisk as a special prosecutor with the responsibility to investigate Whitewater and the death of Vince Foster. Improper use of FBI files and the firing of White House travel agents also were to be investigated. Fisk was a partner in a prominent New York law firm and a U.S. attorney for the Southern District of New York. He had been appointed U.S. attorney by President Ford and had served throughout the term of President Carter.

On June 30, 1994 Fisk issued a preliminary report that cleared Clinton of any criminal involvement with Whitewater, any attempt to interfere with the Resolution Trust Corporation in its investigation of the failure of Madison Guaranty, and of any involvement in the death of Vince Foster. Predictably, congressional Republicans were outraged, charging that the investigation was a whitewash and that congressional Democrats, who were in the majority, were coordinating with the White House in failing to convene any congressional investigations of the matter.[25]

Because the Whitewater special prosecutor was appointed by the attorney general who was, in turn, appointed by the president, there appeared to be a conflict of interest in the Fisk investigation. Consequently, Congress passed the Independent Counsel Reauthorization Act of 1994. This law resurrected Title VI of the Ethics in Government Act of 1978, which had authorized the appointment of an independent counsel to investigate alleged crimes of the executive branch. Unlike the special prosecutor, who was selected by the attorney general, the independent counsel was appointed by a panel of three federal judges and could only be impeached and removed by Congress or fired by the attorney general.[26]

Once President Clinton signed the bill into law, Attorney General Reno immediately petitioned the court to appoint Robert Fisk as independent counsel on the Whitewater investigation. Instead, the court appointed Kenneth Starr, who had been a judge on the DC Circuit Court of Appeals (appointed by Ronald Reagan) and, after that, solicitor general under President George H. W. Bush. Initially, Starr's charge was to investigate the death of Foster and the Whitewater land deal. Later, he would be assigned the added responsibility of investigating perjury charges against the president in the case *Paula Jones v. Clinton.*

In May 1991 Paula Jones, who was then an employee of the State of Arkansas, claimed that she was escorted (by state police) to a hotel room in Little Rock where she met Governor Clinton who proceeded to proposition her and expose himself to her. Three years later, in May 1994, she filed suit against Clinton for sexual harassment. The charges were dismissed by a federal district court on the grounds that she could not prove any damages. But on appeal, her attorneys convinced an appellate court that the case should proceed and that they had the right to depose Clinton even though he was by this time president of the United States. Clinton's lawyers appealed that decision to the Supreme Court, arguing that because the presidency had a unique set of responsibilities, sitting presidents could not be required to testify in civil suits, especially involving incidents that occurred prior to their time in office. In May 1997, by a unanimous vote, the Supreme Court rejected Clinton's appeal and the president was forced to testify.[27]

In that deposition, Clinton was asked point blank about his sexual history including his relationship with Monica Lewinsky, a White House intern. Clinton then lied under oath, claiming that he had not had sexual relations with Lewinsky. Physical evidence was then produced to counter Clinton's claim. The president had clearly perjured himself. Starr, as independent counsel, went to court to ask that his jurisdiction be expanded to include charges of perjury against the president.[28]

The House Moves to Impeach

In their book *How Democracies Die*, authors Steven Levitsky and Daniel Ziblatt argue that one of the characteristics of a democracy in decline is the willingness of public officials to play "hardball politics" in opposition to their political opponents. In most mature democracies, participants adhere to a set of norms that transcend formal constitutional boundaries. In fact, norms are part of a constitution in a broader sense. But in democracies under stress, politicians toss aside the niceties of tradition and attempt to win by any means.[29]

But norms are every bit as important to the operation of a Constitution as are formal constitutional grants of power because no constitution, not matter how finely written, can account for the myriads of circumstance faced by government across space and time. Furthermore, there are some things in a constitutional system that are just never done. For example, in the British political system constitutionalism is formally understood as encompassing things that theoretically could happen—for instance, it might be theoretically possible for the queen to veto an act of Parliament (or for the House of Lords to reject an act of the House of Commons), but it would be "unconstitutional." In the mid-nineteenth century British journalist and author Walter Bagehot compared the American Constitution to the British Constitution. He was generally predisposed toward (with apologies to the Scots, Welsh, and Irish) the English Constitution, which had the flexibility and durability to adjust to evolutionary change. Americans, on the other hand, under their written Constitution would have to resort to what Bagehot called "absurd fictions" to justify the constitutionality of actions of government under extraordinary circumstances for which there was no precedent and no written text.[30]

American history is rife with circumstance that requires the U.S. government to twist the Constitution into knots to explain and justify its actions, with the Supreme Court leading the way. But in the case of impeachment, the reference to high crimes and misdemeanors remains the province of Congress to decide. Thus, it was possible that the president's lie, under oath, in regard to an extramarital affair between consenting adults rose to the level of an impeachable offense in the meaning of the Constitution.

By the late 1990s the trend toward hyperpartisanship, especially in Congress, was already well established, with the Republicans leading the way.[31] There had been plenty of presidents prior to Bill Clinton who had faced a Congress controlled by the other party. But in the absence of crimes rising to the level of the Watergate Affair, no president had been subject to impeachment since Andrew Johnson. And, as we have seen, Johnson faced a Congress that was overwhelmingly controlled by the other party, in a period of deep division in the country. Consequently, the Republican Congress in Andrew Johnson's time was emboldened by the size of its majority and the weight of its anger to play hardball politics, but, even so, the Radical Republicans still lost. Similarly, by 1997, the partisan divide had become so profound that opposition to a president of the other party transcended traditional norms, resulting in the first impeachment proceedings since 1868. So began a new era of hardball politics.

Several months prior to the uproar over the Whitewater and the Jones and Lewinsky scandals, a Republican congressman (and former federal prosecutor) from Georgia, Bob Barr, sent a letter to Henry Hyde, chair of the House Judiciary Committee. In it he stated that Clinton had used his office in a "pay for play" scheme and that there was a clear historical precedent for the committee to investigate the president on the "use of his high office to amass a campaign war chest" and that selling access was an "impeachable offense under Article II, Section 4 of the Constitution." He went on to say that "we must remain mindful as members of the House and as members of the Committee that by House rule we have always been the vehicle to investigate charges of impropriety and must undertake impeachment inquiry when there is a systematic subversion of lawful political processes."[32] The next day, Barr fired off correspondence to Attorney General Janet Reno to the effect that President Clinton had overseen illegal contributions to the Democratic National Committee by foreign individuals and corporations. He requested that an independent counsel be established to investigate these activities "under section 591 (c) of the Independent Counsel Act."[33] It is not so much that Barr expected the committee or the attorney general to respond immediately to his requests, but he was hoping to get Congress to seriously think about impeachment.[34]

Barr continued to press his claim. Barr complained to Chairman Hyde, reporting that Reno was not instigating an investigation.[35] He sent similar correspondence to House Speaker Newt Gingrich.[36] He then went to the press and began to draft a House resolution directing the House Judiciary Committee to conduct an inquiry into impeachment of the president. Interestingly, Hyde then contacted Barr, stating his displeasure over public comments made by Barr to the effect that there was "reluctance by me as Chair of the House Committee on the Judiciary to proceed on the investigation of the president and vice president." Hyde further stated that the "Committee will move quickly warranted by the circumstances, [but] there are four investigations underway. It seems prudent to await results of the investigations before starting what could be a constitutional crisis."[37] Impeachment at that point was the province of bomb throwers like Barr. Even Barr's hometown paper, the *Atlanta Journal-Constitution*, stated in an editorial that he was so "blinded by partisanship that he is willing to use any means available to inflict damage on his enemies."[38]

Barr's attempts to initiate an impeachment in the House failed, but the investigation went on. As Clinton's sexual indiscretions were leaked to the press, the president was forced to respond. At a press conference in January 1998, Clinton famously stated that "I did not have sexual relations with that woman," referring to Lewinsky. In the investigation Starr subpoenaed the president, who reluctantly agreed to appear before a grand jury. The president went on to acknowledge misconduct, but angrily stated that the inquiry was a political witch hunt seeking to discredit him based on a personal matter.

On September 9, 1998, Starr issued his report. Starr suggested in his report that the president had committed acts that in several instances constituted grounds for impeachment:

> "There is substantial and credible information that President Clinton's actions since January 17, 1998, regarding his relationship with Monica Lewinsky have been inconsistent with the President's constitutional duty to faithfully execute the laws. . . .
>
> A. Beginning on January 21, 1998, the President misled the American people and Congress regarding the truth of his relationship with Ms. Lewinsky.
>
> B. The First Lady, the Cabinet, the President's staff, and the President's associates relied on and publicly emphasized the President's denial.

C. The President repeatedly and unlawfully invoked the Executive Privilege to conceal evidence of his personal misconduct from the grand jury.

D. The President refused six invitations to testify to the grand jury, thereby delaying expeditious resolution of this matter, and then refused to answer relevant questions before the grand jury when he testified in August 1998.

E. The President misled the American people and the Congress in his public statement on August 17, 1998, when he stated that his answers at his civil deposition in January had been "legally accurate."

Starr concluded:

"In this case, the President made and caused to be made false statements to the American people about his relationship with Ms. Lewinsky. He also made false statements about whether he had lied under oath or otherwise obstructed justice in his civil case. By publicly and emphatically stating in January 1998 that "I did not have sexual relations with that woman" and these "allegations are false," the President also effectively delayed a possible congressional inquiry, and then he further delayed it by asserting Executive Privilege and refusing to testify for six months during the Independent Counsel investigation. This represents substantial and credible information that may constitute grounds for an impeachment."[39]

In order to buttress their case, on September 21 the Republican leadership released the videotaped testimony of the president before the grand jury.

Two days later the president and his legal team issued a seventeen-point response to the Starr Report:[40]

"September 11, 1998

EXECUTIVE SUMMARY

Summary of Key Points of the President's Case in Anticipation of the Starr Report

1. The President has acknowledged a serious mistake—an inappropriate relationship with Monica Lewinsky. He has

taken responsibility for his actions, and he has apologized to the country, to his friends, leaders of his party, the cabinet and most importantly, his family.

2. This private mistake does not amount to an impeachable action. A relationship outside one's marriage is wrong—and the President admits that. It is not a high crime or misdemeanor. The Constitution specifically states that Congress shall impeach only for "treason, bribery or other high crimes and misdemeanors." These words in the Constitution were chosen with great care, and after extensive deliberations.

3. "High crimes and misdemeanors" had a fixed meaning to the Framers of our Constitution—it meant wrongs committed against our system of government. The impeachment clause was designed to protect our country against a President who was using his official powers against the nation, against the American people, against our society. It was never designed to allow a political body to force a President from office for a very personal mistake.

4. Remember—this report is based entirely on allegations obtained by a grand jury—reams and reams of allegations and purported "evidence" that would never be admitted in court, that has never been seen by the President or his lawyers, and that was not subject to cross-examination or any other traditional safeguards to ensure its credibility.

5. Grand juries are not designed to search for truth. They do not and are not intended to ensure credibility, reliability, or simple fairness. They only exist to accuse. Yet this is the process that the Independent Counsel has chosen to provide the "evidence" to write his report.

6. The law defines perjury very clearly. Perjury requires proof that an individual knowingly made a false statement while under oath. Answers to questions that are literally true are not perjury. Even if an answer doesn't directly answer the question asked, it is not perjury if it is true—no accused has an obligation to help his accuser. Answers to fundamentally ambiguous questions also can never be perjury. And nobody can be convicted of perjury based on only one other person's testimony.

7. The President did not commit perjury. Most of the illegal leaks suggesting his testimony was perjurious falsely describe his testimony. First of all, the President never testified in the Jones deposition that he was not alone with Ms. Lewinsky. The President never testified that his relationship with Ms. Lewinsky was the same as with any other intern. To the contrary, he admitted exchanging gifts with her, knowing about her job search, receiving cards and notes from her, and knowing other details of her personal life that made it plain he had a special relationship with her.

8. The President has admitted he had an improper sexual relationship with Ms. Lewinsky. In a civil deposition, he gave narrow answers to ambiguous questions. As a matter of law, those answers could not give rise to a criminal charge of perjury. In the face of the President's admission of his relationship, the disclosure of lurid and salacious allegations can only be intended to humiliate the President and force him from office.

9. There was no obstruction of justice. We believe Betty Currie testified that Ms. Lewinsky asked her to hold the gifts and that the President never talked to her about the gifts. The President admitted giving and receiving gifts from Ms. Lewinsky when he was asked about it. The President never asked Ms. Lewinsky to get rid of the gifts and he never asked Ms. Currie to get them. We believe that Ms. Currie's testimony supports the President's.

10. The President never tried to get Ms. Lewinsky a job after she left the White House in order to influence her testimony in the Paula Jones case. The President knew Ms. Lewinsky was unhappy in her Pentagon job after she left the White House and did ask the White House personnel office to treat her fairly in her job search. He never instructed anyone to hire her, or even indicated that he very much wanted it to happen. Ms. Lewinsky was never offered a job at the White House after she left—and it's pretty apparent that if the President had ordered it, she would have been offered a position.

11. The President did not facilitate Ms. Lewinsky's interview with Bill Richardson, or her discussions with Vernon

Jordan. Betty Currie asked John Podesta if he could help her with her New York job search which led to an interview with Bill Richardson, and Ms. Currie also put her in touch with her longtime friend, Mr. Jordan. Mr. Jordan has made it clear that this is the case, and, as a private individual, he is free to offer job advice wherever he sees fit.

12. There was no witness tampering. Betty Currie was not supposed to be a witness in the Paula Jones case. If she was not called or going to be called, it was impossible for any conversations the President had with her to be witness tampering. The President testified that he did not in any way attempt to influence her recollection.

13. There is no "talking points" smoking gun. Numerous illegal leaks painted the mysterious talking points as the proof that the President or his staff attempted to suborn the perjury of Monica Lewinsky or Linda Tripp. The OIC's [Office of the Independent Counsel] spokesman said that the "talking points" were the "key" to Starr even being granted authority to investigate the President's private life. Yet in the end, Ms. Lewinsky has apparently admitted the talking points were written by her alone [or with Ms. Tripp's assistance], and the President was not asked one single question about them in his grand jury appearance.

14. Invocation of privileges was not an abuse of power. The President's lawful assertion of privileges in a court of law was only made on the advice of his Counsel, and was in significant measure validated by the courts. The legal claims were advanced sparingly and as a last resort after all attempts at compromise by the White House Counsel's office were rejected to protect the core constitutional and institutional interests of this and future presidencies.

15. Neither the President nor the White House played a role in the Secret Service's lawful efforts to prevent agents from testifying to preserve its protective function. The President never asked, directed or participated in any decision regarding the protective function privilege. Neither did any White House official. The Treasury and Justice Departments independently decided to respond to the historically unprecedented subpoenas

of Secret Service personnel and to pursue the privilege to ensure the protection of this and future presidents.

16. The President did not abuse his power by permitting White House staff to comment on the investigation. The President has acknowledged misleading his family, staff and the country about the nature of his relationship with Ms. Lewinsky, and he has apologized and asked for forgiveness. However, this personal failing does not constitute a criminal abuse of power. If allowing aides to repeat misleading statements is a crime, then any number of public officials are guilty of misusing their office for as long as they fail to admit wrongdoing in response to any allegation about their activities.

17. The actions of White House attorneys were completely lawful. The White House Counsel attorneys provided the President and White House officials with informed, candid advice on issues raised during this investigation that affected the President's official duties. This was especially necessary given the fact that impeachment proceedings against the President were a possible result of the OIC's investigation from Day One. In fact, throughout the investigation, the OIC relied on the White House Counsel's office for assistance in gathering information and arranging interviews and grand jury appearances. The Counsel's office's actions were well known to the OIC throughout the investigation and no objection was ever voiced.

This means that the OIC report is left with nothing but the details of a private sexual relationship, told in graphic details with the intent to embarrass. Given the flimsy and unsubstantiated basis for the accusations, there is a complete lack of any credible evidence to initiate an impeachment inquiry concerning the President. And the principal purpose of this investigation, and the OIC's report, is to embarrass the President and titillate the public by producing a document that is little more than an unreliable, one-sided account of sexual behavior.

Where's Whitewater? The OIC's allegations reportedly include no suggestion of wrongdoing by the President in any of the areas which Mr. Starr spent four years investigating: Whitewater, the FBI files and the White House travel office. What began as an inquiry into a 24-year-old land deal in Arkansas has ended as an inquest into brief, improper personal encounters between the President and Monica Lewinsky. Despite the exhaustive nature of the OIC's investigation into the Whitewater, FBI files and travel office matters, and a constant stream of suggestions of misconduct in the media over a period of years, to this day the OIC has never exonerated the President or the First Lady of wrongdoing."

Public opinion polls immediately following the release of the Starr Report were largely opposed to impeachment and removal. On September 8–10, in response to the question, "Based on what you know, do you think Congress should or should not impeach Clinton and remove him from office?," 64 percent of the respondents were opposed, 31 percent were in favor. The same poll asked the same question six times over the next two months, and in the first week of December 1998, 64 percent were still opposed.[41]

As if to reinforce the public opinion polls, in the congressional elections of 1998, the Democrats lost no seats in the Senate, despite the fact that nineteen Democratic-held seats were open for that cycle, versus fifteen Republican seats. Furthermore, in the House elections, the Republicans actually lost five seats to maintain a very thin majority, 223 to 211. This result was significant in that the second midterm election for any president is generally bad for the party in power. Furthermore, the elections were, in effect, a referendum on impeachment. Impeachment was highlighted by Republicans as one of the central issues of the campaign. Nevertheless, the Democrats actually gained seats overall. This disappointing result led to the removal of Speaker Newt Gingrich from the leadership by his fellow Republicans. Gingrich resigned from Congress soon thereafter amid his own mounting scandals and infidelities.[42]

In that same month, November 1998, ignoring public sentiment, and in a lame-duck session of Congress, the Republican majority voted two articles of impeachment against Bill Clinton, one based on perjury and the other on obstruction of justice. The House Judiciary Committee never did an independent investigation of its own, but instead relied almost exclusively on the Starr Report. The votes on the floor were largely, albeit not exclusively, along party lines. Republican House members knew there was little chance of convicting the president in the Senate, but they went ahead anyhow.

Given that the chances for removal were almost nil, why were Republicans willing to proceed? Even when presented with a compromise solution that was likely to pass and was just as likely to end the investigation in its tracks, Republicans demurred. Moderate Republicans Chris Shays of Connecticut and Paul McHale of Pennsylvania argued that the president should not be impeached unless it was certain that he would be removed from office. They proposed that it was in the best interest of the nation to get the matter resolved quickly and that censure would be more appropriate.[43] But their attempt at mediation was ignored. The fact that, against all odds, House Republicans were willing to proceed meant that they saw some political advantage in fighting the battle. Perhaps the public could be convinced that Clinton's lie rose to the level of an impeachable offense? Or maybe Clinton could be convinced to resign? There were still hard feelings on the Republican side over Nixon's resignation. Finally, if worse came to worst from the Republican perspective, and Clinton was acquitted, a trial in the Senate could damage the Clinton presidency badly enough to make him less effective, as well as influence the outcome of the next presidential election.

There really wasn't much support for impeachment in the Senate. According to the current U.S. Senate historian, Betty Koed, at the time of the Clinton impeachment the then historian of the Senate did explore the possibility that the Senate simply fail to act on an impeachment resolution by the House. But there was no such precedent, except when, under pressure, the target of the impeachment effort had resigned and there was no longer a need for a trial. And the fact that the impeachment resolutions were adopted by a lame-duck House didn't make any difference either. Again, according to the U.S. Senate historian, impeachments, like treaties (but unlike regular legislation), do not expire at the end of a particular Congress. It appears that the Constitution instructs the Senate to decisively dispose of impeachments in one way or another. Thus, from the Senate perspective, House impeachment resolutions, no matter how improbable, cannot be ignored.[44]

Forced to act, the Senate dusted off the record of the Johnson impeachment from 130 years before. The Senate also had a modern guide to impeachments that had been adopted in the twentieth century and had been utilized in the impeachment of several judges in the modern era.[45] In January 1999, one of the first things that the new Senate did when it was sworn in was to adopt procedures designed to try the impeachment in the modern context. The impeachment proceeded in four stages.[46]

The Senate Trial

On January 7, 1999, the Senate and the presiding officer of the impeachment, Chief Justice of the Supreme Court William Rehnquist, formally received the House Resolution of Impeachment and supporting materials. The Senate sent a summons to the president asking that he formally respond to the charges and designate a floor manager for his defense.

On January 14–16, the House managers presented their case. The House was represented by thirteen members of the Judiciary Committee who acted as prosecutors. All were attorneys, and several were former federal and state prosecutors including the aforementioned Barr.

The president was represented by eight attorneys, including some of the top trial lawyers in the country. They presented their case on January 19 and 20.

Both sides made arguments similar to the case made in Starr's Report and the president's response as presented above. The two main questions were whether Clinton had perjured himself and, if so, did that perjury rise to the level of an impeachable offense?

After the two sides presented their case, the floor was opened to questions of counsel and the House managers on January 22 and 23. Under the rules, the questions were written down and were posed by Chief Justice Rehnquist. There were over 150 questions.

As soon as both sides rested, Senator Robert Byrd (D-WV) introduced a motion that the charges be dismissed. The motion was rejected 56–44, mostly along party lines with the exception of Senator Russ Feingold (D-WI) who voted with the majority Republicans. By the same margin the Senate then voted to continue the trial by calling witnesses in the case.

The vote on the Byrd Resolution was a key moment in the Clinton impeachment. The Republicans had always needed twelve Democratic votes (plus the fifty-five Republicans) in the Senate to convict. If after the presentations of the House managers and the president's counsel, the Republicans managed to turn only one Democratic vote, the chances of conviction were essentially zero. As if to reinforce that point, the resolution of dismissal was sponsored by Senator Byrd, who had previously been targeted as a possible vote for conviction. This meant that conviction and removal were impossible. Just as the House Republicans had rallied around an unpopular and unlikely resolution to impeach, Senate Democrats rallied around a doomed motion to dismiss, if only to demonstrate to the Republicans that they didn't have a chance.[47] The impeachment of Clinton had become a strictly symbolic, partisan debate.

As the Senate wound its way toward a desultory conclusion, witnesses were deposed on videotape including Lewinsky and presidential advisors Vernon Jordan and Sidney Blumenthal, the latter two regarding the obstruction of justice charge. Susan Collins of Maine proposed that the Senate take a two-step approach, vote first on whether the president was guilty of perjury and obstruction of justice and then vote whether to remove him from office. But here also the Constitution provides for only a single vote on removal.

The outcome of the final votes for removal was preordained. The president was going to be acquitted; the only question was by how much. How many senators would break with their party? Members could vote their conscience and still vote with the party, but would every member do so on every charge? Was it really possible that on the merits of the case, fifty-five Republicans and forty-five Democrats were diametrically opposed to one another and unanimous in that conviction? As it turns out, on February 12, 1999, the vote on perjury was 55–45, with a majority for acquittal. Thus, a number of Republicans did vote for acquittal, most of whom were moderates. No Democrats voted the other way. On the obstruction of justice charge the Senate split 50–50, but it was still nowhere near the two-thirds vote needed to convict. The Clinton presidency survived.[48]

Analysis—Why No Conviction?

I. Opposite Party Control of the House

In this historical chapter, we see a politically successful and popular president impeached on scant constitutional grounds by a House majority composed of an opposition party bitterly opposed on a partisan basis. This opposing majority, in a lame-duck session, and with little political capital to lose, was intent on sending a message to the president that although he might not be removed from office, through impeachment there would be an energetic denunciation of his policies and character. Congressional Republicans, who watched while Democrats set the impeachment wheels in motion against Nixon, were all too willing to return the favor against the Clinton administration and his liberal allies.

At the time of the vote on articles of impeachment against Clinton, the Republicans held a 230 to 204 majority in the House. If the House had adjourned and waited for the next Congress to act, that majority would have fallen slightly to 226 to 207. But, given that a majority in the House is 218, the House Republicans in 1998 had to know that their chances for success were worse in 1999 should they decide to wait. As it was, two articles of impeachment voted by the House passed (two others failed). The first article of impeachment relating to perjury passed the House by a mere 228–206 vote. Five Republicans defected as did five Democrats. Any combination of votes that reduced the majority by eleven votes, and the motion would have failed. As it was, there were thirty-three retirements from Congress that year, sixteen Republicans and seventeen Democrats. Of those retirees, only one defected (voting for impeachment) from the party majority, and that was Democrat Paul McHale from Pennsylvania. Assuming that all five Republicans who lost their seats to a Democrat plus the one defector means that the Democrats would have still lost the vote; it just would have been closer. On the second article of impeachment, relating to obstruction of justice, the vote was closer, 221–212. Given that five Republican members had lost their seats to Democrats, it's a virtual certainty that this article would have failed in the new Congress.[49]

Finally, probably the most important retirement of them all was Speaker Newt Gingrich. While it was not clear at the time who would replace Gingrich, Bob Livingston, the heir apparent, was forced to pass on the Speakership when his own marital infidelities came to light. The eventual successor to Gingrich was Dennis Hastert. Whether Speaker Hastert would have been as aggressive in pursuing a vote on impeachment, we will never know. Interestingly, Hastert would later be involved in a criminal sexual scandal himself. Thus, there is good reason to believe that the House articles of impeachment against Bill Clinton were Gingrich's swan song.

2. OPPOSITE PARTY CONTROL OF THE SENATE

The Republicans had a comfortable but not overwhelming majority in the Senate, 55–45. That means that even if all the Republicans voted to convict, they would still need another twelve Democratic votes. Consequently, as long as impeachment was perceived as a partisan issue, there was no chance for conviction in the Senate.

Any hope that the Republicans had that the evidence presented in trial would change public opinion and pressure Senate Democrats into voting to remove the president went up in flames as the poll numbers continued to overwhelmingly oppose impeachment and removal. Furthermore, the

Democratic voters who elected these Democrats to the Senate were even more opposed than the general public to the impeachment of Clinton.[50] Finally, by the time the case went to the Senate trial, basically all the evidence was known. Starr, if nothing else, was thorough in his investigation; as a result, everyone involved had already made up their minds.

Nevertheless, the Senate went through the motions of a trial. The problem for Republicans in this case was that their insistence on pursuing a matter that was basically a waste of time is a dangerous tactic in the Senate. The ever-present threat of a filibuster means that senators must get along to go along. Most bills in the Senate require a sixty-vote supermajority for approval. Therefore, the Senate is not a majoritarian institution (in contrast to the House). To inconvenience the minority for no good reason in the Senate invites retaliation. The Republicans were playing a dangerous game.

As if to reinforce the pyrrhic nature of the impeachment, after the two sides presented their case, a motion to dismiss sponsored by a Democratic senator, Robert Byrd, who was believed most likely to turn, failed, but with forty-five votes in support. At that point, there was no chance of conviction.[51]

3. IMPORTANT POLICY DIFFERENCES BETWEEN THE PRESIDENT AND CONGRESSIONAL LEADERS

In 2009 a team of six political scientists published an article that established a spatial measure for the ideological distance between members of Congress.[52] Basically, these researchers collect the roll-call votes of all members of Congress, determining the similarity in voting (or distance) of each member of Congress from all other members of Congress. Then the researchers establish a median score for both houses of Congress and the distance of individual members from that midpoint. This "DW-Nominate Score"[53] has become the gold standard of measurement of ideology in American political science.

If Congress has a median, ideological score, so does the president. Royce Carroll and his colleagues have established a DW-Nominate score for American presidents (based on legislation considered by Congress on which the president has established a clear position). In comparison with other modern presidents (up to and including Obama), President Clinton was a liberal relative to modern Republican presidents but was a center moderate compared to other Democratic presidents. In other words, in the ideological sense Clinton wasn't out of the ordinary.[54]

But the real difference was not in the position of the president, it was in the position of the House. After 1992, House Republicans took a hard turn to the right. By 1998, Republicans in the House were more "right" of center than they had been in the entire twentieth century. The Senate, which operates on a six-year electoral cycle, lagged the House. Senate Republicans took a hard turn to the right after the election of 2004. But as far as ideological distance between the branches was concerned and its effect on the propensity to impeach, it wasn't Clinton who moved to the left; it was the House that moved to the right.[55]

4. TIME OF NATIONAL CRISIS OR SOCIAL UNREST

In relative terms, 1998–99 was a quiet period in American political history. The economy was growing. According to the Organization for Economic Co-operation and Development, U.S. unemployment in 1998 was below 5 percent and dropping. Government spending was down, wages were up, the federal government was running a surplus, and the United States was not engaged in a major foreign war.[56] There was no policy reason that the Congress and the president should have been in fierce opposition at this time.

5. PERSONAL ANIMOSITY BETWEEN THE PRESIDENT AND CONGRESSIONAL LEADERS

Surprisingly, President Clinton's relationship with congressional leaders wasn't all that bad. In fact, it is rumored that, by 1997, President Clinton had made a secret deal with Speaker Gingrich to try to cooperate to reshape policy, when possible, in the last few years of the Clinton presidency.[57] Gingrich and Clinton worked closely together on NAFTA, welfare reform, and the Mexican debt crisis. Unfortunately for them both, the Lewinsky scandal intervened. The Clinton presidency was wounded, and Gingrich was eventually forced to leave. Even when Bob Livingston was named as Speaker and Gingrich's replacement, and was forced to withdraw because of his own marital infidelity, Clinton actually urged Livingston to tough it out.

Clinton didn't get along badly with Senate Majority Leader Trent Lott either. Lott and Clinton had a lot in common. The two were born a couple of hundred miles apart in just about the same era. Lott worked with Clinton on the signature achievements of the latter part of the Clinton administration: welfare reform, children's health insurance, and the chemical weapons ban.

Here, again, the problem wasn't policy, it wasn't clashing personalities, and it wasn't even the law. The impeachment of Bill Clinton was hardball politics.

6. Climate of Public Animosity toward the President

The public had a very subtle and complex view of the president during the impeachment. Not only was the public, as previously noted, firmly and consistently opposed to impeachment and removal, the public did not even have much of a negative reaction to the president's personal behavior.

First, regarding lying. After the release of the Starr Report and the videotaped testimony of the president before the Grand Jury, a September 1998 ABC News Poll asked,

> As you may know, the video of Clinton's grand jury testimony shows prosecutors asking about details of Clinton's sexual activity with Lewinsky. In the tape, Clinton says he had improper sexual activity with Lewinsky but refused to discuss any of the details of that activity. Do you think Clinton was right not to talk about these sexual details or wrong to not talk about them?[58]

Seventy percent of the respondents said the president was right not to talk about the details, and 68 percent of those respondents who had viewed the tape answered "yes" it was appropriate for the president to lie as well. Even when they were asked how they felt about the lie in the personal sense, they were generally willing to give Clinton a "bye."[59]

Before the release of the Starr Report, the release of videotaped testimony before the grand jury, and the impeachment, according to the periodic Gallup Poll, the public gave the president an approval rating in the low to mid 60s (August 1998). After the acquittal, Clinton's approval ratings were in the mid to high 60s (March 1999).[60] Not only were the president's approval ratings exceptionally high through the impeachment, but they stayed that way afterward.

7. The President Accused of Criminal Behavior—Actual

President Clinton was accused of perjury and obstruction of justice. These are felonies under the law. But here is where the politics of impeachment kick in. We started out this book asking the question, what type of crime rises to the constitutional standard of "high crimes and misdemeanors"? As the impeachment process is not the same as a criminal trial, an individual can be impeached and not brought to trial for criminal acts or the other way around. This is because an impeachment refers to the abuse of the powers of the office. So, for example, President Clinton was accused of trying to arrange for a job for Lewinsky in order to buy her silence.[61] If Clinton had arranged for such a job, especially in the government, that may have been grounds for impeachment, as the president, according to the Constitution, is the chief executive of the federal government.[62]

On the charge of perjury, there seems to be very little here in the way of an impeachable offense. A lie under oath about a consensual sexual affair, even if that affair occurred in the West Wing, hardly rises to level of an impeachable offense as defined above. And if the public was willing to overlook it, so was the Senate. If Clinton had pressured Lewinsky or assaulted her, that would be a different matter. And, in the modern context, in the environment of the #MeToo movement, Clinton's actions could have been, and are, seen in a different light. Whether a president committing such acts today would be able to avoid impeachment and escape conviction remains to be seen. Such is the changing nature of the politics of impeachment.

8. The President Accused of Criminal Behavior—Political

About the only political transgression that Bill Clinton could be accused of is being too moderate. The president's attempt to triangulate in a bipolar political environment threatened the electoral chances of the Republicans on the right and softened support from the Democrats on the left. This was a particular problem for President Clinton. As noted above, in the years that Clinton served as president, the Republican Party took a sharp turn to the right. The Democratic Party took a corresponding, if not as radical, turn to the left and Clinton was left in the middle.

According to Duverger's Law, in a winner-take-all political system, candidates for office tend to move to the center of the political spectrum. Therefore, winner-take-all structured political systems tend to have a moderating effect on political discourse. But there is an important exception to this rule. In a highly partisan political environment, where the parties have sorted themselves into separate camps, to try to split the difference between the parties, to try to find the middle of the political spectrum, is a losing proposition because there is no one in the center remaining.[63] For the first four years of the Clinton presidency, the president was able to split the difference in policy terms. Triangulation worked. But in his second term, the division between the parties became so profound that triangulation no longer worked. It would have been to Clinton's benefit to move to the left, but after years as a southern politician, that just wasn't his instinct.

If there was any actual political crime related to the Lewinsky scandal it might have been a cover-up or obstruction of justice. The problem is that that sort of thing is hard to prove. It is not hard to believe that if Nixon hadn't taped his conversations in the Oval Office and had not been forced to turn over those tapes to the court, he wouldn't have had to resign. Without a "smoking gun," obstruction is hard to prove. Even if, in the case of the Lewinsky scandal, Vernon Jordan tried to find Lewinsky a job, just because that effort was concurrent with the breaking news of a sexual relationship between the president and Lewinsky, does not mean this was a crime. Criminal behavior, for a very good reason, requires a substantial burden of proof. Without a "smoking gun," the fact that the president helped a friend (even a "special" friend) does not rise to the level of a criminal or impeachable offense. Finding employment for friends is what politicians do. It is called patronage, and patronage is as old as the Republic.

Should Bill Clinton Have Been Impeached?

Offenses perceived as impeachable should be based on an abuse of office, not a private wrong, and not where there is a disagreement over policy. The majority in the Senate did their job in refusing to remove a president based on what were technical wrongs used by political enemies to remove a rival. Impeachment is as much a political as a constitutional proceeding, and there was no popular groundswell to remove the president. Clinton was as popular after he was impeached as he was before. Even after it became clear that there was no chance that Clinton would be removed, congressional Republicans insisted on staying the course. And there wasn't really a political price to pay. Except for a brief downturn in support for the Republican Party from November 1998 to March 1999, the GOP suffered no lasting political harm. They even won the 2000 presidential election. In fact, in the long run, the Clinton impeachment paid political benefits, perhaps contributing to the defeat of Al Gore in 2000 and even to the defeat of the Hillary Clinton candidacy in 2016.

And even if they expected to lose, they could have taken heart from Edmund Burke's pursuit before Parliament of the 1787 impeachment trial of Warren Hastings, the famous trial that may have influenced the authors of the Constitution that we referred to in the opening chapter of this book. By the time Hastings went to trial, he was already out of office, having resigned under pressure. Thus, the case was in its particulars moot. Nevertheless, Burke pursued the impeachment on principle *and even though he expected to lose.* He conceived of the trial as an important discussion of the appropriate obligations of a public official.[64]

So, if there is a political lesson to be learned from the Clinton impeachment, it is that in a polarized political environment, hardball politics are more likely to occur because they work. The Republicans didn't pay a price for pursuing a scorched earth strategy in the face of insurmountable odds. The Democrats would have every reason to take note and respond in kind. The problem for our democracy, then, is to break the cycle. Political prosecutions, including impeachments, are likely to continue as long as there isn't a price to pay.

CHAPTER SEVEN

Conclusion

The Politics of Impeachment

This book had two major goals. First, we wanted to determine, using a small set of case studies, what factors increase the likelihood of a presidential impeachment. Second, we set out to demonstrate that the use of impeachments, particularly against presidents, is a political, not a legal, process. Given this premise, we suggest that the correct way to view impeachments is through a political and not a legal or historical lens. In this concluding chapter, we compare our cases to illustrate our findings through the use of both qualitative and quantitative analysis.

Presidential Impeachments: Qualitative Analysis

As discussed in chapter 2, there are certain structural conditions for impeachment. One of the most obvious is divided government. It is hard to imagine the impeachment of a president whose party holds a significant majority in the House of Representatives. And since congressional elections occur on a biennial basis, the House remains a reasonably good indicator of the mood of the public including attitudes toward impeachment. But because of the constitutional thresholds of a majority in the House for impeachment and a two-thirds vote in the Senate for conviction, except under extraordinary circumstances divided government is a necessary, but not sufficient, condition for impeachment.[1] Indeed, even when the opposition had the necessary votes in the Senate, as it did in the case of Andrew Johnson, it could not muster enough votes to convict. That is because Johnson was clearly on his way out of office. Johnson had been denied the nomination in both parties and there simply wasn't enough support for an independent candidacy. All Congress needed to do was wait the president out. Not only was Johnson a lame duck but also there was a very legitimate question as to whether he had committed an impeachable offense. And was it worth subverting the will of the voters and setting a drastic precedent over a "technicality" such as a violation of the Tenure of Office Act (which was of questionable constitutionality in and of itself)?

After all, policy disagreements between the president and Congress are inevitable. As Lyndon Johnson once said when asked why he changed his position as president on an issue opposite to the position he held as Majority Leader in the Senate, "I've changed my constituency." A president with a national perspective will see things differently than a member of Congress or a governor of a state.

Andrew Johnson thought the Tenure of Office Act was unconstitutional, and he was right. At first glance it may seem that the Radical Republicans thought to bring the country to a constitutional crisis over such a small issue, but that wasn't what the Johnson impeachment was about anyhow. For some very legitimate reasons, Republicans in Congress could see their control of Reconstruction slipping away and they were desperate to do something about it, which highlights a problem in our constitutional system.

As the Andrew Johnson case illustrates, even in the nineteenth century, well before the rise of the "imperial presidency," the president was in a position to subvert national policy on his own authority as Johnson did in subverting "radical" Reconstruction. But this is a problem of a government that has failed to become, as the Framers had hoped, a government of laws and not of men. The presidency has simply become too powerful under the existing constitutional structure. The impeachment tool is much too blunt an instrument to address the problems of the imperial presidency. There is not an intermediate remedy available, short of waiting for the next election, for reining in a runaway presidency. Besides, even though the imperial presidency presents its own problems, sometimes a president might just be right.

What should presidents do when they see that Congress has taken an action that is tragically ill advised? This was Reagan's dilemma in the case of Iran-Contra, particularly on the Contra side of the transaction. Reagan failed to veto the appropriations bills that included the Boland Amendment. If he had wanted to confront Congress on the issue of Nicaragua, he should have done it then. But even so, as the latitude for the president in the conduct of foreign policy is so broad, a plausible argument could be made that supplying the Contras and even trading arms for hostages was in pursuit of a legitimate national security goal. However, when it came to lying and other forms of obstruction of justice, Reagan and his minions were out of their constitutional depth and for that there was no legitimate excuse.

Indeed, there were a number of prosecutions and convictions on those grounds. Unfortunately (or fortunately for Reagan himself) for the country, this president could plausibly argue that he was unaware of what was happening on his behalf as these actions were carried out by an overzealous staff. We find that excuse, as did Congress, difficult but not impossible to believe and perhaps a convenient fiction. What was the point of removing a president who was reasonably popular, clearly in pursuit of legitimate foreign policy goals whether we agree with them or not, and certainly not in pursuit of any personal or political gain? Furthermore, by the time Iran-Contra was thoroughly investigated, Reagan was in his final term and could never run for president again.[2]

But such was not the case in the impeachment of President Nixon. Nixon got caught up in the cover-up of a felony that, if discovered, would have been to his personal and political detriment. To add to his predicament, his crimes were caught on tape. Even while Nixon was in his last term in office, the scandal blossomed at the beginning and not the end of his second term. Nevertheless, in a different era, Nixon might have been able to brazen it out. The key moments on the path to the Nixon resignation were not the acts of the opposition, but the acts of the president's own party. When many House Republicans on the Judiciary Committee broke with their party and voted to impeach, the progression of events was set in motion. Their defection from the party lent legitimacy to a process that, under other circumstances, could have been perceived as entirely partisan. But to add to Nixon's problem and to seal his doom were the defections of Senate Republicans. When Senator Barry Goldwater went to the White House at the head of a Senate delegation to tell the president that he was inclined to vote for removal, the jig was up. If that same set of events were to occur today, would the opposition be so willing to go along? In our hyperpartisan environment, what would it take for senators from the president's party seriously to consider removal of the president?

That was certainly the issue at the core of the Clinton impeachment. What Clinton had done was wrong, but did it constitute a "high crime and misdemeanor" in the meaning of the Constitution? Because there was no real legal guidance on the question, it was a judgment call. At that point, partisanship prevailed. As long as Clinton's supporters could define the impeachment in partisan terms, there would never be enough votes in the Senate to convict.

So, the picture that emerges is that each impeachment, or the failure to impeach as was the case in Iran-Contra, has both institutional and idiosyncratic foundations. Divided government is key to an impeachment as it is hard to imagine an impeachment resolution in the House much less a conviction in the Senate if the president's party is in the majority. What also matters is the nature of the illegal act (i.e., political, procedural, or actual).

Theoretically, there is no reason that the president couldn't be removed from office but never be convicted in a court of law. That actually happened in the case of Florida judge Alcee Hastings who in 1989 was impeached and removed from office but never convicted of a crime. In fact, Hastings was later elected to the House of Representatives.

It is also the case that the president could be acquitted and later face some kind of punishment after leaving office, as was the case with President Clinton. Clinton was acquitted by the Senate but later disbarred for having lied under oath regarding the Lewinsky affair.

Consequently, there is some kind of crime that exists in the middle ground between actual criminal behavior and what constitutes an impeachable offense. We don't have an example of a president who has committed an obvious and heinous crime, bank robbery, murder, and the like. Should that happen, the seriousness of the crime would probably trump all other matters and lead to removal. This is especially true given that, in the modern era, there are few costs in succession. Vice presidents are chosen with the thought in mind that should they come to the presidency, they can continue the administration's policies in spirit if not in the person of the elected president. Modern vice presidents are unlikely to be chosen for geographical balance regardless of ideological similarity, as John Tyler and Andrew Johnson were chosen for their tickets.[3]

Thus, the crime that constitutes an impeachable offense appears to be one that encompasses an abuse of office for personal gain. Reagan abused his office for the purpose of protecting national security. Whether we agree or disagree, the threat from the Soviet Union during the Cold War was plausible enough that we were willing to give the president a bye. But in the case of Nixon, the wiretapping of an opponent's party headquarters, a burglary, the paying of hush money, the use of government agencies to harass political enemies, all of these constitute an abuse of the office for personal gain.

There are other important factors that contribute to but are not determinate of impeachment. It appears that ideological distance between parties may be a contributing factor. In the United States, parties represent broad coalitions, and while a president and Congress may be of the same party, there could remain deep ideological divisions indeed. This worked to President Reagan's favor in Iran-Contra. By the time Reagan was elected, the House was already turning from blue to purple, presaging the Republican takeover in 1993. But at the same time, that fact may have hurt Clinton, who may have been too close to the center to elicit anything but tepid support from the left wing of his own party and rabid opposition from the right.

Consequently, party politics are changing, as partisan polarization is another factor that contributes to impeachments. Polarization accentuates both the possibilities and impossibilities of impeachment. When both parties see the other as an existential threat, hardball politics are the result. The Clinton impeachment was the first impeachment pursued mostly for ostensibly partisan purposes. It seems likely that others will follow, especially when the House is controlled by the party opposite. But as a function of the same partisan political environment, unless the Senate comes to be controlled by a supermajority of the party opposite the president, conviction seems even less likely than before. Thus, in the modern era of partisan polarization, impeachments are both more likely to occur, while convictions and removal are less likely to be voted than ever before. Thus, President Trump practically invited the House to impeach as he could be reasonably certain that he would never be convicted in the Senate. At that point, an unsuccessful impeachment was an argument for total exoneration. Thus, we had the strange spectacle of a Democratic Speaker, Nancy Pelosi, reluctant to impeach and a Republican president apparently eager to face a trial. Under such conditions, impeachment is no longer even a useful threat.

Other Influences on Impeachment

Along with the systematic institutional factors, each impeachment is idiosyncratic. What were the themes of each of the five cases discussed in this volume?

THE JOHNSON IMPEACHMENT

The Johnson impeachment was a function of the national stress created by Reconstruction. The Civil War was fought at a ghastly price. Congressional Republicans could see the fruits of victory slipping away in the failure of Reconstruction. Johnson was at best inept and at worst malign in his handling of the reunification of the country. And in 1866–67, with the demobilization or reassignment of the U.S. Army to other regions, the window on Reconstruction was closing fast.

Congressional Republicans were desperate to try anything they could to pursue the policies they thought would work to facilitate Reconstruction. But to do that, they had to get rid of Johnson. But Johnson, in the end, was merely wrong, not criminal, and the Republicans had to construct an excuse to impeach. That is why from the perspective of the modern era, a violation of the Tenure of Office Act seems such a flimsy basis for the Johnson impeachment. But the Constitution at the time (the Twenty-Fifth Amendment wasn't yet adopted) didn't authorize the removal of a president any other way (at least at that time) short of impeachment.

But the fact is that Reconstruction of the South was going to be difficult if not impossible in any event. Even if Lincoln had lived, it is unlikely that he would have been able to pull it off. It took forty years of occupation to turn Germany and Japan into liberal democracies. But in the absence of a standing army and with the South in its antebellum form readmitted to the Union, it seems unlikely that any single president could have restructured the social fabric of the South. Perhaps then what the Johnson impeachment was all about was the helplessness the congressional Republicans felt in winning a war but losing the peace.

THE NIXON IMPEACHMENT

President Nixon broke the law. He didn't just break the law, but he did so for personal and political gain. Not only that, there was incontrovertible evidence of Nixon's lawlessness. The presence of a "smoking gun" made Nixon's impeachment and removal almost a certainty.

The president wasn't above breaking the law in other areas. The secret bombing of Cambodia and Laos was probably illegal as was the impoundment of appropriated funds. But these disagreements were about policy and the president could make a case, albeit flawed, on the constitutional merits of his actions. While Congress and the courts never pushed back very hard on foreign policy, the courts did rule on a number of occasions that the impoundment of appropriated funds was illegal. At that point, the president obeyed the courts and released the funds. Had the president refused to obey the court, that would have been another matter and one day we may see if that rises to the level of an impeachable offense.[4]

Besides the three articles of impeachment the House Judiciary Committee approved, it also considered two other articles of impeachment based on President Nixon's secret bombing of Cambodia and his failure to pay and perhaps evade income taxes. Ultimately, the committee wasn't willing to challenge the president's decision as commander in chief, even an action as ill-considered as the secret bombing of a sovereign country not at war with the United States. That may have been an abuse of office, but it was just as possible that in the places he bombed there was no national sovereignty and there were certainly the lives of American troops at risk. This was certainly a matter of dispute and it wasn't the place of the committee to second guess the president's decisions as commander in chief. And if Congress was willing to challenge the president in this regard, impeachment was the wrong tool.

On the issue of tax evasion, the Committee was unwilling to impeach as well. Many of us have disputes with the IRS. In those cases, the government has a number of intermediate actions short of a criminal prosecution. The president had yet to exhaust his options in regard to the disputed taxes and, therefore, should not have been subject to an impeachment. Besides, such matters in the case of the president did not rise to the level of a presidential impeachment because they did not represent an abuse of office. Here, impeachment wasn't the right tool.[5]

The signature feature of the Nixon impeachment was the president's misuse of office associated with the Watergate burglary cover-up, in violation of the law, for the purpose of personal gain, in this case, for reelection, which was accompanied by solid evidence.

IRAN-CONTRA AND THE RELUCTANCE TO IMPEACH

In a system of separation of powers there will often be disagreements between the branches. In fact, such disagreements are hardwired into the system. It cannot be the case that disagreements over policy should result in impeachment and removal. The proper way to settle those disagreements would be through the legislative process, the courts, and the ballot box.

The CIA station chief in Beirut had fallen into the hands of an enemy organization. The potential for a massive intelligence breach was imminent. President Reagan, in exploring all options, contacted the Iranian government, which he believed had some influence over Hezbollah, the group that held the CIA station chief hostage.

The Iranian government was desperate too. It was engaged in a brutal war with the Iraqis and needed resupply of its American-made weapons.

Even though Iran was classified as a terrorist state and, therefore, on the embargo list for the purchase of American weapons, the Reagan administration arranged a back-channel sale; and then it redirected the proceeds to fund the Contra rebels in Central America. This too was in violation of the law.

The question here was the role of the American president in the conduct of foreign affairs. The president, pursuant to his oath of office, is obligated to protect and defend the Constitution of the United States. If Congress passes a law that, in the moment, is a threat to national security, is the president of the United States obligated to obey that law at the risk of national security? Furthermore, on the claim of secrecy, the president has a reasonable national security claim to make related to the abduction of a CIA station chief and actions to counter the threat of Soviet influence in Central America.[6]

We want to emphasize that while we may or may not agree with the president's judgment in this regard, we do not believe these actions rise to the level of an impeachable offense. Had the president's actions been challenged in the courts and had the case gone against the president, the president would have been obligated to follow the ruling of the court. More likely the case would have gone to the public through the electoral process, and because of the president's relative popularity, he or his party would have won (as it did in 1988). Had the president failed to obey the ruling of the courts or had the president intentionally misled Congress, he may have been subject to impeachment. But as it was, he did as he was required to do, and when his staff did not, they were prosecuted for crimes and some of them were convicted.

As with the question of impoundments during the Nixon impeachment, disagreements over policy in the Iran-Contra Affair did not rise to the level of an impeachable offense.

THE CLINTON IMPEACHMENT AND TRIAL

What constitutes an impeachable offense? If an impeachable office is the misuse of office for personal gain, then Clinton should not have been impeached or removed. Clearly, he lied under oath in relation to a sexual affair that he had with a White House intern. But how that constituted an impeachable offense is hard to say. *Not every illegal act is impeachable, and not every impeachable offense is an illegal act.* Nevertheless, congressional Republicans impeached Clinton and took the case to trial. Why, in the face of certain failure, did they decide to proceed?

The basis of the Clinton impeachment was an institutional change. Between the time Clinton took office and the initiation of his impeachment, Republicans in the House had taken a hard turn to the right. Clinton was, by nature, a relative centrist. But the political world around him had begun to change.

Around 1993, with the election of a Republican majority in the House, the ideological median in the House began to move to the right. Movement in the House ideological median represents not only the number of members elected from the party opposite to the president but also the ideological position of those members. Articles of impeachment were voted by the lame-duck 105th House of Representatives elected in 1996. The Republicans held a rather slim majority, 226–207, before the election and had, in fact, lost three seats in 1996. Overall, however, the House Republicans at about that time took a hard turn to the right. That means that the ideological change in the House was a function of a change in the makeup of the House Republican Caucus and not the number of members in the House Republican caucus. As noted in the previous chapter, Clinton hadn't changed; the House had.[7]

There was a dramatic and permanent move to the right on the part of House Republicans starting in about 1976 but accelerating in the mid-1990s. We hypothesize that because impeachments are in part a function of the ideological distance between presidents and the House, the relative frequency of modern presidential impeachments is a function of partisan polarization. And as polarization is likely to continue, so should the likelihood of impeachments.[8]

So, the grounds for impeachment, in this case, don't matter. If it wasn't Lewinsky, it would have been something else. The conditions were there for a Clinton impeachment.

Presidential Impeachments: Quantitative Analysis

In chapter 2, we introduced a matrix of variables as a framework to analyze presidential impeachments. Table 7.1 reintroduces this matrix with values filled in for each variable across presidential impeachments. For each variable for each of the impeached presidents, we fill in the value with a yes or no. A "yes" indicates that the variable was present, while a "no" indicates that the variable is not present for that impeachment. We have left the row for ideological distance between the president and Congress blank as we will discuss this variable below. We present each variable in order from most prevalent to least prevalent.[9]

Table 7.1. Impeachment Contributing Factor Matrix

	Andrew Johnson	Richard Nixon	Ronald Reagan	Bill Clinton
Divided Government	Yes	Yes	Yes	Yes
Ideological distance between president and Congress	Not available	0.529 (House) 0.574 (Senate)	0.866 (House) 0.885 (Senate)	0.709 (House) 0.556 (Senate)
Major Personality Conflicts with Congressional Leaders	No	No	No	No
National Crisis/ Social Upheaval	Yes	Yes	No	No
Unpopular President	Yes	Yes	No	No
Presidents in Their Final Term	Yes	Yes	Yes	Yes
Accused Criminal Behavior—Actual	No	Yes	No	Yes
Accused Illegal Behavior— Procedural	Yes	Yes	Yes	No
Accused Illegal Behavior— Political	No	Yes	No	No

DIVIDED GOVERNMENT

What is most noticeable from the matrix is that divided government is present for all four impeachments (100%). This demonstrates that divided government seems to be a prerequisite condition for impeachments to occur. Because the president and Congress are of opposite parties, it creates a scenario in which party conflict exacerbates differences between the two branches. The presence of divided government in all four impeachments also demonstrates that impeachment is largely a political weapon that members of Congress will wield against presidents who fail to follow the will of Congress. In other words, if we observed that unified or quasi-divided government existed in some or all of the impeachment case studies, we would not be able to conclude that partisan (political) differences affect the use of impeachment. Rather, we would have to say that impeachment is a principled (legal) matter that occurs when presidents violate the letter of the law.

This finding regarding divided government is particularly important when considering the current political climate in the United States. Since 1936, divided government has occurred in forty out of eighty-two years (48.7%), and thirty-three out of forty-eight years (68.75%) since 1970. Because an impeachment demands action by both the House and the Senate, this means that divided government, one of the primary conditions for impeachments to occur, has become the norm and not the exception in modern politics. In other words, given the increased frequency of opposite party control of Congress, we should expect more instances of impeachment.

IDEOLOGICAL DIFFERENCES BETWEEN CONGRESS AND THE PRESIDENT

Divided government provides some of the conditions necessary for impeachment. However, divided government only means that the president and Congress are controlled by the opposite party. It does not mean that the ideological divide between Congress and the president will be wide enough to incentivize impeachment. Moderate Republicans might be quite tolerant of moderate Democrats and vice versa. We are not suggesting that divided government is not a cause, but rather that ideological differences between the branches might present a more nuanced picture of the mechanisms at work.

Poole and Rosenthal have developed a measure of political ideology that falls on a scale ranging from −1 to 1, where a move toward −1 represents a move in a liberal direction and a move toward 1 represents a move in a conservative direction.[10] These measures are referred to as NOMINATE scores and are useful because the ideology of actors can be compared across institutions and across time. For chambers of Congress, political scientists typically rely on the ideology score of the median member of the chamber to represent the ideology of that chamber for that Congress. The median member represents the swing vote that is needed to gain a majority in either chamber.

For the 1st through 113th Congress, the average ideological distance between the president and the House was .358 and the average distance between the president and the Senate was .366. If we examine the ideological distance between the House and the president and the Senate and the president for the presidents presented in the book (data on Johnson is not available), we see that the average ideological distance is .708 and .672, respectively. Thus, we see that the ideological distance, on average, is much larger when impeachments occur than the average ideological distance for all presidents and each chamber.

In fact, we can track the ideological distance between presidents and each chamber. Figure 7.1 presents the ideological distance between the president and the House for all Congresses for which data is available. To remind, the Andrew Johnson era DW-Nominate scores are unavailable.

Ideological Distance Between House and President by Congress Number

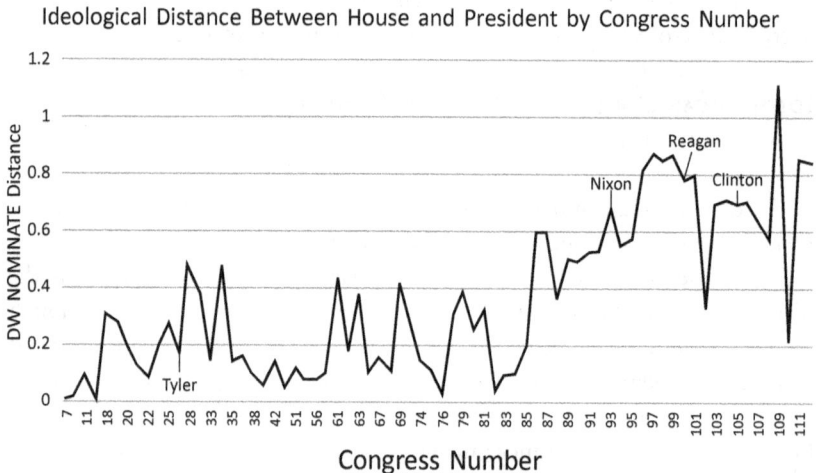

Figure 7.1. Ideological (DWNOMINATE) distance between the House and the President by Congress.

Figure 7.1 highlights four major points for which significant impeach-ment actions were taken (Tyler, Nixon, Reagan, and Clinton).[11] Data for Johnson are not available for direct comparison, but the data provide a strong visual example of how ideological differences play a role in impeachment actions. However, these data by themselves do not provide enough evidence as differences between averages can be skewed by sample size and the stan-dard deviation of each sample. Thus, we delve further into the numbers.

Using Poole and Rosenthal's DW-Nominate scores that were available for presidents and House medians, we calculated the absolute value of the ideological distance between the median member of the House and the president by Congress number. We then conducted a difference of means t-test, otherwise known as a Satterthwaite's t-test, to determine whether there was a statistically significant difference between the *average* ideological distance between the president and the House for all available presidents by Congress (N = 73), and for the ideological distance between the House and the presidents for whom the impeachment process was exercised (N = 3, Andrew Johnson DW-Nominate not available). Supposing that ideological distance for impeached presidents would be greater than that of all presidents, results for a one-tailed test produced a p-value of .03. Said differently, we can say with 97 percent confidence that the difference between the means of the two samples is not due to random chance and that impeached pres-idents had greater ideological distance from the House than all presidents.[12] We find the results here to be quite compelling given the small sample size. This provides further support to the qualitative results we discussed above that ideological differences play a key role in the likelihood of impeachment.

As we noted in chapter 2, ideological division between the parties is growing. When combined with the fact that divided government is becoming the norm, this means that not only will the branches have partisan differences, but the ideological differences between branches will grow when Congress and the presidency are controlled by opposite parties. Clearly, ideological differences play a role in the use of impeachment against presidents.

But this effect will not necessarily lead to a greater likelihood of the removal of a president as the consequence of an impeachment. For the same reasons that impeachments are more likely to be voted in the House, in a highly partisan environment the supermajority requirement makes conviction less likely in the Senate. What evidence would it take to convince members of the president's own party, who are likely to hold at least a third of the Senate plus one (that is, enough to block a conviction), that the removal of one of their own is justified? We have noted that the pattern of polarization in the Senate very much parallels the same progression in the House (but with a lag both because of the longer Senate terms and the fact that only a third of the Senate is elected in any given cycle and senators represent much more amorphous constituencies).[13] Under these circumstances it is going to be harder than ever to find the votes necessary to convict in the Senate.

PRESIDENTS IN THEIR FINAL TERMS

In chapter 2, we discussed the counterintuitive nature of presidential experience and the power presidents enjoy in different stages of their term. Presidents enjoy the most influence and power at the beginning of their presidency (the honeymoon phase), when they possess the least amount of experience, while lame-duck presidents enjoy the least amount of power despite their acquired knowledge. In short, on average, the longer a president goes into their term, particularly a second term, the less political power the president will wield.[14]

From a political standpoint, it would make sense that Congress would act to impeach when presidents are in their second term as that period presents less political risk to members who will be seeking reelection. Impeaching a newly elected president or a president who may be seeking an additional term would present a greater political risk. Mayhew explains that because the primary motivation of members is to get reelected, they will act with this interest in mind as they consider a variety of actions.[15] Thus, with regard to impeachment, strategically it would make sense for members of Congress to move to impeach when presidents are in their final term.

We observe that all of the attempts at presidential impeachment discussed in this book occurred when the presidents were in their final terms either because of term limits or because the president had no real prospect of getting elected. Therefore, the stage of the president's term is a factor that increases the likelihood of an impeachment.[16] It also demonstrates, again, that impeachment is a political matter as members of Congress weigh the political benefits of the use of impeachment. Members want to minimize the risks to their own political careers. Thus, members will be more likely, as demonstrated by all four case studies, to use impeachment when presidents are weakened and in their final term.

ACCUSED OF ILLEGAL BEHAVIOR—PROCEDURAL

In chapter 2, we distinguish procedural crimes from other types of crimes as they involve violations by presidents that interfere with the process of lawmaking, rulemaking, or the law enforcement function of government. But, as we have noted above, to break the law is not necessarily a crime. Thus, the president can commit an illegal act that while not a crime could be an impeachable offense. That was the main question in the Reagan and Johnson impeachments. Reagan had violated the Boland Amendment in providing arms to the Contras and Johnson had failed to enforce the Reconstruction statutes with vigor. These actions, strictly speaking, were illegal but not criminal. Nevertheless, they could be impeachable offenses.

The question then goes to motive. Did Reagan and Johnson misuse the powers of office to make those decisions for personal remunerative or political gain? In those cases, it appears they did not. Thus, impeachment was not the appropriate remedy.

We find that in three out of four impeachments presidents (Johnson, Nixon, and Reagan) engaged in procedural violations that resulted in impeachment proceedings.

All Other Factors

For factors in the matrix that were not present in only 50 percent of impeachment cases presented in chapters 3–6, we cannot say with any degree of certainty that they will have any impact on presidential impeachments. To explain, even if a factor is present in 50 percent of cases, this represents a statistical coin flip as to whether this has an impact. Thus, we cannot say with any degree of certainty that national crises (50%) and the popularity of the president (50%) have an impact on the likelihood of impeachment occurring. However, we can say with certainty that major personality conflicts with congressional leaders (0%) do not have an impact on presidential impeachments based on the case studies here.

Political crimes, or illegal actions to win elections, were present in only 25 percent of cases, but the absence of political crimes in the majority of impeachments does not necessarily negate the influence of this factor. We do not include criminal behavior with the variables discussed in the previous paragraph as it is clear under the Constitution that criminal behavior is impeachable.

We observe that actual criminal behavior is present in 50 percent of cases, while political crimes are present in only 25 percent of cases. While we cannot draw conclusions on the impact of these factors on the likelihood of impeachment, it does support our primary thesis that impeachments are largely political. For if actual and political crimes are only present in

50 percent and 25 percent of cases, respectively, then that would suggest something other than criminal behavior is driving the use of impeachment.

The Future of Presidential Impeachments

THE RISE OF THE IMPEACHMENT ERA

The inclusion of the Iran-Contra scandal as a case study demonstrates that we have not exhausted all possible cases of impeachment. Impeachment activity doesn't have to just include full-fledged Senate trials but can manifest itself in other forms. In other words, just because the number of actual impeachments is small doesn't mean that frustrated legislators don't often mention the word when they see no other recourse.

Impeachment activity can come in several stages from introducing articles of impeachment in the House, to impeachment investigations in the Judiciary Committee, to voting actual articles of impeachment and trials in the Senate. Prior to Ronald Reagan, we found impeachment activity involving only seven presidents, including Johnson and Nixon, dating back to the founding of the country. However, every president since Ronald Reagan has faced articles of impeachment introduced by one or more members of Congress.[17] We expect that these other forms of impeachment activity will expand the data set in the future.

While the introduction of articles of impeachment may simply represent posturing and symbolic actions by opposition members of Congress, we think the more likely scenario, given the rise of divided government and increasing ideological polarization, is that impeachment will become a tool that is used more often in the political process. This represents the new norm, an age in which impeachment will more likely be wielded as a political weapon against the president.

FINAL THOUGHTS—ON IMPEACHMENT, THE CONSTITUTION IS FLAWED

The Framers got a lot right, but on impeachment they may have got it wrong. Impeachment as a check on the executive is no longer useful because it is hard to imagine, given the degree of partisan polarization in Congress, the circumstances under which it will result in removal. Without the threat of a real sanction, part of the checks and balances is stripped away. Of course, the hyperpartisanship of the modern era may just be an aberration. But even if it is, it is precisely at times when the parties are most at odds that there needs to be a realistic constitutional check on the presidency. That is something we don't have now. The modern era has highlighted the weakness of the Constitution is this regard.

It is true that the Framers wanted presidents to have a long enough term to pursue policies that might, in the short term, prove unpopular, but that in the long term were good for the country. The problem is that, in a single term, an incompetent or malign president can do a lot of damage. This is particularly true in the modern era, with the advent of the imperial presidency. In the modern era, therefore, impeachment may not be the right tool.

And, in the technical sense, incompetence or evil may not be an impeachable offense, but it is a pretty good cause for removal. However, that doesn't mean that impeachment can't be adapted to the circumstances. But then we're back to relying on the "absurd fictions" that Bagehot warned us about in comparing the strengths of the unwritten British to the written American Constitution. It is absurd to suggest that Clinton should have been removed from the American presidency for lying about an adulterous affair. It is absurd to accept the excuse that President Reagan didn't know about the details of the Iran-Contra Affair. And, yet, it was convenient to believe that Reagan, a popular president on his way out of office, shouldn't be removed for doing what he sincerely thought was good for the country. And in the case of Johnson, it was absurd to think that a dispute over who got to be secretary of war was cause for impeachment and removal when the real disagreement was over something that was a great deal more important. And, in the end, Johnson stayed to the end of his term and did a considerable amount of damage.

In a parliamentary system, a vote of no confidence provides a mechanism whereby incompetent or malign prime ministers can be removed. But all we've got in the United States is impeachment, and with the advent of heightened partisanship, while it is more likely that there will be more impeachments, it is just as likely that there will be fewer convictions. Thus, with increasing frequency, we're saddled with presidents who preside without a governing majority for much of their only two terms in office. Gridlock is the result, and just as Andrew Johnson was able to derail Reconstruction for the want of removal, some other future president, to the detriment of the nation, will either fail to act on matters crucial to the country or will be allowed to create excuses for unilateral action that border on the absurd.

The Trump Impeachment

Now that the House has impeached President Trump and the President was acquitted, it would be instructive to go back and analyze current events in light of the metrics we provide in the previous chapters.

We believe given the current context characterized by extreme partisanship that the Trump impeachment was almost inevitable. Furthermore, had Hillary Clinton been elected, she would have been impeached as well. Divided government now means that when the House of Representatives is controlled by the party opposite to the President, impeachment is much more likely. On the other hand, given the two thirds vote requirement in the Senate required for conviction and removal, it is even less likely that an impeachment trial in the Senate will end in removal.

To put all these strands together let's go back to the impeachment metrics we provided in Chapter Two:

Impeachment: Contributing Factors

1. Opposite Party House Control

2. Opposite Party Senate Control

3. Critical Policy Difference between the President and Congressional Leaders

4. Time of National Crisis/Social Upheaval

5. Personal Animosity between President and Congressional Leaders

6. Climate of Public Animosity toward the President

7. Accused of Criminal Behavior—Actual

8. Accused of Criminal Behavior—Procedural

9. Accused of Criminal Behavior—Political

Opposite Party House Control

In the election of 2018, the Democrats picked up 40 seats and took control of the House of Representatives. Newly elected Speaker Nancy Pelosi was asked almost immediately whether she planned to move to the impeachment of President Trump. She demurred, citing the impending release of the Mueller Report. She also opposed the impeachment of President Trump for "political reasons" but kept her options open depending on the contents of the Report.[1] She knew as well as many others that were the House to impeach and the President was acquitted, the political fallout might be to the detriment of her new House majority.

Parenthetically, had Secretary of State Clinton been elected in 2016, when the House was controlled by Republicans, she would have certainly faced at least an impeachment investigation. Prior to the 2016 election, several prominent House Republicans had already stated their intention to investigate further the Clinton e-mails with the goal being impeachment and removal.[2]

Opposite Party Senate Control

If one thing has been clear all along, in the current context, should the House vote articles of impeachment, it is very unlikely that the Senate will vote to convict. The partisan make-up of the Senate has always been an important consideration in the decision of the House to impeach, but even more so now. Partisanship hit a peak in Congress after 2016 with more party unity votes than ever before. In 2017, 69 percent of all votes in the Senate were "party unity" votes (76 percent of all votes in the House were along party lines, a record). That means that in those cases, no members from either side voted against their party.[3]

In 2018, however, party unity votes made a dramatic decline. Members of Congress could read the polls and they knew that not only was Congress unpopular in general, but that the polls were trending against the Republicans who at that point became much more interested in bipartisan cooperation. In addition, several Democratic members of the Senate were planning on running for president and were interested in burnishing their bi-partisan records. Party unity votes dropped from 69 to 50 percent in the Senate as Congress passed two major bipartisan pieces of legislation on prison reform and financial regulation.

This could have been bad news for President Trump because the more bipartisan the character of the Senate, the greater the chance of a vote for impeachment and removal. However, bipartisanship does not extend to the decision to impeach. While the substance of the allegations that President Trump solicited the aid of a foreign power in investigating one of his political opponents were egregious, in announcing her decision to launch an impeachment investigation, Speaker Pelosi had to take into consideration the likelihood of conviction and removal in the Senate. Consequently, members of the Democratic leadership in the House were reluctant, all along to impeach. After all, as of the initiation of the impeachment hearings, the presidential election was only a year away. Perhaps for the Democrats it would have been better to "slow walk" the investigation and let the voters decide?[4] On the other hand, the Democrats could have hoped that it might be in the interest of the Republicans if the political environment changed (or Trump's poll numbers dropped), to dump the President either by voting for impeachment and removal or nominating another candidate for the 2020 ticket. But none of this happened. The impeachment and trial of Donald Trump neither swayed many voters nor changed the mind of the Parties.

Critical Policy Difference between the President and Congressional Leaders

Not only has Donald Trump been highly partisan in his policy recommendations, he has also challenged Republican Party orthodoxy. Democrats had no reason to expect anything different from the policy pursuits of this Republican president. The policy foundation of the Trump Administration was the appointment of conservative, pro-business, anti-abortion judges, promote tax cuts for corporations and the wealthy, and repeal of the previous administration's signature achievement, Obamacare. President Trump has been enormously successful in the first two pursuits and may have even succeeded in the long run on the third with the repeal of the individual mandate and the introduction of low-cost alternatives (with limited coverage) to the mandated Obama health insurance care plans. It is understandable, therefore, that Democrats were unalterably opposed to this administration and were receptive to allegations of wrongdoing that might end with impeachment and removal.

What makes the Trump administration unique, however, is his rejection of bedrock Republican Party principles as well. Trump has broken with various factions in his own party in his immigration policies, his rejection of free trade, his reluctance to support U.S. military intervention abroad, his embrace of dictatorships over democracies, his rejection of international organizations and even his denial of climate change. In each one of these policies there is a base of support within the Republican Party but taken as a whole, Trump in the policy sense is out of the Republican mainstream. That means that for one reason or another practically everyone, save his closest associates and family, have a grievance with the President. In the short run, the President's support in the Republican base insulates him against the objections of the various factions of the Party he as abandoned. But in the long run, his decision to eschew some of the bedrock principles of the Republican Party means that his support could be characterized as broad but shallow. Should the President show any signs of political weakness (an erosion of his base), his support would likely melt away and in that case he could be vulnerable to conviction and removal in the Senate. For most Republicans, in the policy sense, Vice President Pence would be a much more palatable option.

As far as Hillary Clinton is concerned, her policies were much more likely to be conventional. Republicans would have been opposed to her presidency from a policy perspective, but Democrats would have not. Therefore, it is unlikely that even had she been impeached by the House, she would have been convicted and removed by the Senate. Senate Democrats would have had no policy reason to defect.

Time of National Crisis/Social Upheaval

Was the United States in the midst of a national crisis when Donald Trump was elected? Donald Trump certainly thought so. In his inaugural address, the President said:

> "But for too many of our citizens, a different reality exists: Mothers and children trapped in poverty in our inner cities; rusted-out factories scattered like tombstones across the landscape of our nation; an

education system, flush with cash, but which leaves our young and beautiful students deprived of knowledge; and the crime and gangs and drugs that have stolen too many lives and robbed our country of so much unrealized potential. This American carnage stops right here and stops right now."

The President's reference to "carnage" belied the rather placid status of the American economy and its place in the world. When President Trump took office, growth in U.S. GDP was at 1.6%, the inflation rate was at 1.3% and unemployment was at just under 5%. These were less than optimal results, but they hardly equated with the Great Recession. Furthermore, the trends which are just as important in the political sense as the "snapshots," if not particularly robust, were moving in the right direction. In other words, the situation in the United States could hardly be described as "carnage."

In retrospect, however, it was not just happenstance that Hillary Clinton lost in Midwestern states that had in the past been fairly reliable strongholds for the Democrats. Furthermore, she lost badly in the swing states, such as Iowa and Ohio, in the same region. In fact, recovery from the Great Recession of 2008 had been slow and spotty. If we look at the GINI index, a standard measure for income inequality, for the period from 1980 to 2016, inequality in the United States reached record levels the year that Trump was elected president.[5] Clearly some segments of the population were suffering even as the overall economy showed growth.

In addition, evangelical Christians were becoming increasingly alarmed with the secularization of the "public square." Trump's promises to appoint conservative judges that would not, from their perspective, allow the murder of unborn babies was enough to overlook the personal peccadillos of a serial philanderer. These two factors formed and continue to form the base of President Trump's support. Maybe there was "carnage" in the United States but it was not apparent in a thorough reading of *The New York Times.* Furthermore, it was clear that had Hillary Clinton been elected, not much would have changed. Consequently, if there were a split in the country that was not contained within the traditional geographic boundaries of the states, it might well be that a populist candidate, in this instance of the Right, was electable in the American context (especially given the idiosyncrasies of the electoral system featuring the Electoral College).

Furthermore, if the election of Donald Trump reflected a fault line in the country, there is another side to that split. If Trump represents dispossessed Right, there are those on the Left who would be just as alarmed by the election of Hillary Clinton to the presidency. In 2016, there was a surprising level of support for the Trump candidacy from disaffected supporters of Bernie Sanders, the champion of the far American left. Surveys showed that more than 10 percent of Sanders' voters, voted for Candidate Trump in the November election. Those votes alone, strategically placed, could have swung the general election to Trump.[6] In other words, besides disagreements in policy terms with tradition candidates of both parties, there is a significant level of anomie in the population that led to the election of Donald Trump.

Personal Animosity between President and Congressional Leaders

From the day he was inaugurated President Trump did little to cultivate a good relationship with congressional leaders. President Trump is a political novice. He had not held public office before he became president and he had certainly not had a lot of Washington experience. He had testified before Congress on issues such as Native American casinos, but he was not an insider. Even as a private citizen, he was rarely included in quasi-governmental decision making as would have been indicated by membership on the board of quasi-public institutions such as the Smithsonian.

Prior to his decision to run for president, Trump had neither identified strongly with the Republican nor the Democratic Party. He had made campaign contributions to candidates from both sides. Therefore, he was hardly a party insider. In fact, the Republican Party fought hard against his nomination and a number of prominent party insiders and conservatives including the Bush family, Mitt Romney, William Kristol and George W. Will refused to support his candidacy. During the campaign Trump had insinuated that Senator Ted Cruz's (Rep. – Texas) father was in on the Kennedy Assassination as well as referring to Cruz himself as "Lyin' Ted." Other nicknames included "Pocahontas" in reference to Senator Elizabeth Warren (Dem. – Massachusetts), "Little Marco" in reference to Senator Marco Rubio (Rep. – Florida), "Crazy" Rep. Maxine Waters (Dem. – California), "Foul Mouthed" Rep. Ilhan Omar (Dem. – Minnesota), Senator (Minority Whip) "Dicky" Durban (Dem. – Illinois), "Little" Adam Schiff (Chair of the House Intelligence Committee),[7] "Cheatin Obama" in reference to his predecessor, "Crazy Bernie" in reference to Senator Bernie Sanders (Dem. – Vermont), "Nervous Nancy" in reference to Speaker of the

House Nancy Pelosi, Senator "Sleepin" Bob Casey (Dem. – Pennsylvania), Senator "Liddle" Bob Corker (Rep. – Tennessee), Senator "Sneaky/Leakin" Diane Feinstein (Dem. – California), "Rejected" Senator Jeff Flake (Rep. – Arizona), "Lightweight" Senator Kirsten Gillibrand, Senator "Puppet" Doug Jones (Dem. – Alabama) and the list goes on.[8]

This is not a way to endear oneself to a group of people he needs. His comment about Senator John McCain's capture and imprisonment by the North Vietnamese, "I like people that [*sic*] weren't captured," may well have cost him the repeal of Obamacare. McCain with what appeared a wry smile, cast the deciding vote against repeal. Nevertheless, in his first two terms, Trump enjoyed a more or less typical legislative success rate of a president in his honeymoon with substantial if not overwhelming majorities of his own party in both houses of Congress.[9]

These results are preliminary scores based on the president's first half term in office. Given the high degree of partisan polarization currently in Congress, we would expect that as good as the President's success rate was in the first half of his first term, it will be much worse in the after the election of 2018 in which the Republicans lost their majority in the House. Nevertheless, in that same election Republicans actually increased the number of seats they held in the Senate. Consequently, on items, such as judicial appointments, that are under the Constitution, the sole province of the Senate, President Trump can expect to maintain or even increase his success.

Nevertheless, as the House entered its impeachment investigation stage, relations between Democratic leaders and the President already strained, had gotten worse. Even Republicans chafed at some of the decisions made by the White House, most notably the President's decision to abandon the Kurds. In another political context, this development may have boded badly for the President's chances to survive an impeachment trial in the Senate. However, partisanship ultimately trumped any policy differences within the parties.

Climate of Public Animosity toward the President

The President has a low but not historically low popularity rating. As of February 2020, the President's approval rating in the Gallup poll is 49%. His administration average is 40 and his lowest rating has been 35%. By contrast, the last eight presidents starting with Eisenhower averaged an approval rating of 53% at this point in their presidencies. This is hardly a disastrous result for President Trump and one from which he can easily recover.[10] And more importantly for President Trump, his support amongst self-identified Republicans is unwavering. His approval rating among Republicans is in excess of 90%.

This is probably the most important factor in protecting the President from impeachment and removal in the Senate. In our interview with Dagmar Hamilton, staff attorney to the House Judiciary Committee for the investigation of the Watergate Affair, she commented that public opinion had begun to run strongly against President Nixon after the 1972 election and in the aftermath of the revelations contained on the White House tapes. Not only were Democratic members of Congress under pressure from their constituents to impeach but so were Republicans. That pressure led to Republican defections on the House Judiciary Committee and, more importantly, Republican defections in the Senate.

In the polarized environment of 2020, concern for public policy has been eclipsed by the force of party politics. President Trump's (presumed) jest that he could shoot someone on Fifth Avenue and get away with it, is probably not altogether true but is close enough to being true that the President is unlikely to commit an act as president that is a serious enough breach to convince his supporter to abandon him. On the Republican side, only Senator Mitt Romney was willing to vote for impeachment and removal and by all appearances survive the blowback in his state. The fact of the matter is that of this writing, in the aftermath of impeachment and acquittal, President Trump enjoys the support of his party. Thus, impeachment and removal in this political environment is highly unlikely.

Accused of Criminal Behavior—Actual

While the President has been accused of criminal behavior including tax evasion, violation of the campaign finance laws (in approving payments to Stormy Daniels in exchange for her silence) and sexual assault, the actual articles of impeachment had more to do with procedural than actual crimes. The Democrats did suggest that the President had committed a crime when he solicited in the form of a bribe when he proposed to a foreign leader a trade of foreign aid paid for by tax dollars, in exchange for something of personal value to the President's campaign for reelection, political dirt on Democratic rival for president Joe Biden. The President's allies had a number of defenses for the President's actions, some of them very thin and others quite novel.

Some Republicans argued that the President's telephone conversation with President Zelensky of the Ukraine did not contain an explicit offer of a quid pro quo. Just because the President says one thing and then in the same conversation implies another, doesn't mean the two things are connected. In addition, the fact that the "bribe" was never actually paid, and that the foreign aid was released before any investigation of the Bidens or even announcement of an investigation occurred, is an indication that there was never an expected trade. Furthermore, it was argued, that in asking for an investigation of Joe Biden and his son Hunter, the President was actually pursuing was a legitimate policy goal, proof that the Ukrainian government was battling corruption. The fact is that Hunter Biden *had* engaged in some nefarious activity in the Ukraine, probably with the knowledge of his father who at the time was Vice President of the United States. Ultimately, in one of the more extreme arguments in defense of the President, Alan Dershowitz argued that since the President believed that his own reelection was in the nation's interest, that any action taken in that pursuit was justified in the cause of national defense.[11]

These arguments, particularly the one made by Dershowitz, may seem absurd to the neutral observer. But as we argued in previous chapters, in the impeachment process, absurd fictions are often promoted to justify the actions of the participants. President Johnson was impeached because he supposedly violated the Tenure of Office Act, but the real cause of his impeachment was his foot dragging on reconstruction. Ironically, Nixon was impeached and removed because it was no longer possible to rely on the absurd fiction that he did not know of and approve the cover up of the Watergate burglary. This, especially after the release of the Watergate tapes. Reagan was exonerated, or at least not charged in the Iran Contra affair because, in part, he could maintain the absurd fiction that he didn't know what his staff was doing in his name. Clinton was impeached for lying under oath about an adulterous affair, but he was really being impeached because in the highly partisan environment that had exploded in the aftermath of his election, his triangulation strategy threatened the prospects of the newly elected Republican majority in the House and the Republican's prospects in the presidential election of the year 2000. Finally, the Trump impeachment, while ostensibly about a single phone call made by President Trump to the President of Ukraine was really about the behavior of a president who roughly 60% of the public believes to be fundamentally dishonest.[12]

It has been said, "it is difficult to get a man to understand something when his salary depends upon his not understanding it."[13] Whether the

President's phone call and subsequent action rose to an impeachable offense is in the eye of the beholder. So, for example, would the evidence presented by the House in its investigation be enough to convict in a criminal trial? Probably not. And even so, as impeachment is not a criminal trial, was the evidence presented cause to convict? This is essentially a political question and the answer to a political question is based on more than just evidence. President Trump was and is supported by less than 50% of the public, but only at times a bit less than 50%. Is the removal of President Trump supported by enough of the voters to justify negating the public's choice in the 2016 election? Probably not. At any given time in the impeachment process, conviction and removal was almost never supported by a majority of the voters. The Democrats simply did not do a good enough job in the prosecution. The public decides who gets to be president. And in this case, the public decided. Congress was more or less reflecting that choice and the ambiguity of the situation in its more or less split decision to acquit.

Accused of Criminal Behavior—Procedural

The second of two articles of impeachment against President Trump titled, Obstruction of Congress, was based on the refusal of the Administration to cooperate with the congressional investigation into the Ukrainian affair. Specifically, the indictment reads in part:

"In response, without lawful cause or excuse, President Trump directed Executive Branch agencies, offices, and officials not to comply with those subpoenas. President Trump thus interposed the powers of the Presidency against the lawful subpoenas of the House of Representatives and assumed to himself functions and judgments necessary to the exercise of the 'sole Power of Impeachment' vested by the Constitution in the House of Representatives."

This article of impeachment goes to the matter of whether Congress will be able in the future to fulfil its oversight function. In some ways, this article is more important than the first because it establishes a precedent that will either enable Congress to collect evidence pursuant to its oversight function or allow future presidents to simply refuse to cooperate with Congress if they so choose. And, so far, the Courts seem to support the President's position. On January 3, 2020, the DC Circuit ruled in a 2-1 decision that former White House attorney Don McGahn did not have to obey a subpoena of the House Judiciary Committee to testify before the Committee on the matter of President Trump's impeachment. Simply put, according to the Court, "The Committee's suit asks us to settle a dispute that we have no authority to resolve."[14] This is a stunning decision because the Court has negated much of Congress' ability to enforce its own subpoenas. That is, unless, Congress enforces the subpoena's itself by, for example, withholding funding to the Executive Branch. Practically, the only real remedy then is impeachment and removal.[15] If the Supreme Court upholds the lower court, the only option left for Congress will be impeachment. Thus, this second article of impeachment becomes more important than the first because it constitutes a broad precedent that can presumably be applied in other cases in the future. On the other hand, the Senate's decision to acquit is not a legal precedent in the formal sense and with a different composition of the Senate, a future president could be impeached for the same cause.

Accused of Criminal Behavior—Political

In some sense, the accusation contained in the first article of impeachment was a political crime. Clearly, President Trump in his capacity as president, was looking for dirt on a political opponent for purposes connected to his 2020 reelection campaign. While the President's lawyers argued that the President's concern about the activities of Hunter Biden were related to general questions about corruption in Ukraine, there is very little evidence to back that up. As per standard operating procedures, the Ukrainian Government's capacity and willingness to distribute the aid as intended had already been vetted and approved by the State Department. There was no evidence, prior to the President's phone call to the Ukrainian leader, that President Trump had been particularly concerned about Ukrainian corruption in general.

But, then again, the President's lawyers argued, there wasn't any evidence that the President wasn't concerned about Ukrainian corruption and it was a well-known fact that Trump was opposed to foreign aid in general, for precisely the reasons his lawyers stated. Furthermore, the United States Government had been concerned about Ukrainian corruption in previous administrations and there was no reason not to assume the same in the current U.S. administration. Furthermore, Hunter Biden's "employment" at Burisma Holdings, the (Cypriot based) Ukrainian oil company did seem suspicious to say the least.

Thus, the President's investigation into the Biden family's involvement in the Ukraine had just enough credibility to serve as an excuse and a cover for voting against Article One of the impeachment. Besides, as the president's lawyers argued, everybody does it. Presidents have often used their institutional offices to further their political fortunes. But, in the end, given the President's popularity within the Republican Party, it was hard to convince Republican senators that the President had committed an impeachable offense when their livelihood depended on voting to acquit.

The Meaning of the Trump Impeachment and Trial

Throughout much of the Trump presidency much of what the President has done has been characterized by his opponents as an existential threat. But now that we face as a world an indisputably existential crisis, the corona virus, the Trump impeachment seems as much a gauzy memory. But on occasion it does rear its' ugly head. For example, as the Senate was putting the final touches on a $2.2 trillion pandemic relief package, the bill was held up for several days because Senate Democrats refused to pass a bill without independent supervision of the distribution of the funds. If the President could make the claim that he had no obligation to respond to congressional subpoenas in relation to impeachment and, in fact, other congressional investigations as well (and was to this point backed by the Courts), congressional Democrats had no choice but to install a mechanism into the legislation itself that included an independent oversight board to review the expenditure of funds.

Consequently, congressional Democrats favored a mechanism in the legislation itself that included an independent oversight board to review the expenditure of funds. The head of this Board, a Special Inspector General for Pandemic Recovery, would be appointed by the President and confirmed by the Senate.[16] Senate Republicans agreed, and the revised legislation quickly passed the House and was signed by the President. However, hours after the President signed the Bill into law, he issued a "signing statement" to the effect that his Administration disputed the authority of the independent oversight board and pledged to limit the Administration's cooperation with the Board.[17]

As of this writing, the President has nominated Brian Miller, a White House Attorney as Inspector General for Pandemic Recovery. There has been some controversy related to the appointment as Miller was on the White House Staff and was a member of the President's defense team during the impeachment trial. On the other hand, Miller served for ten years as

Inspector General in the General Services Administration, a post which confers just the type of experience necessary for this job. On the other hand, a few days after Miller's appointment, the President fired without cause the Inspector General of the Department of Defense, Glenn A. Fine, who was slated to be the Executive Director of the Pandemic Relief Oversight Board. The President in his attacks on this and other Inspectors General has showed a renewed and invigorated opposition to independent oversight of his Administration. Certainly, this is in part a function of the absence of impeachment as a realistic check on presidential power.

If the President challenges the legitimacy of Congress' power to investigate the activities of the Executive Branch, what option is left in Congress' oversight toolkit? If access to the activities of the Administration is not forthcoming and if the courts won't order the President to comply, what is left for the legislative branch to do? The only tool left is impeachment and that tool is broken. There is, we suppose always another election, but with the swiftness of the spread of the corona virus and with the sheer size of the pandemic bailout comes a unique potential for the abuse of presidential power unchecked now at least until January of 2021.

When viewed in that light, the President's impeachment and acquittal becomes a very important precedent indeed. The impeachment of Donald Trump and the events unfolding related to disaster relief continue to underscore the trends we have highlighted in this book. With divided government becoming the new norm and the ideological gap between Republicans and Democrats continuing to grow, the fact that Congress is left with fewer options through which to check the president means that presidential impeachments are more likely than ever to occur. Because we know that presidential impeachments in their essence are not a legal but political process given the current environment, the time is ripe for the politics of impeachment.

Notes

Chapter One

1. See James Madison, Federalist 53.

2. It is a comment on the gravity of impeachment proceedings that senators are required to swear an oath beyond their oath of office in order to proceed to trial of an impeachment.

3. According to precedents set in 1862 and 1913 in the impeachment trials of Judges West Humphreys and Robert Archibald, impeachment and removal required a two-thirds vote in the Senate. But disqualification required only a majority vote.

4. In 1797, William Blount, senator from Tennessee, was impeached by the House for having conspired with the British to take control of territories in Florida and Louisiana that were held by the Spanish. The case was dismissed as Blount had already been expelled from the Senate. There is no constitutional provision for the impeachment of members of Congress. Rather, the houses of Congress are responsible for the discipline of their own members. See U.S. House of Representatives, "List of Individuals Impeached by the House of Representatives," accessed October 19, 2018, https://history.house.gov/Institution/Impeachment/Impeachment-List/.

5. U.S. House of Representatives, "List of Individuals Impeached by the House of Representatives," accessed October 19, 2018, https://history.house.gov/Institution/Impeachment/Impeachment-List/.

6. See *Cannon's Precedents of the House of Representative* (1936).

7. This was an issue regarding Vice President Spiro Agnew who as governor of Maryland was accused of accepting kickbacks for construction contracts. Currently, President Trump is under investigation for violation of campaign finance reporting requirements regarding payments made to porn star Stormy Daniels. Whether that is potentially an impeachable offense is a decision to be made by Congress. See Richard M. Cohen and Jules Witcover, *A Heartbeat Away: The Investigation and Resignation of Vice President Spiro T. Agnew* (New York: Viking, 1974). For Agnew's own view of the question, see Spiro T. Agnew, *Go Quietly . . . or Else* (New York: Morrow, 1980).

8. Alexander Hamilton, Federalist 65; see also Calvin C. Jillson, *Constitution Making: Conflict and Consensus in the Federal Convention of 1787* (New York: Agathon Press, 1988).

9. See Neil Kinkopf, "The Scope of 'High Crimes and Misdemeanors' after the Impeachment of President Clinton," *Law and Contemporary Problems* 63, nos. 1–2 (2000): 201–21, www.jstor.org/stable/1192449. In particular, see his discussion summarizing James Wilson's discussion of the clause at the Pennsylvania Ratifying Convention (211).

10. One contemporary reading of the meaning of high crimes and misdemeanors comes from the House report on the *Impeachment of William Jefferson Clinton*, H.Rept. 105–830 at 110–18 (1998). Here it defines high crimes and misdemeanors as "Such offenses surely include most of the 'great' political infractions recognized under English common law, including misapplication of funds, abuse of official power, neglect of duty, or encroachment on the prerogatives of another co-equal branch of government" (207).

11. See Richard M. Pious, "The Constitutional and Popular Law of Presidential Impeachment," *Presidential Studies Quarterly* 28, no. 4 (1998): 806–15, www.jstor.org/stable/27551935.

12. For an extended version of this discussion, see Peter Charles Hoffer and N. E. H. Hull, *Impeachment in America, 1635–1805* (New Haven: Yale University Press, 1984).

13. For an excellent review of the translation of the English use of impeachment to the colonial context, see Jonathan Turley, "Senate Trials and Factional Disputes: Impeachment as a Madisonian Device," *Duke Law Journal* 49, no. 1 (1999): 1–146.

14. For example, in 1757 the Pennsylvania Assembly impeached and removed William Moore, a justice of the peace. The King's Privy Council restored Moore to his position, making it clear that they did not believe that the colonies had the authority to impeach at all. See Jonathan Turley, "Senate Trials and Factional Disputes: Impeachment as a Madisonian Device," *Duke Law Journal* 49, no. 1 (1999): 27.

15. See Michael Edwardes, *Warren Hastings: King of the Nabobs* (London: Hart-Davis, MacGibbon, 1976), or Patrick Turnbull, *Warren Hastings* (London: New English Library, 1975).

16. Chris Monaghan, "In Defence of Intrinsic Human Rights: Edmund Burke's Controversial Prosecution of Warren Hastings, Governor-General of Bengal," *Law, Crime & History* 1, no. 2 (November 2011): 58–107.

17. See James Madison, *Notes on Debates in the Federal Convention of 1787*, ed. Adrienne Koch (Athens: Ohio University Press, 1966). Also see Michael J. Gerhardt, *The Federal Impeachment Process: A Constitutional and Historical Analysis* (Princeton: Princeton University Press, 1996), for a more focused discussion on the origins of the impeachment provisions in the U.S. Constitution.

18. Benjamin Franklin as quoted by James Madison, *Debates on the Adoption of the Federal Constitution*, ed. Jonathan Elliot, vol. 5, 340–41 (1845).

19. See mainly Federalist 65, but also 39, 47, 66, 69, 74, 79 and 84.

20. Federalist 66, accessed October 23, 2018, http://www.constitution.org/fed/federa66.htm.

21. To quote some of the charges:

- Chase failed to correctly apply Virginia law dealing with the prosecution of a misdemeanor—Callender should not have been tried in the same term of court in which he was indicted, but rather in the next term.

- Chase improperly refused to grant Callender's lawyers a continuance until the following term so they could assemble needed witnesses (from distant states) and documents.

- Chase required the defense to put questions to Taylor in writing, to be examined in advance by the court, rather than allowing them to be asked extemporaneously.

- Repeatedly interrupted and harassed Callender's defense in their presentation.

All these charges may have constituted judicial errors but were certainly not an impeachable offense.

22. See Buckner F. Melton, *The First Impeachment: The Constitutional Framers and the Case of Senator William Blount* (Macon, GA: Mercer University Press, 1998).

23. Robert J. Morgan, *A Whig Embattled: The Presidency under John Tyler* (Lincoln: University of Nebraska Press, 1954).

24. See Edward P. Crapol, "John Tyler and the Pursuit of National Destiny," *Journal of the Early Republic* 17, no. 3 (1997): 467–91, www.jstor.org/stable/3123944.

25. Edward P. Crapol, *John Tyler, the Accidental President* (Chapel Hill: University of North Carolina Press, 2006).

26. *Myers v. United States*, 272 U.S. 52 (1926).

27. See Michael Les Benedict, "A New Look at the Impeachment of Andrew Johnson," *Political Science Quarterly* 88, no. 3 (1973): 349–67, www.jstor.org/stable/2148988.

28. Howard Fields, *High Crimes and Misdemeanors: Wherefore Richard M. Nixon Warrants Impeachment: The Dramatic Story of the Rodino Committee* (Toronto: W. W. Norton, 1978).

29. In an ironic twist of fate, during his confirmation hearings, Kavanaugh, who had been a strong advocate of airing all the sordid details of the Lewinsky scandal, faced charges of sexual indiscretions of his own.

30. See Karl G. Brandt, *Ronald Reagan and the House Democrats* (Columbia: University of Missouri Press, 2009); Peter Kornbluth and Malcolm Byrne, *The Iran/Contra Scandal: The Declassified History* (New York: New Press, 1993).

31. See David E. Kyvig, *The Age of Impeachment: American Constitutional Culture since 1960* (Lawrence: University Press of Kansas, 2008).

32. John A. Ferejohn and Randall L. Calvert. "Presidential Coattails in Historical Perspective," *American Journal of Political Science* 28, no. 1 (1984): 127–46, www.jstor.org/stable/2110790.

33. See Matt Golder, "Presidential Coattails and Legislative Fragmentation," *American Journal of Political Science* 50, no. 1 (2006): 34–48, www.jstor.org/stable/3694255.

34. Stephen Ansolabehere, David Brady, and Morris Fiorina, "The Vanishing Marginals and Electoral Responsiveness," *British Journal of Political Science* 22, no. 1 (1992): 21–38, www.jstor.org/stable/193860; Gary C. Jacobson, "Polarized Politics and the 2004 Congressional and Presidential Elections," *Political Science Quarterly* 120, no. 2 (2005): 199–218, www.jstor.org/stable/20202515.

35. For examples of the constitutional legal approach, see Laurence H. Tribe and Joshua Matz, *To End a Presidency: The Power of Impeachment* (New York: Basic Books, 2018); Michael J. Gerhardt, *Impeachment: What Everyone Needs to Know* (Oxford: Oxford University Press, 2018); Cass R. Sunstein, *Impeachment: A Citizen's Guide* (Cambridge: Harvard University Press, 2017); Barbara A. Radnofsky, *A Citizens Guide to Impeachment* (New York: Melville House, 2017); Charles L. Black, *Impeachment: A Handbook* (New Haven: Yale University Press, 1998); and for the historical approach, see Michael J. Gerhardt, *The Federal Impeachment Process: A Constitutional and Historical Analysis* (Princeton: Princeton University Press, 1996).

36. These remarks were made regarding the impeachment of Justice William O. Douglas on April 15, 1970 and were recorded in the *Congressional Record*, vol. 116, p. 11913.

37. John R. Labovitz, *Presidential Impeachment* (New Haven: Yale University Press, 1978); Charles L. Black Jr., *Impeachment: A Handbook* (New Haven: Yale University Press, 1974); Steven D. Strauss and Spencer Strauss, *The Complete Idiot's Guide to Impeachment of the President* (New York: Alpha Books, 1998); Arnold H. Leibowitz, *An Historical-Legal Analysis of the Impeachments of Presidents Andrew Johnson, Richard Nixon, and William Clinton: Why the Process Went Wrong* (Lewiston, NY: Edwin Mellen Press, 2011).

38. John Gerring, "The Case Study: What It Is and What It Does," in *The Oxford Handbook of Political Science* (Oxford: Oxford University Press), September 5, 2013; Oxford Handbooks Online, accessed April 23, 2019, http://www.oxfordhandbooks.com/view/10.1093/oxfordhb/9780199604456.001.0001/oxfordhb-9780199604456-e-051.

Chapter Two

1. Paul M. Kellstedt and Guy D. Whitten, *The Fundamentals of Political Science Research* (New York: Cambridge University Press, 2009).

2. Janet Buttolph Johnson and H. T. Reynolds, *Political Science Research Methods*, 7th ed (Thousand Oaks, CA: Sage/CQ Press, 2012).

3. Lawrence S. Rothenberg and Mitchell S. Sanders, "Lame-Duck Politics: Impending Departure and the Votes on Impeachment," *Political Research Quarterly* 53, no. 3 (September 2000): 523–36; Brian R. Fry and John S. Stolarek, "The Impeachment Process: Predispositions and Votes," *Journal of Politics* 42: 1118–34; Gregory A. Caldeira and Christopher Zorn, "Strategic Timing, Position-Taking, and Impeachment in the House of Representatives," *Political Research Quarterly* 57 (2004): 517–27; Christopher N. Lawrence, "Of Shirking, Outliers, and Statistical Artifacts," *Political Research Quarterly* 60 (2007): 159–62; Brian R. Fry and John S. Stolarek, "The Nixon Impeachment Vote: A Speculative Analysis," *Presidential Studies Quarterly* 11, no. 3 (Summer 1981): 387–94.

4. Michael R. Kagay, "Public Opinion and Polling during Presidential Scandal and Impeachment," *Public Opinion Quarterly* 63 (1999): 449–63; Carol L. Silva, Hank C. Jenkins-Smith, and Richard Waterman, "Why Did Clinton Survive the Impeachment Crisis? A Test of Three Explanations," *Presidential Studies Quarterly* 37 (2007): 468–85.

5. Alan L. Abramowitz, "It's Monica, Stupid: The Impeachment Controversy and the 1998 Midterm Election," *Legislative Studies Quarterly* 26 (2001): 211–26; Gary Jacobson, "Impeachment Politics in the 1998 Congressional Elections," *Political Science Quarterly* 114 (1999): 31–51.

6. Richard L. Cole, *Introduction to Political Science and Policy Research* (New York: St. Martin's Press, 1996).

7. Jarol B. Manheim and Richard C. Rich, *Empirical Political Analysis: Research Methods in Political Science* (White Plains, NY: Longman Publishers, 1995).

8. Keith Whittington, *Constitutional Construction: Divided Powers and Constitutional Meaning* (Cambridge: Harvard University Press, 1999).

9. Joel Silbey, "Divided Government in Historical Perspective 1789–1996," in *Divided Government, Change, Uncertainty, and the Constitutional Order*, ed. Peter F. Galderisi, Roberta Q. Herzberg, and Peter McNamara (New York: Rowan and Littlefield, 1996). Morris Fiorina's *Divided Government* (New York: Pearson, 2002) also provides an in-depth analysis of the consequences of divided government.

10. David R. Mayhew, *Divided We Govern: Party Control, Lawmaking, and Investigations, 1946–1990* (New Haven: Yale University Press, 1991). See also Leroy Rieselbach, "It's the Constitution Stupid! Congress, the President, Divided Government, and Policy Making," in *Divided Government, Change, Uncertainty, and the Constitutional Order*, ed. Peter F. Galderisi, Roberta Q. Herzberg, and Peter McNamara (New York: Rowan and Littlefield, 1996).

11. Keith T. Poole and Howard Rosenthal, "Patterns of Congressional Voting," *American Journal of Political Science* 35 (1991): 228–78. Basically, this measure is derived by scoring the votes of a member of Congress (there are about five hundred roll-call votes a year) relative to the votes of all other members of the chamber. This establishes a continuum along which all members of Congress can be placed

relative to one another. Those members who are the most extreme, whose votes are farthest away from the median member (the one most likely to vote one way or the other in the issue space), are the ends of the ideological spectrum identified as Liberal or Conservative. To establish a DW-Nominate score for the president, the presidents' stated preferences are scored as if they were votes relative to all members of Congress.

12. Poole and Rosenthal consider members of Congress with ideology scores within +.25 and −.25 to be moderate; see www.voteview.org for more information.

13. However, any member of the House can introduce articles of impeachment, even if only as a symbolic gesture.

14. On September 21, 2001, Gallup polls showed a 90% approval rating for George W. Bush.

15. Richard F. Fenno Jr., *Home Style: House Members in Their Districts* (New York: Longman, 2003). See also David R. Mayhew, *Congress: The Electoral Connection* (New Haven: Yale University Press, 1974).

Chapter Three

1. Eric Foner, *Reconstruction: America's Unfinished Revolution, 1863–1877* (New York: Harper Perennial, 2014).

2. For a particularly nuanced discussion of this, see Frederick Douglass, "Reconstruction," *Atlantic Monthly,* December 1866, https://www.theatlantic.com/magazine/archive/1866/12/reconstruction/304561/.

3. Eric Foner, "If Lincoln Hadn't Died . . . ," *American Heritage* 58, no. 6 (Winter 2009): 47–54.

4. See J. G. Randall and Richard Nelson Current, *Lincoln the President: Last Full Measure* (Champaign: University of Illinois Press, 1991); Peyton McCrary, *Abraham Lincoln and Reconstruction: The Louisiana Experiment* (Princeton: Princeton University Press, 1978).

5. For this section we rely on several biographies of Andrew Johnson, including James E. Sefton, *Andrew Johnson and the Uses of Constitutional Power* (New York: Little, Brown, 1980); Eric L. McKitrick, *Andrew Johnson and Reconstruction* (Oxford: Oxford University Press, 1988); Hans L. Trefousse, *Andrew Johnson: A Biography* (New York: W. W. Norton, 1989); and Paul H. Bergeron, *Andrew Johnson's Civil War and Reconstruction* (Knoxville: University of Tennessee Press, 2011).

6. For a comprehensive history of this era, see Eric Foner, *Reconstruction: America's Unfinished Revolution, 1863–1877* (New York: Harper Perennial, 2014).

7. Robert Orr, *President Andrew Johnson of Greeneville, Tennessee* (Knoxville, TN: Tennessee Valley Publishing, 2005).

8. Hans L. Trefousse, *Andrew Johnson: A Biography* (New York: W. W. Norton, 1989).

9. Matt Speiser, "The Ticket's Other Half: How and Why Andrew Johnson Received the 1864 Vice Presidential Nomination," *Tennessee Historical Quarterly* 65, no. 1 (2006): 42–69, www.jstor.org/stable/42628582.

10. For this section, see Eric L. McKitrick, *Andrew Johnson and Reconstruction* (Chicago: University of Chicago Press, 1960); Kenneth M. Stampp, *The Era of Reconstruction, 1865–1877* (New York: Knopf, 1965); and Patrick W. Riddleberger, *1866, the Critical Year Revisited* (Carbondale: Southern Illinois University Press, 1979).

11. Historically only about 7% of presidential vetoes are overridden (110/1,505).

12. See Claude G. Bowers, *The Tragic Era: The Revolution after Lincoln* (New York: Halcyon, 1929), or George Fort Milton, *The Age of Hate: Andrew Johnson and the Radicals* (New York: Coward-McCann, 1930). See also Michael Benedict, "A New Look at the Impeachment of Andrew Johnson," *Political Science Quarterly* 88, no. 3 (1973): 349–67, doi:10.2307/2148988.

13. Patrick W. Riddleberger, *1866, the Critical Year Revisited* (Carbondale: Southern Illinois University Press, 1979).

14. John Hope Franklin and Eric Foner, *Reconstruction after the Civil War* (Chicago: University of Chicago Press, 2013).

15. See Francis W. Schruben, "Edwin M. Stanton and Reconstruction," *Tennessee Historical Quarterly* 23, no. 2 (1964): 145–68; William Marvel, *Lincoln's Autocrat: The Life of Edwin Stanton* (Chapel Hill: University of North Carolina Press, 2015).

16. This effectively meant that no former slaves could have the right to vote. How many former slaves could be expected to own property?

17. For a good discussion of this issue, see Martin E. Mantell, *Johnson, Grant, and the Politics of Reconstruction* (New York: Columbia University Press, 1973).

18. In the nineteenth (and early twentieth) century, the new Congress was sworn in during March of the year after the election. This resulted in a formal third or lame-duck session of Congress following the national election. It was this lame-duck Congress that initiated impeachment proceedings against Johnson.

19. The law was substantially weakened in 1869 and repealed in its entirety in 1887. The issue of the president's power to fire Senate-confirmed officials in his administration was settled once and for all in 1903 in *Shurtleff v. United States*, 189 U.S. 311. In that case the court ruled that the president had the power to remove administrative appointments whether or not they required Senate confirmation. See also *Myers v. United States*, 272 U.S. 52 (1926), which specifically negated a law similar to the Tenure of Office Act. Also see *Humphrey's Executor v. United States*, 295 U.S. 602 (1935). It is interesting to speculate as to whether the court would have found the same way in 1867 as it did in 1903 and 1926 had Congress done what it should have done and gone to court to defend the Tenure of Office Act instead of impeaching the president. But, of course, the impeachment wasn't really about the Tenure of Office Act, it was really about Reconstruction.

20. The added benefit of removing Johnson was that because Johnson had no vice president, were he removed, according to the Succession Act of 1792, he

would be replaced by the president pro-tempore of the Senate. The "Unity" candidate and a Democrat, Johnson would be replaced by Republican senator Benjamin F. Wade of Ohio. Ironically, Wade's unpopularity may have undone the Johnson impeachment. Wade had been the sponsor of draconian Reconstruction legislation, the Wade-Davis Act, that had been vetoed by Abraham Lincoln. Thus, when faced with the choice of a too lenient Andrew Johnson and a too radical Benjamin Wade in the presidency, at least one and maybe more moderate Republicans preferred the former. For a contemporary account of Reconstruction that includes this argument, see J. R. Lynch, *The Facts of Reconstruction* (New York: Arno Press, 1968).

21. U.S. Senate, The Tenure of Office Act, *Statutes at Large*, 39th Congress, Session II, Ch. 153 and 154, 1867. Accessed December 24, 2018, https://www.senate.gov/artandhistory/history/resources/pdf/Johnson_TenureofOfficeAct.pdf.

22. This account of the Johnson impeachment relies heavily on two excellent books on the topic, Michael Les Benedict, *The Impeachment and Trial of Andrew Johnson* (New York: W. W. Norton, 1973), and David O. Stewart, *Impeached: The Trial of President Andrew Johnson and the Fight for Lincoln's Legacy* (New York: Simon and Schuster, 2009).

23. Eight seats were vacant.

24. For a good brief narrative of the trial, see U.S. Senate, "The Impeachment of Andrew Johnson (1868) President of the United States," accessed May 28, 2019, https://www.senate.gov/artandhistory/history/common/briefing/Impeachment_Johnson.htm.

25. Mary Land, " 'Bluff' Ben Wade's New England Background," *New England Quarterly* 27, no. 4 (1954): 484–509, www.jstor.org/stable/362115. The first sentence of this article reads, "When the Radical Republicans picked 'Bluff' Ben Wade to succeed Andrew Johnson as President, they signed the death-warrant of impeachment."

26. There is also some evidence to suggest that several of the seven Republican senators to vote against conviction were bribed. See D. O. Stewart, *Impeached: The Trial of President Andrew Johnson and the Fight for Lincoln's Legacy* (New York: Simon and Schuster, 2009), 240–49.

27. See C. A. Jellison, *Fessenden of Maine: Civil War Senator* (Syracuse, NY: Syracuse University Press, 1962), and R. Cook, *Civil War Senator: William Pitt Fessenden and the Fight to Save the American Republic* (Baton Rouge: Louisiana State University Press, 2011).

28. David Greenberg, "Andrew Johnson: Saved by a Scoundrel: Edmund Ross Cast the Deciding Vote to Acquit, but His Was No 'Profile in Courage,' " *Slate*, January 21, 1999, http://www.slate.com/articles/news_and_politics/history_lesson/1999/01/andrew_johnson_saved_by_a_scoundrel.html.

29. With the exception of the top leadership.

30. "Andrew Johnson: Impact and Legacy," by Elizabeth R. Varon, accessed July 24, 2017, https://millercenter.org/president/johnson/impact-and-legacy.

31. Johnson had asked Grant to accompany him on a speaking tour. Grant took that as an order from the commander-in-chief. But when it became clear to

Grant that the president was using the general as a prop for his presidential campaign, Grant feigned illness and went back to Washington.

32. David Mayhew, *Congress: The Electoral Connection* (New Haven: Yale University Press).

33. See Patrick W. Riddleberger, *1866: The Critical Year Revisited* (Carbondale: Southern Illinois University Press, 1979).

34. This is not to say that Johnson's conduct in the presidency didn't help him at all in mapping his political future. Eight years after leaving the presidency, in January 1875, Johnson was elected by the Tennessee legislature to the United States Senate. By 1875 almost no African Americans could vote in Tennessee.

35. At his request, he was buried in Greeneville, Tennessee with a copy of the U.S. Constitution under his head.

36. A very similar situation occurred during the Nixon administration when the president impounded, or refused to spend, duly appropriated funds. In multiple court cases, parties with standing sued the president to release the funds, and when the plaintiffs prevailed, the administration released the funds. The House Judiciary Committee in the Nixon impeachment considered and rejected articles of impeachment based on procedural malfeasance. These articles were rejected as the administration, albeit somewhat reluctantly and sometimes incompletely (see the Nixon tapes), always obeyed court orders. On impoundment, see *Train v. City of New York*, 420 U.S. 35 (1975); *Train v. Campaign Clean Water*, 420 U.S. 136 (1975); *State Highway Comm'n of Missouri v. Volpe*, 479 F.2d 1099 (8th Cir. 1973); and *Pennsylvania v. Lynn*, 501 F.2d 848 (D.C. Cir. 1974).

37. Alexander Hamilton, Federalist 65.

Chapter Four

1. There are many accounts of the Watergate Affair. Our short description of the Watergate scandal is a distillation of a number of sources including Carl Bernstein and Bob Woodward, *All the President's Men* (New York: Simon and Schuster, 1974); Marlyn Aycock, et al., *Watergate: Chronology of a Crisis* (Washington, DC: Congressional Quarterly, 1975); Fred Emery, *Watergate: The Corruption of American Politics and the Fall of Richard Nixon* (New York: Times Books, 1994); Keith W. Olson, *Watergate: The Presidential Scandal That Shook America* (Lawrence: University Press of Kansas, 2003); and Stanley I. Kutler, *Watergate: A Brief History with Documents* (Malden, MA: Wiley-Blackwell, 2010).

2. *United States v. Nixon*, 418 U.S. 683 (1974).

3. Melvin Small, *The Presidency of Richard Nixon* (Lawrence: University Press of Kansas, 1999.

4. Richard M. Nixon, *The Memoirs of Richard Nixon* (New York: Grosset and Dunlap, 1978).

5. Hiss was probably lying. U.S. intelligence intercepts of Soviet espionage communications released after his death reveal that Hiss was probably a Soviet agent

codenamed ALES. See Allen Weinstein, *Perjury: The Hiss-Chambers Case* (Stanford, CA: Hoover Institution Press, 2013). This conclusion has been consistently disputed by, among others, Victor Navasky, "Allen Weinstein's Docudrama," *Nation* 265, no. 14 (November 1997), 11–16. The significance of this debate goes to heart of the dispute over Nixon's character. Was Richard Nixon an ambitious, paranoid schemer capable of ruining the lives of innocent victims, or was he a shrewd politician slandered by the Liberal Establishment in a way that led to his resignation from the presidency?

6. David Greenberg, "Was Nixon Robbed?," *Slate (USA)*, October 17, 2000, https://slate.com/news-and-politics/2000/10/was-nixon-robbed.html; Josh Seitz, "Worried about a Rigged Election? Here's One Way to Handle It," *Politico*, October 2016, https://www.politico.com/magazine/story/2016/10/donald-trump-2016-rigged-nixon-kennedy-1960-214395. Was Nixon robbed? The answer is, "Who knows?" But what we do know is that Nixon conceded the election without a recount because he probably knew he would lose. Ironically, that decision may have burnished his reputation for his 1968 run.

7. See Richard M. Nixon, *In the Arena: A Memoir of Victory, Defeat, and Renewal* (New York: Simon and Schuster, 1990). Besides, he believed that Lyndon Johnson would be almost impossible to beat.

8. D. Segal, "Partisan Realignment in the United States: The Lesson of the 1964 Election," *Public Opinion Quarterly* 32, no. 3 (1968): 441–44, http://www.jstor.org/stable/2747649.

9. For more on Nixon's philosophy of administrative governance, see Joel D. Aberbach and Bert A. Rockman, "Clashing Beliefs within the Executive Branch: The Nixon Administration Bureaucracy," *American Political Science Review* 70, no. 2 (1976): 456–68, www.jstor.org/stable/1959650; Dwight Ink, "Nixon's Version of Reinventing Government," *Presidential Studies Quarterly* 26, no. 1 (1996): 57–69, www.jstor.org/stable/27551550; Margaret C. Rung, "Richard Nixon, State, and Party: Democracy and Bureaucracy in the Postwar Era," *Presidential Studies Quarterly* 29, no. 2 (1999): 421–37, www.jstor.org/stable/27551997.

10. There are many discussions of the expansion of presidential power including Clinton Rossiter, *The American President* (New York: Harcourt, Brace, 1962); Arthur M. Schlesinger, *The Imperial Presidency* (Boston: Houghton Mifflin, 1973); and Joseph M. Bessette and Jeffrey K. Tulis, *The Constitutional Presidency* (Baltimore: Johns Hopkins University Press, 2009).

11. On Richard Nixon and the administrative state, see Robert Maranto, "The Administrative Strategies of Republican Presidents from Eisenhower to Reagan," *Presidential Studies Quarterly* 23, no. 4 (1993): 683–97; and Larry S. Luton, "Administrative 'Interpretation' as Policy-Making: An Abuse of Discretion by Presidential Administrations," *Administrative Theory & Praxis* 31, no. 4 (2009): 556–76. It should be noted that a lot of what Nixon did in this regard was objectionable at the time, but in the modern era has become a common practice.

12. See Kevin J. McMahon, *Nixon's Court: His Challenge to Judicial Liberalism and Its Political Consequences* (Chicago: University of Chicago Press, 2011).

13. Dean J. Kotlowski, "Trial by Error: Nixon, the Senate, and the Haynsworth Nomination," *Presidential Studies Quarterly* 26, no. 1 (1996): 71–91, www.jstor.org/stable/27551551.

14. Rehnquist had served as a law clerk early in his career for Supreme Court justice Robert Jackson in 1952–53.

15. See Louis Fisher, "Presidential Spending Discretion and Congressional Controls," *Law and Contemporary Problems* 37, no. 1 (1972): 135–72, www.jstor.org/stable/1191125; John P. Mallan, "Washington: The Impoundment Controversy," *Change* 5, no. 5 (1973): 10–61, www.jstor.org/stable/40161767; Christopher Wlezien, "The Politics of Impoundments," *Political Research Quarterly* 47, no. 1 (1994): 59–84, www.jstor.org/stable/448902.

16. The courts had ruled that the president was not required to spend money that for one reason or another was no longer needed. For example, in the case of President Jefferson, money had been allocated to build patrol boats on the Mississippi River, which at the time was an international boundary. But after the Louisiana Purchase, the river was entirely within the territory of the United States. What distinguished President Nixon's impoundments was that he was withholding funds, funds he was required by law to spend, for exclusively policy purposes. See *Train v. City of New York*, 420 U.S. 35. See William Bradford Middlekauff, "Twisting the President's Arm: The Impoundment Control Act as a Tool for Enforcing the Principle of Appropriation Expenditure," *Yale Law Journal* 100, no. 1 (1990): 209–28, www.jstor.org/stable/796769.

17. Just, for example, see Bob Woodward and Carl Bernstein, *The Secret Man: The Story of Watergate's Deep Throat* (New York: Simon and Schuster, 2005); Bob Woodward, *The Last of the President's Men* (New York: Simon and Schuster, 2015); John W. Dean, *The Nixon Defense: What He Knew and When He Knew It* (New York: Viking, 2014); John W. Dean, *Blind Ambition: The White House Years* (New York: Open Road Media, 2016). There is even a fictionalized account of the scandal by Thomas Mallon, *Watergate: A Novel* (New York: Pantheon Books, 2012).

18. Carl Bernstein and Bob Woodward, *All the Presidents Men* (New York: Simon and Schuster, 1974).

19. Jim Hougan, *Secret Agenda: Watergate, Deep Throat, and the CIA* (New York: Random House, 1984).

20. For a self-serving account of this incident, see G. Gordon Liddy, *Will: The Autobiography of G. Gordon Liddy* (New York: St. Martin's Press, [1980] 1997), and for some perspective on that book, see Alan M. Dershowitz, "Will (Book)," *New Republic* 182, no. 22 (May 1980): 25–28.

21. Richard M. Nixon, *RN: The Memoirs of Richard Nixon* (New York: Grosset & Dunlap, 1978).

22. For a good outline of the Watergate scandal, see "The Watergate Story: Timeline," *Washington Post*, accessed June 5, 2019, https://www.washingtonpost.com/wp-srv/politics/special/watergate/timeline.html.

23. Carl Bernstein and Bob Woodward, *All the President's Men* (New York: Simon and Schuster, 1974).

24. John W. Dean, *The Nixon Defense: What He Knew and When He Knew It* (New York: Viking, 2014).

25. See the full text of "Louis Patrick Gray III: Hearings, Ninety-Third Congress, First Session, on Nomination of Louis Patrick Gray III, of Connecticut, to Be Director, Federal Bureau of Investigation," accessed June 5, 2019, https://archive.org/stream/louispatrickgray00unit/louispatrickgray00unit_djvu.txt.

26. The Supreme Court unanimously rejected these arguments. The definitive settlement on this issue was the Supreme Court's 8–0 decision in *United States v. Nixon*, 418 U.S. 683 (1974). In that case the court "threaded the needle" by recognizing the existence of the principle of executive privilege while, at the same time, rejecting the president's arguments in that particular case and ordering President Nixon to turn over the tapes.

27. Pursuant to the Presidential Succession Act of 1947, *61 Stat. 380.*

28. 418 *US* 683 (1974)

29. For a transcript of that June 23, 1972 conversation, see https://www.nixonlibrary.gov/sites/default/files/forresearchers/find/tapes/watergate/trial/exhibit_01.pdf.

30. For a good discussion of the findings and controversies faced by the House Judiciary Watergate investigations unit, see John R. Labovitz, *Presidential Impeachment* (New Haven: Yale University Press, 1978). Also see the interview with House Watergate Committee staffer Professor Dagmar S. Hamilton conducted by Daniel P. Franklin of Georgia State University in September 2017. The transcript of that interview is forthcoming through the Oral History Project at the Nixon Presidential Library in Loma Linda, California. It should be noted that Professor Hamilton shared an office and responsibilities with William Weld, a future Republican governor of Massachusetts, and Hillary Rodham, a future First Lady and Democratic nominee for president of the United States. In order to avoid any taint of partisanship Rodham was not allowed by the special Committee's staff director to visit her husband, William Jefferson Clinton, in Arkansas as he was running as a Democrat for Congress from that state. Instead, Clinton had to come to Washington to visit his wife.

31. It is probably the case that Howard Hunt ordered the break-in, but whether it was at the prompting of someone in the White House remains unknown. John Dean has speculated that Nixon was haunted by the possibility that he had ordered the break-in but had forgotten about it. For a discussion of this, see Timothy Noah, "Did Nixon Really Order the Watergate Break-in?," MSNBC, August 9, 2014, http://www.msnbc.com/msnbc/nixon-40th-anniversary-order-the-watergate-break.

32. This was according to Nixon's own account. Richard M. Nixon, *The Memoirs of Richard Nixon* (New York: Grosset and Dunlap, 1978).

33. This would change in the next two decades as the southern wing of the Democratic Party basically disappeared. In the modern era of partisan polarization, partisan divisions in the House are a more accurate reflection of ideological divisions in the House. See Byron E. Shafer and Richard G. C. Johnston, "The Transformation of Southern Politics Revisited: The House of Representatives as a Window," *British Journal of Political Science* 31, no. 4 (2001): 601–25, or Seth Charles McKee, *Republican Ascendancy in Southern U.S. House Elections* (Boulder, CO: Westview Press, 2010).

34. See *Train v. City of New York*, 420 U.S. 35 (1975) or *Train v. Campaign Clean Water*, 420 U.S. 136 (1975).

35. There were two independents in the Senate, one of whom caucused with the Democrats and one with the Republicans. Thus, the Democratic majority was more accurately 53–47.

36. See the United States Senate, Office of the Senate Historian, *The Senate's Impeachment Role*, accessed November 7, 2017, https://www.senate.gov/artandhistory/history/common/briefing/Senate_Impeachment_Role.htm. According to the Senate historian, there is no record of a Senate ignoring an article of impeachment received from the House. Sometimes the target individual, as did Nixon, resigned before the trial and sometimes the Senate voted to acquit. But according to the U.S. Senate historian, the Senate has always disposed of impeachment articles transmitted from the House. Furthermore, articles of impeachment do not expire at the end of a Congress (as is the case with unfinished legislation). There have been times in which articles transmitted by the House in one Congress have been taken up for trial by the Senate in the next. Office of the Senate Historian, personal communication, November 9, 2017.

37. See Lyn Ragsdale and John J. Theis, "The Institutionalization of the American Presidency, 1924–92," *American Journal of Political Science* 41, no. 4 (1997): 1280–1318.

38. See Arthur M. Schlesinger Jr., *The Imperial Presidency* (Boston: Houghton Mifflin, 1973), for an argument typical of the time.

39. Two of the most prominent being the "pink sheet" smear of Helen Gahagan Douglas, his (incumbent Democratic) opponent in his first election to Congress, and his role in the investigation of Alger Hiss, a State Department official accused of espionage. Nixon's role as a member of the investigating committee became synonymous with McCarthyism.

40. Carl B. Albert and Danney Goble, *Little Giant: The Life and Times of Speaker Carl Albert* (Norman: University of Oklahoma Press, 1999). In fact, it is reported that Albert contemplated resigning the Speakership and recommending that Ford be elected Speaker had the nomination not been confirmed by the time Nixon was either removed or resigned the presidency. See

Joseph J. Fins, "Secret Memo Shows Bipartisanship during Watergate Succession Crisis," *The Conversation*, January 22, 2018, http://theconversation.com/secret-memo-shows-bipartisanship-during-watergate-succession-crisis-90211.

41. See Gallup, Presidential Approval, President Richard Nixon, accessed July 8, 2019, https://news.gallup.com/poll/116677/presidential-approval-ratings-gallup-historical-statistics-trends.aspx.

42. See Tim Weiner, *One Man against the World: The Tragedy of Richard Nixon* (New York: Henry Holt, 2015).

43. Kenneth Franklin Kurz, *Nixon's Enemies* (Los Angeles: Lowell House, 1998).

44. Jon Marshall, *Watergate's Legacy and the Press: The Investigative Impulse* (Evanston, IL: Northwestern University Press, 2011).

45. See *Articles of Impeachment, Adopted by the House of Representatives Committee on the Judiciary, July 27, 1974.* Accessed November 8, 2017, http://www.presidency.ucsb.edu/ws/?pid=76082.

46. The target was Anna Chennault who was probably acting as an operative for the Nixon campaign. She was trying to undermine peace talks that might have resulted in a cease-fire in the Vietnam War a month before the election of 1968. It appears that she succeeded. See https://www.politico.com/magazine/story/2017/08/06/nixon-vietnam-candidate-conspired-with-foreign-power-win-election-215461.

Chapter Five

1. Ronnie Dugger, *On Reagan: The Man and His Presidency* (New York: McGraw-Hill, 1983), 6, 9.

2. Dugger, *On Reagan*, 23.

3. Bill Boyarsky, *Ronald Reagan: His Life and Rise to the Presidency* (New York: Random House, 1981), 106–13, 153–54.

4. Boyarsky, *Ronald Reagan*, 138.

5. Boyarsky, *Ronald Reagan*, 194.

6. See Gary Sick, *October Surprise: America's Hostages in Iran and the Election of Ronald Reagan* (New York: Times Books; Toronto: Random House, 1991).

7. The Logan Act, U.S.C. 18 § 953. The Logan Act forbids private citizens from engaging in diplomacy on behalf of the United States government.

8. See Neil A. Lewis, "New Reports Say 1980 Reagan Campaign Tried to Delay Hostage Release," *New York Times*, April 15, 1991, http://www.nytimes.com/1991/04/15/world/new-reports-say-1980-reagan-campaign-tried-to-delay-hostage-release.html. These charges are systematically refuted by Steven Emerson and Jesse Furman, "The Conspiracy That Wasn't," *New Republic* 205, no. 21 (November 18, 1991), 16–31. But like the charges made by Sick, the refutation is circumstantial as well.

9. Quoted in Gary Sick, *October Surprise: America's Hostages in Iran and the Election of Ronald Reagan* (New York: Times Books; Toronto: Random House,

1991), 220. For the record, Reagan wasn't diagnosed with Alzheimer's disease until 1994, three years after this interview. For more information, see Bruce Kuniholm, "There You Go Again? Gary Sick, Ronald Reagan, and the Iranian Revolution: A Review Article," *Iranian Studies* 24, nos. 1–4 (1991): 61–69, www.jstor.org/stable/4310756.

10. United States Congress, House, Committee on Foreign Affairs, Task Force to Investigate Certain Allegations Concerning the Holding of American Hostages by Iran in 1980, *Joint Report of the Task Force to Investigate Certain Allegations concerning the Holding of American Hostages by Iran In 1980 ("October Surprise Task Force")* (Washington, DC: U.S. Government Printing Office, 1993).

11. Stephen Skowronek, *Presidential Leadership in Political Time: Reprise and Reappraisal* (Lawrence: University Press of Kansas, 2011).

12. Kathleen Schalch, "1981 Strike Leaves Legacy for American Workers," NPR, August 3, 2008, https://www.npr.org/2006/08/03/5604656/1981-strike-leaves-legacy-for-american-workers.

13. Bill Boyarsky, *Ronald Reagan: His Life and Rise to the Presidency* (New York: Random House, 1981), 189.

14. Fact Checker, "Did Ronald Reagan's 1981 Tax Cut Supercharge the Economy?," *Washington Post*, November 8, 2017, https://www.washingtonpost.com/news/fact-checker/wp/2017/11/08/did-ronald-reagans-1981-tax-cut-supercharge-the-economy/.164.

15. See Daniel Paul Franklin and Michael P. Fix, "The Best of Times and the Worst of Times: Polarization and Presidential Success in Congress," *Congress & the Presidency* 43, no. 3 (September–December 2016): 377–94.

16. United States Department of State, "The Reagan Doctrine," January 20, 2009, https://2001-2009.state.gov/r/pa/ho/time/rd/17741.htm.

17. Dick Wirthlin and Winston Hall, *The Greatest Communicator: What Ronald Reagan Taught Me about Politics, Leadership, and Life* (Hoboken, NJ: Wiley Press, 2004), 131–64. See also 270 to Win, https://www.270towin.com/1984_Election.

18. Wirthlin and Hall, *The Greatest Communicator*, 110.

19. P.L. 98–473, 98 Stat. 1935–1937, signed October 12, 1984. The relevant provision in the law states, "During fiscal year 1985, no funds available to the Central Intelligence Agency, the Department of Defense, or any other agency or entity of the United States involved in intelligence activities may be obligated or expended for the purpose or which would have the effect of supporting, directly or indirectly, military or paramilitary operations in Nicaragua by any nation, group, organization, movement or individual." S.960, which became Public Law 99–83, extended the policy to 1986.

20. Furthermore, the Nicaraguans used the incident as an opportunity to sue the U.S. government in the International Court of Justice at The Hague. The court found in favor of the Nicaraguans, but the United States neither recognized the jurisdiction of the court nor paid the judgment.

21. See Peter Kornbluth and Malcolm Byrne, *The Iran-Contra Scandal: The Declassified History* (New York: New Press, 1993), 214.

22. Peter Wallison, *Ronald Reagan: The Power of Conversation and the Success of His Presidency* (Cambridge, MA: Westview Press, 2003), 171, 177–78, 211.

23. Wallison, *Ronald Reagan*, 193–96, 201–2, 252.

24. Quoted in Peter Kornbluth and Malcolm Byrne, *The Iran-Contra Scandal: The Declassified History* (New York: New Press, 1993), 352.

25. Peter Wallison, *Ronald Reagan: The Power of Conversation and the Success of His Presidency* (Cambridge, MA: Westview Press, 2003), 195, 197–201.

26. Quoted in Daniel K. Inouye and Lee H. Hamilton, *Report of the Congressional Committees Investigating the Iran-Contra Affair: With the Minority Views* (New York: Random House, 1988), 18.

27. Peter Wallison, *Ronald Reagan: The Power of Conversation and the Success of His Presidency* (Cambridge, MA: Westview Press, 2003), 198–200.

28. "The Price of Iran-Contra Immunity," *New York Times*, June 12, 1988, https://www.nytimes.com/1988/06/12/opinion/the-price-of-iran-contra-immunity.html.

29. Lawrence E. Walsh, *Iran-Contra: The Final Report* (New York: Random House, 1994).

30. Peter Wallison, *Ronald Reagan: The Power of Conversation and the Success of His Presidency* (Cambridge, MA: Westview Press, 2003), 270.

31. Wallison, *Ronald Reagan*, 168.

32. In some sense there was precedent for this as President Ford had pardoned Richard Nixon before his indictment in relation to Watergate. The pardon, at least as it was envisioned in the eighteenth century when the Constitution was written, was intended to be an act of mercy on the part of the president that, at the same time, served as an admission of guilt. The subject was guilty and, thus, was pardoned. For the president to pardon Weinberger (or Nixon for that matter) before he was convicted could itself serve as a cover-up as a Weinberger trial may have revealed heretofore unknown information including the degree of culpability of President Reagan and even George H. W. Bush himself. Parenthetically, President Bill Clinton did the same thing on his way out of office in pardoning financier Marc Rich.

33. Peter Kornbluth and Malcolm Byrne, eds., *The Iran-Contra Scandal (The National Security Archive Document)* (New York: New Press, 1993), 215.

34. Caspar W. Weinberger, Diary Entry for December 7, 1985 (Washington, DC: National Archives); available from the National Security Archive, *The Iran-Contra Affair 20 Years On*, http://www.gwu.edu/~nsarchiv/NSAEBB/NSAEBB210/index.htm.

35. Weinberger, Diary Entry for December 7, 1985.

36. Peter Kornbluth and Malcolm Byrne, eds., *The Iran-Contra Scandal (The National Security Archive Document)* (New York: New Press, 1993), 305. When he finally admitted that weapons had in fact been traded for hostages in his March 5, 1987 speech, Reagan maintained that his earlier denials were based on the fact

that he didn't know. But he did know as early as December 7, 1985, according to the Weinberger diaries.

37. See David Hoffman, "Bush, CBS' Rather Clash over Iran," *Washington Post*, January 6, 1988, https://www.washingtonpost.com/archive/politics/1988/01/26/bush-cbs-rather-clash-over-iran/fdf4e8ee-e566-484b-bc5e-ead6f496813e/?utm_term=.d6e8b194edbe.

38. Bush diary entry, November 24, 1986, from Richard Harwood, "A Quick Peek at the Bush Diaries," *Washington Post*, January 23, 1993, www.highbeam.com/doc/1P2-929091.html?refid=easy_hf.

39. *The Tower Commission Report*, "Tower Commission Report Excerpts," Tower Commission, 1987, http://www.presiddency.ucsb.edu/PS157/assignment%20files%20public/TOWER%20EXCERPTS.htm. President Reagan sometimes relied on his perceived infirmities to duck the questions of the press. For example, the president acted as if he couldn't hear the questions of the press for the noise created by the propellers of his helicopter *Marine One*. It is possible that he knew about the entire Iran-Contra operation from beginning to end, but just acted as if he didn't know. Presidents are often called upon to prevaricate especially when discussing ongoing operations or in the midst of negotiations with other states. Henry Kissinger coined the phrase "constructive ambiguity" to describe a technique of negotiation designed to create uncertainty in the minds of the opposing negotiating team.

40. Richard Meislin, "Iran-Contra Hearings: A Majority in New Poll Still Find Reagan Lied on Iran-Contra Issue," *New York Times*, July 18, 1987, https://www.nytimes.com/1987/07/18/world/iran-contra-hearings-majority-new-poll-still-find-reagan-lied-iran-contra-issue.html.

41. Meislin, "Iran-Contra Hearings."

42. Daniel K. Inouye and Lee H. Hamilton, *Report of the Congressional Committees Investigating the Iran-Contra Affair: With the Minority Views* (New York: Random House, 1988), 13.

43. Lawrence E. Walsh, *Iran-Contra: The Final Report* (New York: Random House, 1994), 187–91.

44. An appeals court ruled that North (and later Poindexter's) conviction was affected by the fact that the two men had testified before Congress under a grant of immunity. That congressional testimony may have influenced the testimony of witnesses in the criminal trial and, thus, unfairly weighted the government's case against the accused. See David Johnston, "North Conviction Reversed in Part; Review Is Ordered," *New York Times*, July 21, 1990.

45. Walsh, *Iran-Contra*, 120, 173–78, 179–80, 183–86.

46. Daniel K. Inouye and Lee H. Hamilton, *Report of the Congressional Committees Investigating the Iran-Contra Affair: With the Minority Views* (New York: Random House, 1988).

47. Inouye and Hamilton, *Report of the Congressional Committees Investigating the Iran-Contra Affair*, 33.

48. H. Res 111, 133 Cong. Rec. 4899–900, 4918 (1987).

49. See Mack C. Shelley, "Presidents and the Conservative Coalition in the U.S. Congress," *Legislative Studies Quarterly* 8, no. 1 (1983): 79–96, www.jstor.org/stable/439472; or Bernard Grofman, William Koetzle, Samuel Merrill, and Thomas Brunell, "Changes in the Location of the Median Voter in the U.S. House of Representatives, 1963–1996," *Public Choice* 106, nos. 3/4 (2001): 221–32, www.jstor.org/stable/30026217.

50. Stephen W. Stathis and David C. Huckabee, "Congressional Resolutions on Presidential Impeachment: A Historical Overview," *CRS Report for Congress*, Penny Hill Press, September 16, 1998. https://www.everycrsreport.com/files/19980916_98-763_9d27a8aa0761f1bf0148170a80258d47a16e2dc7.pdf.

51. Daniel Inouye and Lee Hamilton, *Report of the Congressional Committees Investigating the Iran-Contra Affair: With the Minority Views* (New York: Random House, 1988).

52. "Iran-Contra Redux," *Progressive* 54, no. 6 (June 1990), 9. Seymour M. Hersh, "The Iran-Contra Committees: Did They Protect Reagan?" *New York Times*, April 29, 1990.

53. Associated Press, "Iran-Contra Revisited: Fears of Impeachment," *New York Times* (October 27, 1993), https://nyti.ms/29e1i8H.

54. See, for example, the *Prize* Cases, 67 U.S. 635 (1862), and, of course, the infamous *Korematsu v. United States*, 323 U.S. 214 (1944).

55. Michael J. Glennon, "Foreign Affairs and the Political Question Doctrine," *American Journal of International Law* 83, no. 4 (1989): 814–21, www.jstor.org/stable/2203370.

56. Center for Arms Control and Nonproliferation, "Fact-Sheet: Intermediate-Range Nuclear Forces (INF) Treaty," February 14, 2017, https://armscontrolcenter.org/intermediate-range-nuclear-forces-inf-treaty/.

57. "A Brief History of U.S. Unemployment," *Washington Post*, http://www.washingtonpost.com/wp-srv/special/business/us-unemployment-rate-history/.

58. Country Studies, "The UNO Electoral Victory," http://countrystudies.us/nicaragua/19.htm.

59. Ronald Reagan and Douglas Brinkley, *The Reagan Diaries* (New York: HarperCollins, 2007). But before 6 p.m., according to O'Neill, it was all politics. Martin Tolchin, "Thomas P. O'Neill Jr., a Democratic Power in the House for Decades, Dies at 81," *New York Times*, January 7, 1994. Reagan said that when he received a Valentine's card from O'Neill he knew who had sent it because the heart was bleeding, https://archive.nytimes.com/www.nytimes.com/learning/general/onthisday/bday/1209.html.

60. For a discussion of the relationship between Reagan and O'Neill, see Christopher Matthews, *Tip and the Gipper: When Politics Worked* (New York: Simon and Schuster, 2013).

61. See Gallup, "Presidential Job Approval Center," accessed July 9, 2019, https://news.gallup.com/interactives/185273/presidential-job-approval-center.aspx.

62. 22 U.S.C. § 2778, the Arms Export Control Act.

63. 22 U.S.C. § 2776.

64. Eugene R. Wittkopf and James M. McCormick, "The Domestic Politics of Contra Aid: Public Opinion, Congress, and the President," in *Public Opinion in U.S. Foreign Policy: The Controversy over Contra Aid*, ed. Richard Sobel, 73–103 (Lanham, MD: Rowman and Littlefield, 1993).

65. David G. Savage, "Hyde View on Lying Is Back Haunting Him," *Los Angeles Times*, December 4, 1998, 3, http://articles.latimes.com/1998/dec/04/news/mn-50567.

66. Evan Thomas, "Questions of Age and Competence," *Time*, October 22, 1984, 3.

67. Daniel Inouye and Lee Hamilton, *Report of the Congressional Committee Investigating the Iran-Contra Affair: With the Minority View* (New York: Random House, 1988), 52.

Chapter Six

1. See Bill Bishop and Robert G. Cushing, *The Big Sort: Why the Clustering of Like-Minded America Is Tearing Us Apart* (Boston: Mariner Books, 2009); or Alan Abramowitz, *The Disappearing Center: Engaged Citizens, Polarization, and American Democracy* (New Haven: Yale University Press, 2010).

2. The practice of constitutional hardball has three characteristics: it involves arguments and behavior by political actors (including judges, although their role is less interesting than that of other political actors) that are defensible—though sometimes only barely so—by standard constitutional doctrine; it is inconsistent with settled preconstitutional understandings; and it involves extremely high stakes (control over the national government as a whole). Mark Tushnet, "Constitutional Hardball," 37 *J. Marshall L. Rev.* 523 (2004); see also Steven Levitsky and Daniel Ziblatt, *How Democracies Die* (New York: Crown, 2018).

3. James David Barber, *The Presidential Character: Predicting Performance in the White House* (Englewood Cliffs, NJ: Prentice-Hall, 1977).

4. Russell L. Riley, "Bill Clinton: Life before the Presidency," University of Virginia Miller Center, https://millercenter.org/president/clinton/life-before-the-presidency.

5. Riley, "Bill Clinton."

6. Riley, "Bill Clinton."

7. Real Clear Politics, "Unlike Obama, Bill Clinton Was a Centrist," August 2, 2012, http://www.realclearpolitics.com/articles/2012/08/02/mr_president_youre_no_bill_clinton_114982.html.

8. Russell L. Riley, "Bill Clinton: Campaigns and Elections," http://miller center.org/president/clinton/campaigns-and-election.

9. Jeffrey H. Birnbaum, *Madhouse, the Private Turmoil of Working for the President* (New York: Random House, 1998), 50.

10. Russell L. Riley, "Bill Clinton: Campaigns and Elections," http://miller center.org/president/clinton/campaigns-and-elections.

11. Sidney Blumenthal, *The Clinton Wars* (New York: Farrar, Straus and Giroux, 2003), 261.

12. Jeffrey Birnbaum, *Madhouse: The Private Turmoil of Working for the President* (New York: Random House, 1996), 6, 9.

13. Birnbaum, *Madhouse*, 27–28.

14. For a good discussion of this lack of coordination drawn extensively for the William Clinton Oral History Project, see David A. Graham, "How Trump Can Fix His Troubled White House," *Atlantic*, March 21, 2017, https://millercenter. org/issues-policy/governance/atlantic-how-trump-can-fix-his-troubled-white-house.

15. Morris's relationship with a prostitute was probably outed by liberals in the White House who resented his access to the president. Such is the "court politics" of the White House. Morris would go on to become a conservative media political commentator, and a harsh critic of the Clintons.

16. Charles O. Jones, "Campaigning to Govern: The Clinton Style," in *The Clinton Presidency: First Appraisals*, ed. Colin Campbell and Burt A. Rockman (Chatham, NJ: Chatham House, 1996), 26, 28.

17. Sally Bedell Smith, *For Love of Politics, Bill and Hillary Clinton: The White House Years* (New York: Random House, 2007), 116–18, 251–52.

18. George Edwards, "Frustration and Folly: Bill Clinton and the Public Presidency," in *The Clinton Presidency: First Appraisals*, ed. Colin Campbell and Bert Rockman (Chatham, NJ: Chatham House, 1996), 234–61.

19. For example, Martin Luther King Jr. in his "Letter from a Birmingham Jail" reserved special opprobrium for moderates who purportedly supported the cause of civil rights but actually delayed justice and made the status quo, segregation, more palatable. So have revolutionaries in the French Revolution, the Bolshevik Revolution, and the rise of Hitler to power in Germany found so-called moderates to be some of the most dangerous groups in opposition.

20. For a discussion of this, see Terry Sullivan, "Bargaining with the President: A Simple Game and New Evidence," *American Political Science Review* 84, no. 4 (1990): 1167–95.

21. Colin Campbell, "Management in a Sandbox: Why the Clinton White House Failed to Cope with Gridlock," in *The Clinton Presidency: First Appraisals*, ed. Colin Campbell and Bert A. Rockman (Chatham, NJ: Chatham House, 1996), 51.

22. Steven M. Gillon, *The Pact: Bill Clinton, Newt Gingrich and the Rivalry That Defined a Generation* (Oxford: Oxford University Press, 2008), 151.

23. Sally Bedell Smith, *For Love of Politics, Bill and Hillary Clinton: The White House Years* (New York: Random House, 2007), 18, 99, 132, 151.

24. Clinton categorically denied David Hale's account. Hale's testimony was never corroborated and Clinton was never charged for any crime associated with this part of Whitewater.

25. Sally Bedell Smith, *For Love of Politics, Bill and Hillary Clinton: The White House Years* (New York: Random House, 2007), 152, 173–74.

26. Congress.gov, "S24-Independent Counsel Reauthorization Act of 1994," http://www.congress.gov/bill/103rd-congress/senate-bill/24.

27. *Jones v. Clinton*, 520 U.S. 681 (1997).

28. Starr knew about the Lewinsky affair because he had been in contact with Lucianne Goldberg who was friends with Linda Tripp, a confidant of Monica Lewinsky's, who without Lewinsky's knowledge had taped their telephone conversations. Tripp had done so at the urging of Goldberg who then obtained the tapes and turned them over to Starr. In her conversations with Tripp, the ones that were taped, Lewinsky discussed her affair with Clinton.

29. Steven Levitsky and Daniel Ziblatt, *How Democracies Die* (New York: Crown, 2018).

30. In regard to the inflexibility of the American Constitution, Bagehot writes, "The consequence is that the most obvious evils cannot be quickly remedied; that the most absurd fictions must be framed to evade the plain sense of mischievous clauses; that a clumsy working and curious technicality mark the politics of a rough and ready people." Walter Bagehot, *The English Constitution* (London: Chapman and Hall, 1867), 268.

31. Christopher Ingraham, "Five Charts That Show How Conservatives Are Driving Partisan Rancor in DC," *Washington Post*, June 12, 2014, https://www.washingtonpost.com/news/wonk/wp/2014/06/12/five-charts-that-show-how-conservatives-are-driving-partisan-rancor-in-dc/?utm_term=.d642d180f2a2; or the Pew Research Center, "Political Polarization in the American Public: How Increasing Ideological Uniformity and Partisan Antipathy Affect Politics, Compromise, and Everyday Life," June 12, 2014, http://www.people-press.org/2014/06/12/political-polarization-in-the-american-public/#ith.

32. Bob Barr, Member, U.S. House of Representatives, Correspondence to Henry Hyde, Chair, House Committee on the Judiciary, U.S. House of Representatives, March 11, 1997a, Special Collection, Ingram Library, University of West Georgia, Carrollton.

33. Bob Barr, Member, U.S. House of Representatives, Correspondence to Janet Reno, Attorney General of the U.S., March 12, 1997b, Special Collection, Ingram Library, University of West Georgia, Carrollton.

34. Bob Barr, *The Meaning of IS* (Atlanta: Stroud and Hall, 2004).

35. Bob Barr, Member, U.S. House of Representative, Correspondence to Henry Hyde, Chair, Committee on the Judiciary, U.S. House of Representatives, April 5, 1997c, Special Collection, Ingram Library, University of West Georgia, Carrollton.

36. Bob Barr, Member, U.S. House of Representatives, Correspondence to Newt Gingrich, Speaker of the U.S. House of Representatives, July 24, 1997d, Special Collection, Ingram Library, University of West Georgia, Carrollton.

37. Henry Hyde, Chair, Committee on the Judiciary, U.S. House of Representatives, Correspondence to Bob Barr, Member, U.S. House of Representatives,

July 24, 1997d, Special Collection, Ingram Library, University of West Georgia, Carrollton.

38. Quoted in Bob Barr, *The Meaning of IS* (Atlanta: Stroud and Hall, 2004), 124.

39. The Starr Report," September 9, 1998, republished in the *Washington Post*, https://www.washingtonpost.com/wp-srv/politics/special/clinton/icreport/icreport.htm.

40. Initial White House Rebuttal to Starr Report ("Preliminary Memorandum Concerning Referral of Office of Independent Counsel"), September 11, 1998, republished in the *Washington Post*. http://www.washingtonpost.com/wp-srv/politics/special/clinton/stories/whreport.htm. The next day, the White House issued a more detailed brief.

41. ABC–Washington Post Poll reported by *Pollingreport.com*, accessed May 11, 2018, http://www.pollingreport.com/scandal2.htm.

42. U.S. House of Representatives, "Statistics of the Congressional Election of November 3, 1996," http://clerk.house.gov/member_info/electioninfo/1998/98Stat.htm.

43. Steven M. Gillon, *The Pact: Bill Clinton, Newt Gingrich and the Rivalry That Defined a Generation* (Oxford: Oxford University Press, 2008), 62, 269.

44. Betty Koed, United States Senate historian, personal interview, November 13, 2017. There was a suggestion made at the time that the president be found "guilty" but not subject to removal or, failing that, that the president be censured for his behavior, but, as noted above, as far as the Senate is concerned, impeachments must be tried. Thus, there is no substitute for a trial and a definitive outcome.

45. U.S. Senate, Rules of Procedure and Practice in the Senate When Sitting on Impeachment Trials, S. Res. 479, 99–2, August 16, 1986, accessed May 16, 2018, https://www.gpo.gov/fdsys/pkg/SMAN-104/pdf/SMAN-104-pg177.pdf.

46. See U.S. Senate, Proceedings of the United States Senate in the Impeachment Trial of President William Jefferson Clinton, vols. I–IV, S. Doc. 106–4, February 12, 1999, accessed May 16, 2018, https://www.gpo.gov/fdsys/pkg/CDOC-106sdoc4/pdf/CDOC-106sdoc4-vol1.pdf.

47. Sidney Blumenthal, *The Clinton Wars* (New York: Farrar, Straus and Giroux, 2003), 537; Susan Bedell Smith, *For Love of Politics, Bill and Hillary Clinton: The White House Years* (New York: Random House, 2007), 367–77.

48. CNN, "How the Senators Voted on Impeachment," http://www.cnn.com/ALLPOLITICS/stories/1999/02/12/senate.vote/.

49. "The Impeachment Vote," *Washington Post*, 1998, https://www.washingtonpost.com/wp-srv/politics/special/clinton/housevote/sc.htm.

50. In a CBS News national poll conducted between January 30 and February 1, 1999, 89% of Democrats approved of a Senate vote to "not convict" Bill Clinton (64% of Independents agreed). At the same time, 69% of Republicans favored conviction. CBS News poll, February 12, 1999 report by PollingReport.com, https://www.pollingreport.com/scandal1.htm.

51. "The Impeachment Vote," *Washington Post*, 1998. https://www.washington
post.com/wp-srv/politics/special/clinton/housevote/sc.htm.

52. Carroll Royce, Jeffrey B. Lewis, James Lo, Keith T. Poole, and Howard
Rosenthal, "Measuring Bias and Uncertainty in DW-NOMINATE Ideal Point
Estimates via the Parametric Bootstrap," *Political Analysis* 17 (2009): 261–27.

53. Dynamic Weighted Nominal Three-step Estimation.

54. Carroll Royce, Jeffrey B. Lewis, James Lo, Keith T. Poole, and Howard
Rosenthal, "Measuring Bias and Uncertainty in DW-NOMINATE Ideal Point
Estimates via the Parametric Bootstrap," *Political Analysis* 17 (2009): 261–27. See
Nate Silver, "How Liberal Is President Obama," *FiveThirtyEight*, April, 11, 2011,
https://fivethirtyeight.com/features/how-liberal-is-president-obama/.

55. Silver, "How Liberal Is President Obama."

56. https://data.oecd.org/unemp/unemployment-rate.htm (accessed May 20,
2018).

57. Steven M. Gillon, *The Pact: Bill Clinton, Newt Gingrich, and the Rivalry
That Defined a Generation* (Oxford: Oxford University Press, 2008), 116.

58. ABC News Poll, September 21, 1998, republished by Pollingreport.com
http://www.pollingreport.com/scandal3.htm.

59. See ABC News/*Washington Post* poll, August 19–21, 1998. N=1,015
adults nationwide.

Question: "How did you feel when you first heard that Clinton had
admitted he misled the country about his relationship with Monica
Lewinsky? Did you feel [see below] or not? How about [see below]?"
In response, 45% answered that they were "disgusted."

http://www.pollingreport.com/scandal3.htm.

60. Gallup/CNN/USA Today poll, republished on Pollingreport.com http://
www.pollingreport.com/clinton-.htm.

61. The job never appeared, and it wasn't apparently necessary to buy her
silence anyhow.

62. Postscript: Linda Tripp, who recorded her phone conversations with
Monica Lewinsky and turned those tapes over to Kenneth Starr, was transferred
from the White House to the Department of Defense. There, on the last full
day of the Clinton administration, she was fired from her job. She later sued the
government for wrongful termination and was awarded a substantial settlement.
If Clinton had a role in her firing, that could have been an impeachable offense
in the meaning discussed above. But by the time the firing was generally known,
Clinton was out of office.

63. William Riker, "The Two-Party System and Duverger's Law: An Essay
on the History of Political Science," *American Political Science Review* 76, no. 4
(December 1982): 753–66.

64. See Jonathan Turley, "Senate Trials and Factional Disputes: Impeachment as a Madisonian Device," *Duke Law Journal* 49, no. 1 (1999): 69–70.

Chapter Seven

1. The exception to the rule would be a case similar to that of John Tyler who broke with his own party. When Tyler defied the Whig Party, that increased the probability of his impeachment in the House.

2. Ironically, then, part of what makes impeachment mostly a dead letter is the Twenty-Second Amendment placing term limits on the presidency.

3. Mark Hiller and Douglas Kriner, "Institutional Change and the Dynamics of Vice-Presidential Selection," *Presidential Studies Quarterly* 38, no. 3 (2008): 401–21. www.jstor.org/stable/41219687.

4. In fact, we may be finding that out now as President Trump is likely to ignore court rulings on turning over evidence to congressional investigators. However, given the propensity of congressional Republicans to support the president, it seems likely that impeachment will still not be the result.

5. Nixon had probably evaded taxes, but by the time the president was subject to impeachment, the investigation of his returns was not complete. Furthermore, while the IRS was under some pressure to audit some of those on the president's "enemies list," there is no evidence that the IRS succumbed to that pressure. However, if it had, that would constitute an impeachable offense in the meaning discussed above. For two reviews of Nixon's tax returns, see William D. Samson, "President Nixon's Troublesome Tax Returns," April 11, 2005, published by Tax Analysts, http://www.taxhistory.org/thp/readings.nsf/cf7c9c870b600b9585256df80075b9dd/f8723e3606cd79ec85256ff6006f82c3?OpenDocument, and Joseph J. Thorndike, "JCT Investigation of Nixon's Tax Returns," February 2016, Tax Analysts, Tax History Project, https://uschs.org/wp-content/uploads/2016/02/USCHS-History-Role-Joint-Committee-Taxation-Thorndike.pdf.

6. See *United States v. Reynolds*, 345 U.S. 1 (1953).

7. Source: Keith T. Poole and Howard Rosenthal, "The Polarization of the Congressional Parties," https://legacy.voteview.com/political_polarization_2014.htm (accessed June 13, 2019). Poole and Rosenthal measure the ideological distance between individual members by comparing their roll-call voting records, and the distance between congressional parties by comparing the voting of parties in the aggregate. For more on this, see our discussion of NOMINATE scores below.

8. However, because of the supermajority requirement for conviction and removal in the Senate, the ideological distance between the president and the congressional party in the Senate would have to be much greater to make any difference in the Senate. That was part of the story in the Andrew Johnson impeachment.

9. Our discussion of the prevalence of variables below is not meant to suggest a degree of statistical certainty that is often associated with works in political science. Because we are dealing with a very small sample size, we seek to draw conclusions from the qualitative information discussed in chapter 3–6. We also do not mean to suggest that the presence of any variable means that impeachment will occur, but that the presence of a variable shown to be influential in these impeachments will increase the likelihood of impeachment.

10. Keith T. Poole and Howard Rosenthal, "Patterns of Congressional Voting," *American Journal of Political Science* 35 (1991): 228–78. As a reminder (from chapter 2), this measure is derived by scoring the votes of a member of Congress (there are about five hundred roll-call votes a year) relative to the votes of all other members of the chamber. This establishes a continuum along which all members of Congress can be placed relative to one another. Those members who are the most extreme, whose votes are farthest away from the median member (the one most likely to vote one way or the other in the issue space), are the ends of the ideological spectrum identified as liberal or conservative. To establish a DW-Nominate score for the president, the presidents' stated preferences are scored as if they were votes relative to all members of Congress.

11. Impeachment actions by the Whigs against Tyler were derailed when the Whigs lost the House in the midterm elections of 1842.

12. To check the robustness of these results, we ran several permutations of this analysis. For the House, we also ran a difference of means test for the presidents covered in this book (minus Johnson) with President John Tyler, the first president to have impeachment action taken against him. Results demonstrate a p value of .08 or a 92% probability that the difference of the means is not due to random chance. This falls just below acceptable standards for political science, but still shows strong evidence in support of our theory. In addition, we ran an analysis for presidents for which there was any identifiable impeachment action (investigation, hearing, introduction of resolution of impeachment by a member, or impeachment proceedings). This included eight different presidents (Tyler, Truman, Nixon, Reagan, George H. W. Bush, Clinton, Bush, and Obama) as data were not available for some earlier presidents (Buchanan, Johnson, Grant, and Hoover) and not yet constructed for Trump. The Satterthwaite difference of means test demonstrates a p value of .0076, or a 99.24% chance that the difference of means is not due to random chance. Results for the Senate were similar as well, demonstrating p values of .046 (N = 3) and .04 (N = 8), or a 95.4% and 96% chance, respectively, that the results are not due to random chance. This demonstrates that our results are quite robust.

13. Keith T. Poole and Howard Rosenthal, "Patterns of Congressional Voting," *American Journal of Political Science* 35 (1991).

14. For more on this, see Michael Nelson, "Bill Clinton and the Politics of Second Terms," *Presidential Studies Quarterly* 28, no. 4 (1998): 786–92, www.jstor.

org/stable/27551932; Gregory A. Caldeira and Christopher Zorn, "Strategic Timing, Position-Taking, and Impeachment in the House of Representatives," *Political Research Quarterly* 57, no. 4 (2004): 517–27, www.jstor.org/stable/3219814; David A. Crockett, "The Contemporary Presidency: 'An Excess of Refinement': Lame Duck Presidents in Constitutional and Historical Context," *Presidential Studies Quarterly* 38, no. 4 (2008): 707–21; Kyle Haynes, "Lame Ducks and Coercive Diplomacy: Do Executive Term Limits Reduce the Effectiveness of Democratic Threats?," *Journal of Conflict Resolution* 56, no. 5 (2012): 771–98.

15. David R. Mayhew, *Congress: The Electoral Connection* (New Haven: Yale University Press, 1974).

16. We recognize that there may be an endogeneity problem that exists with certain presidents. Said differently, presidents being in their final term may be the direct result of a failed impeachment by Congress. In the case of Johnson, it could be argued that he did not seek a second term as a direct result of the impeachment action. However, by the time he was impeached and tried in the Senate, he had virtually no chance of being elected to the presidency in his own right. So, for all intents, he was a lame duck.

17. George H. W. Bush, H. Res. 34 and 86 by Rep. Henry B. Gonzalez, January 16 and February 21, 1991. William J. Clinton, H. Res. 304 by Rep. Bob Barr, December 19, 1998. George W. Bush, H. Res. 1258, Rep. Dennis Kucinich and Rep. Robert Wexler, June 10, 2008. Barack H. Obama, H. Con. Res. 107, Rep. Walter B. Jones, March 7, 2012. Donald J. Trump, H. Res. 438, Rep. Al Green and Rep. Brad Sherman, November 15, 2017.

Postscript

1. Davis, Julie Hirschfeld "Nancy Pelosi Elected Speaker as Democrats Take Control of House," *New York Times*, January 3, 2019, https://www.nytimes.com/2019/01/03/us/politics/nancy-pelosi-speaker-116th-congress.html (last accessed 10/1/19).

2. Werner, Erica, "How the GOP is Already Working on How to Impeach Hillary Clinton If She Wins," *Associated Press* reprinted in *The Business Insider*, November 2, 2016, https://www.businessinsider.com/how-the-gop-is-already-working-on-how-to-impeach-hillary-clinton-if-she-wins-2016-11 (last accessed 10/1/19).

3. Miller, Jonathan, "Party Unity on Congressional Votes Takes a Dive: CQ Vote Studies Decline More Dramatic in the Senate," *Roll Call*, Feb. 28, 2019, https://www.rollcall.com/news/congress/party-unity-congressional-votes (last accessed 10/05/19).

4. Fortunately for the Democrats, in that regard, the Trump administration is fighting the release of materials essential to the impeachment investigation in the Courts. That process could take months and there is no reason for the Democrats nor the Administration to rush.

5. Federal Reserve of St. Louis, "GINI Index for the United States," *Economic Research*, https://fred.stlouisfed.org/series/SIPOVGINIUSA (last accessed 4/7/20).

6. John Sides, "The Monkey Cage: Did Enough Bernie Sanders Supporters Vote for Trump to Cost Clinton the Election?" *New York Times*, August 24, 2017, https://www.washingtonpost.com/news/monkey-cage/wp/2017/08/24/did-enough-bernie-sanders-supporters-vote-for-trump-to-cost-clinton-the-election/ (last accessed 04/04/2020.

7. He referred to the Congressman as "Little Adam Schitt" in another tweet.

8. See "List of Nicknames Used by Donald Trump," *Wikipedia*, https://en.wikipedia.org/wiki/List_of_nicknames_used_by_Donald_Trump (last accessed 10/14/19).

9. Bond, Jon R., "Contemporary Presidency: Which Presidents Are Uncommonly Successful in Congress? A Trump Update," *Presidential Studies Quarterly (Early View)*, https://onlinelibrary.wiley.com/doi/abs/10.1111/psq.12614 (last accessed 10/19/19).

10. Gallup, "Presidential Approval Ratings—Donald Trump," https://news.gallup.com/poll/203198/presidential-approval-ratings-donald-trump.aspx (last accessed 2/29/2020).

11. We made the same general argument in relation to the Iran-Contra Affair but never tried to take it this far.

12. See the Quinnipiac University Poll, Question: "Would you say that Donald Trump is honest, or not?" *Polling Report.com*, http://pollingreport.com/trump_ad.htm (last accessed 03/01/2020).

13. There are a variety of attributions to this statement. See *The Quote Investigator*, https://quoteinvestigator.com/2017/11/30/salary/ (Last accessed 3/22/20).

14. *House Committee on the Judiciary v. Don McGahn*, United States Court of Appeals for the District of Columbia, No. 19-5331, January 3, 2020, p. 8.

15. It is also possible that Congress could cut off funding to the Executive Branch. But if Congress cuts off electrical power to the White House, so much else of the country's business suffers, not to mention, the President can retaliate in kind.

16. Coronavirus Aid, Relief, and Economic Security Act, Pub.L. 116–136.

17. Charlie Savage, "Trump Suggests He Can Gag Inspector General for Stimulus Bailout Program," March 27, 2020, *New York Times*, https://www.nytimes.com/2020/03/27/us/trump-signing-statement-coronavirus.html (last accessed 4/1/20).

Index

Note: page numbers in *italics* refer to figures.

www.ingramcontent.com/pod-product-compliance
Lightning Source LLC
Chambersburg PA
CBHW020342270326
41926CB00007B/289